THE BUSHMAN WINTER HAS COME

The true story of the last /Gwikwe bushmen on the Great Sand Face

paul john myburgh

PENGUIN BOOKS

First published by Penguin Books (South Africa) (Pty) Ltd, 2013
A Penguin Random House company

Registered Offices: Block D, Rosebank Office Park, 181 Jan Smuts Avenue, Parktown North,
Johannesburg 2193, South Africa

www.penguinbooks.co.za

Reprinted 2013

ISBN 978-0-14-353066-4
eISBN 978-0-14-352991-0

Cover by MR Design
Printed and bound by CTP Printers, Cape Town

No time can ever return other than in the remembering. For me, the memory of *Kgoatwe* is enormous ... it washes through me in a mix of feelings, sounds, pictures of children, and smells ... voices in my blood ... voices in my blood.

CONTENTS

PROLOGUE

It was one day, thirty-five years ago, and together we sat, two humans in the middle of the Great Sand Face ... in the vast openness of the Kalahari Desert, myself and /Thooshe, a legendary shaman of the //Xo/xei people ... I as a young lion, and he with the countenance of an eagle. We dreamed together, for I could not speak his tongue and he could not speak mine ... I wondered at all that we might share, and I thought of the many things we could never share. It was then that my story began.

ANOTHER SOUL

I was born in Africa with a wind in my head … a wind which held in its breath the knowledge of all life since the beginning, the knowledge of my being and of all beings … it was simply that way. I knew from a young age that I had lived for a long time … such was the nature of my Soul. I knew also that I held the responsibility of choice and consequence, and in the choosing I would find my own relationship with God, and that would be how I stood in this life … my own position of being. So that is where I first came from, my own place on the spirit path … the place where we all begin.

Through my first twelve years I was a silent creature … I stuttered badly, and so chose mostly not to speak. Thoughts to words … when you cannot speak yourself into the outer world you turn the other way, and within that silence I learned to live inside of myself and to find my way in the world of imagination and inspiration.

I have memories from a young age, and some I discussed with my father before his passing to the world of spirit. One, which still seems important … I was about nine months old and I remember crawling across a carpet with a pattern I can still describe, pulling always one record with a white cover from the gramophone cabinet, and crying for that record and no other to be played. It was the first symphony of the Russian composer Rachmaninov, sombre, deep and evocative, and no other music would please or comfort me. Still today, it stirs and moves my Soul to inexplicable depths of longing and sorrow.

Between the ages of four and seven years I would sit every morning in meditation at the foot of my bed … compelled by some deep nostalgia, I would continue with the astral journeys I had undertaken in my sleep dreams the night before … I remember well that childhood ritual. And I have not forgotten the places I visited … travelling always to the north and the east, I remember vast and endless mountains, caves and sacred places, and always the holy man who waited for my visits. I would travel every morning in the spirit world, and my feeling, I recall, was one of reverence, as if I were taking some final instruction, seeking to bring something forward from a past life. And then I would return to the day around me, filled with comfort and a feeling that all was as it should be, and my day would begin.

At that age, as it is with all young humans, I was sheltered within the life-body of my mother, my Spirit held and nurtured by angels and other higher beings. Within this safety net my astral journeys were profound, the memory of which I have carried all through my life … an innate sense of my Soul-journey through many cycles of time, through cycles of life and death and rebirth … for just as we awaken each morning with the same living physical body, so we are born as spiritual beings into each new earthly life.

A child filled with feelings … feelings … a nudging of dreams from my Soul-body, ancient memories held in my blood, my water, and in me the yearning to be a hunter-warrior … a past life unresolved … a circle not closed. In my imaginings it was a vast place from whence I came, a place of soft earth and free wind … I had not forgotten. My hope would always be that I might have the strength of Soul to serve that which I carried as memory.

I knew that I was equal to all creatures and to all of life … I grew to understand that difference between all living creatures is a fact of birth, and that equalness between those same creatures is the spiritual heritage, which each individual, through choice, must claim. My choice was made a long time ago.

And then came the time when my body would manifest those inner feelings, realise my life through muscle, bone and blood … come to understand and express my own young Ego … my sense of my Self. As a young man it was time to live my Soul into the world so that I might one day return, having followed myself when it mattered.

Following always my inclination to explore the outer limits of the physical world, I spent many years in wild and lonely places ... in submarines I explored the belly of the ocean ... in gold mines the heart of the earth. Barefoot across Africa I have walked to many strange and challenging encounters, threading a path through life's jungles and deserts ... memories ... so many humans with hearts opened in kindness ... souls I will always remember ... I could have died a hundred times but I knew no fear, for I journeyed under the wings of strong angels.

Time passed and I came to see that there was more to being a man than just dreams and physical endeavour, and so I felt back inside to my place of beginning to find that which I had always known, my first Soul-rememberings. There was much to learn of my true heart and of my place on the spirit path, my purpose to understand how I stood upon this earth ... who I was and who I could be.

I knew then that I would go to the desert, my heartland ... fuelled by faith and hope, I would go because I remembered and I was born with that wind in my head. Like every young Percival, I set off on a journey that reflects the truth we all seek ... my quest for the Holy Grail.

The Kalahari Desert and the Bushmen ... 'bushman' ... a word and a veiled memory. Outside of my own unconscious blood memory I knew nothing of this stream of humanity. In the little I had read, I recognised a common lack of comprehension and truth. There was the usual array of academic information, much intellectual posturing, but no real understanding of who these people are ... nothing of the Spirit of the First People, and so nothing of our own beginnings.

When the first explorers came to this land from Europe, they brought with them the romantic and prejudiced concept of the 'noble savage'. They had come to patronise, but not to recognise those about whom they would tell tales both interesting and funny back home across the sea. This was the time when 'armchair anthropology' was at its condescending best, its authors happy to borrow what they could from hearsay, synthesise what they had borrowed into more fashionable form, and publish it as their own brave adventure ... a habit that continues to this day. So it was that they were a long way from the truth of Africa, and equally distant from the soul of the earth. And it follows, today, that there are many naive romantics and novelists who insist that the Bushman plays the role of the ideal that they, the authors and their readers, seek in themselves. But there have always been those humans of 'clear vision' ... they are the few who keep the threads of truth alive ... their work stands, and I salute them.

Throughout human history, people and cultures have streamed across the earth from one land to another, hence the process of acculturation that compels human transformation on many levels. There is significant spiritual purpose in this process, for how long can any civilisation sustain if it remains cocooned within its own cultural parameters? Through the imposition of different cultures, one upon the other, we are forced into various states of disparity and conflict ... the very things that cause us to understand, to adapt and grow as humans. And our existence on earth has never been only a question of physical survival, for we are not animals, we are Soul-filled beings, and any cross-pollination of humanity must be seen as an opportunity for transformation and the evolution of Spirit-man ... for such is our purpose.

I remember sometimes being sad in this world filled with people so preoccupied with physical disparity, a global culture that insists that all people are different and therefore unequal. As I began to comprehend the nature of that same prejudice within myself, I came to see that my discomfort was the disparity between my own lower nature and my higher Self, and that mine was the freedom to choose.

As a Soul-body moving through time, I had chosen to be born into the geography of Africa, for it was in this physical realm that I would best learn, and manifest my purpose on earth. The cultural disparities with which people struggle around the world are most extreme in Africa, the obstacles of difference much harder to overcome. In my own endeavour to know more of the 'other', I came to understand a truth that surrounds us all today. We live in a world that encourages prejudice of difference, a condition common to modern humans everywhere ... so let none of us pretend what we are not. Disparity does not ask that we choose one or the other position, but only that we come to understand the nature of the space between the opposites.

As for direction, I had only myself. I knew of the 'bushman' inside of me, and I knew of the Bushmen somewhere in the Kalahari Desert, that Great Sand Face in the southwest of Africa ... and so that was the way I went, for that was my path.

PEOPLE OF THE GREAT SAND FACE

In a time long ago, before the coming of the others, one must try to imagine oneself back into a world inhabited only by the First People, a world within which the lives of animals and humans and all that lived upon the earth were intertwined in a way that we can now barely perceive ... no boundary between visible and invisible worlds ... a time of mystical creatures and nature spirits, of elven-like humans who lived within the realm of spirit as easily as they did within the physical world.

Every now and again you must remind yourself of the time that came before this time ... and think also of the time that is to come ... and when you stand with your eyes nicely open on this long timeline, with all the other souls that have come and gone and come again, then you will best understand this story ... the story of the early race, the First People and yourself.

YGuam/tge ... here on the Great Sand Face it feels like being at the centre of the earth. It is not the people who decide what sort of day it will be, it is the day who decides how the people shall be ... and today we are gentle, like small soft clouds spread across the early African sky.

We are of the First People ... of Africa ... the people of the melon song ... of the healing dance. We are the hunters of the poison arrow sticks ... the story-painters of the rocks, who speak old words with a clicking tongue. We carry the memory of an earlier time when the earth had a different spirit form. We walk the tail end of a time when people were still one with the whole, and the voice of God was not strange … we come from the time of innocence, and we are called the /Gwikwe. In our own language '/Gwi' means 'bush' and 'kwe' means 'people' … and so we are the Bushmen … living in the way that all humanity has lived on earth since the beginning, and we are the last of the first.

Thirty-four people we are, from one year to ninety-five years in age … we share everything. Our relationships are strong and true, with age-old patterns prescribing an inherent respect for each other and for all of life. No one individual pretends or claims to be greater or lesser than another … we are all equal, and it is from this point of equalness that we live our lives.

And I, Paul … for seven years of my life I have lived in the old way of humanity, with a people who inadvertently turn my fundamental perception of life inside out, a people who live by the ethic that all things are different, but equal.

Together we sit on the earth, under the Old Man's Tree … and this is our story.

ARE YOUR EYES NICELY OPEN?

It is late in the summer … moving slowly towards the north, //Gammsa the Sun does not burn as fiercely now, and the earth still produces enough food to keep the band reasonably secure within this area of the Great Sand Face. The rains, which came three moons ago, were small … it is a dry time.

There is no surface water in this part of the Kalahari Desert, and for liquid we depend entirely on whatever melons, tubers and bulbs we find growing in the veld, and that which we can drink from the animals. The old man,

Dzero-O, says that these dry years will kill all the people … I believe it too, but I think also that they will die in a different way if ever they leave this place and this old way of life … their Souls will die, and then there is no life. Perhaps we are thinking of the same thing, he and I.

The //Annsa melons are ripe now, and although not as large and sweet as yesteryear, they are enough. I watch the old man with a juicy melon held between his feet … deftly split in two with his digging stick, the insides hacked out and eaten. He spits the seeds into a fold in his skin cloak, and I know that they will roast well in the coals of his fire.

'Aiee … these seeds are alive,' he says … and so, too, this waterless Kalahari, which holds and nurtures so many lives. I wonder how it would be were it not for this melon, this round liquid womb growing on a vine on the dry earth, filled with pulp and seed … this melon that dances with women, and that feeds gemsbok and lion alike. An entire web of life depends specifically and critically on this green orb carrying the lifeblood that holds together a whole ecosystem, no matter how dry the season … indeed something beautiful, this fruit.

I watch and dream and learn of many things … a large grasshopper walks over my toes … too fat to jump … perhaps she is filled with eggs … the sour berries are still coming … they will be nice … they will help to keep us fat as we go towards winter, if the ostriches do not eat them all as they did last season. Tgoo says that the ostriches are not around Kgoatwe now, and that when he sets his snares he does not think of /Geruma.

Geutwe and /Gaiekwe return from a gathering trip … their carry bags filled to bursting with gemsbok cucumbers, or /Khaa, which, apart from /Gaa roots and bitter melons, are the only other real source of liquid during these last few hot months of summer. I watch as they build up a big fire … placing the spiky, yellow-green cucumbers in a shallow pit and covering them with hot coals. Left to roast until morning, they will be shared and eaten over the next few days, cold and slightly bitter, but filled with fluid for our thirsty bodies. After the melons, the cucumbers and the sour berries are gone we will drink from /Gaa roots, and later in the year when the /Gaa become old and bitter we will drink from the Bie roots, which we share with the animals. By that time it will be dry season, and we will be waiting for the rains … for now, many moons still lie between us and that time … we have enough, and the day has decided how the people will be.

As for the comfort of our existence, there is no conflict among us and no fear, for ours is a culture of sharing and consideration. As humans we are different in manner but equal in Spirit, and safe in that knowledge … for this is the way of the First People, adapted to our environment in all ways … we live as we should.

Voices … laughter … whistling onto the blades of scrapers. Together, some of the men scrape a gemsbok skin pegged out next to the shelters … a cloak against the coming winter for /Gaiekwe, the hunter's wife. Each man is drawn into the patch he scrapes, as if in a trance … soft words, scraping, whistling sounds onto the blades and the clickety-click of sharpening tools take the day away.

Warm in the morning sun, I remember how we first came to this place … it was many moons ago, and it began with /Tgooma the Gemsbok …

IN THE BEGINNING

It was one day in Africa, twelve moons ago. The sun had passed the middle of the sky, and we were four men … Tso/tgomaa, Tgoo, Magu and I. We had walked for many days … it was so very hot, the dry season had ended, the rains had come and the heat of the summer was upon us. Tgoo and Tso/tgomaa had said that we should go towards the east, keeping the sun on our backs, and I had said that we should walk northwards. My feelings were strong that day and so we turned our journey towards the north … Magu walking behind, Tgoo and Tso/tgomaa in the front. Our quest was to find a place where the last of the First People could stay, a place with enough veld food and game to sustain the last band of wild /Gwikwe Bushmen ... thirty-four people still living the old way of life in the central Kalahari Desert of Botswana.

As we walked, the afternoon sky became grey with cloud, and the sand face, now cooling under our feet, sloped gradually down into a shallow basin. A great stillness came to surround us and everything under the sky ... we could feel the rain animal coming from afar, but we could not yet see its face in the sky.

Storms in the Kalahari begin this way ... you find yourself in a calm place, inside and out, compelled to consider your place and purpose on the earth ... inside the waiting ... the acknowledgement ... and then the gift of rain and life!

We moved towards a circle of Giraffe thorn trees for shelter, and there – in the stillness in the centre of the circle – stood a gemsbok bull. A hunter does not easily get close to /Tgooma in the Kalahari Desert, and so, when four men walking get this close, it is no coincidence ... it is a time to listen, a time of revelation.

The gemsbok stood under what was to become the Old Man's Tree, watching us, his eyes filled with solitude and distance ... for he lived here with the wisdom of the earth, from the time of animal-people ... before the separation. We looked at him and he at us for some time, and within us there was no feeling to shoot the animal ... there was another reason for our being there ... the gemsbok was the messenger, and so we waited. I remember the lines between us were strong ... the lines that bind and join all things ... and so we stood transfixed by the certainty with which nature sometimes presents her Soul.

/Tgooma the Gemsbok looked at us for a long time that day, and then he turned and walked away with a great calmness, for this was his place. And so we stayed under the gemsbok's tree because we knew that we should, and Tso/tgomaa pulled the fire sticks from his hunting bag. We gathered food and it rained, big and warm … it was a soft female rain animal that came to wet and nourish our Souls and the earth.

For three days we stayed, washed by the rain and warmed by the fire … with full bellies and good feeling we talked of many things. We talked of /Tgooma the Gemsbok and of what he had come to say, for this was no ordinary encounter … he was a 'power animal', and his coming at this time and in this place was the beginning of our story. I would always remember that gemsbok.

Tgoo told us that this area was called Kgoatwe, and that in the olden days, about fifty years before now, the /Gwikwe people had lived around here. Tso/tgomaa and Magu agreed that the people had lived here within the time of their memories.

For three days we shared our time as men on a long journey can, and we knew that this was a place where the people could live. We had eaten //Annsa melons, sour berries, sweet berries, /Gaa, /Tgara and all of the favourite veld foods … and the spoor of animals lay everywhere. It was as if this Kgoatwe place had been waiting for us, and the gemsbok was the messenger … and that is the way it was when we came to Kgoatwe.

It is now one year and two moons later, and after the rains. /Gowsi, a young hunter, returns to the shelters filled with his own strength. He tells with uplifted tongue how he has chased and run down a full-grown kudu bull. He was out checking snares, and there in his path stood //Gama the Kudu, waiting for him … and so he had given chase and run the legs off the animal in a wide circle over about fourteen kilometres. One of the other hunters heard the noise of the chase, and now stands waiting by the animal, which can run no more. /Gowsi has come to fetch his spear, and quickly we take up our weapons and follow him to where //Gama stands, with legs splayed, in trembling exhaustion … today he will give his heart to the hunters.

/Gowsi throws the first spear ... into the shoulder, but the animal does not even flinch. It stands as if in a trance while Gening/u cautiously retrieves the spear, and then from close range pushes it through the ribs and into the heart. The kudu falls into the entrance gully of an old warthog burrow, kicking and thrashing a last reluctance to leave its physical body ... death throes and dust.

We are enough people, and we easily pull the animal onto the bed of leaves that has been prepared for the skinning ... blood smell on the sand face ... I stand caught in the dichotomy of death and beauty, colours of blood red splattered onto bright green leaves, surrendered under the enormous vault of a blue blue sky. The distance between the physical world and the world of spirit is naught ... with life-death purpose in every moment.

Looking at the now still body of the kudu, I wonder at the force that causes this animal body to function according to its form. What is it that compels the living relationship between one part of the body and any other? What force puts life in the blood and movement in the muscle? What force of life binds the part to the whole, and what compels this force? And if we see this force of life as Spirit, then what is this Spirit? And what do we kill when we kill an animal, do we kill the body? Do we kill the spirit? Do we kill the spirit by killing the body? ... No! I see by what departs the body that we cannot kill Spirit, we only sever the relationship between body and Spirit, but the journey of Spirit continues.

How remarkable this interweaving of Spirit and matter, and how inseparable they are. In this dying today, I see that without Spirit there can be no body – and equally on this earth, without body there can be no Spirit ... and it is this symbiosis that lies at the core of our existence. In this transformation from life to death, I witness the immutable fact of body and Spirit as one, bound by a cosmic principle that lives in everything, absolutely everything ... the force of life which makes whole.

I am awed at the thought of one man running down a fully grown antelope ... a kudu in its prime. The old man, Dzero-O, says that a hunter would not chase any other antelope in this way, only //Gama the Kudu, who cannot run for a whole day like the eland and the gemsbok. The eland runs straight and far, but the kudu runs in a wide territorial circle, and if a hunter runs with this knowledge then he will always intercept the animal before it can rest. 'So … if a man finds a kudu waiting for him on a day when his legs are strong, then he can be lucky.'

Dzero-O is the oldest man at the kill, and it is he who makes the first cut into the animal's foreleg before we begin with the skinning. By cutting open the knee of the kudu in this way he intends for the Soul of the animal to continue forward on its journey … and this is the way it has always been done, for this is the way of the old people.

It is not for nothing that humans throughout the ages have performed rituals that pay homage to the departing of Spirit. We have lived, always, with a deep certainty of the super-sensible, with our various ideas of God, of nature spirits, and of angels and demons … somehow always serving our faith in the world of Spirit. Even today, while shaping our lives around the views of a materialistic science, which in vain denies the existence of much that is invisible … even today, we humans would still believe.

The skinning is done and we wait … they come … first the voices and then the women … laughter … and the promise of full bellies. Together we carry the meat back to the shelters and the waiting children, for they know of //Gama the Kudu who comes to feed their hunger. My share is a generous portion of the liver, roasted in the hot coals of Gening/u's fire … we eat well and the day passes gently.

That evening, the older boys recount the story of /Gowsi and the kudu bull … and then for their ears /Gowsi asks a question of the old man … 'Father,' he asks, 'if a man is chasing a kudu, can he not eat melons for his thirst?'

'Aiee,' says his father. 'No, because the animal-body knows that you are eating, and so it becomes stronger from what you eat and will run away. God has made it this way, and there is no other reason.' The boys listen, for they must know the way in which all things are connected ... like day is to night.

The circle of shelters reflects golden-red from the fire under the Old Man's Tree, and song voices begin to fill the darkness. Young man Seman!ua plays Denku, thumb piano, and the other men have gathered around ... eyes filled with fire and song. Beautiful voices reaching and pulling from the belly through the heart ... atonal sounds ... harmonic overtones whispering through our bodies, drawing us out into that astral realm where we join with all life in joy and sorrow, our Souls soaring into the night, day, darkness, light ... that place of beginning somewhere in the eternal depths of space. This is the sound of true voice, and these songs they have always sung, for these are the story songs that their fathers sang before them.

There is a common thread that runs through the stories and songs of all Bushman culture, the same truth told and sung in many parts of the Kalahari ... among the /Aiekwe, the //Kung, the //Xo, the /Gwikwe and others. These are the story songs of the old people, and all we humans come through the old people, the Kho Kho ... the 'people's people' whom we call the early race. The great grandfathers speak of a time when all the Bushman people were as one, before the splitting into tribes as we know them today ... the time when they alone lived on this land ... before the others came.

At this earlier time, three thousand years ago and before, people living on the earth were more joined in clairvoyant consciousness than today, each Soul in communion with the whole of life ... hence the common thread of wisdom that runs through the core culture of all the world's aboriginal peoples, for all were connected to the same source at the same time in earth history.

Although they no longer wholly access this ancient wisdom, much of the feeling and memory is still alive in Bushmen today, and there are some among them who are able to 'call to life' this inner memory in the way of the old people. It is this ancient relationship with the world of Spirit, which, more than anything else, compels the lives of the last wild Bushmen.

I must make clear that when I talk of the Spirit of Bushmen I speak of pure-blood Bushmen … those who still carry, unimpeached, the ancient threads of 'world wisdom' borne out of that earlier time … the time before the fall of humankind. When one truly gazes into the countenance of a pure-blood Bushman one perceives a quality of Soul before which one can only stand in awe, because what stands before you still reflects the fundamental Soul qualities of what you yourself once were. One beholds a purity of Soul held with unconscious, childlike grace … known, but unknown.

I remember reading a story that wounded me very deeply, for I too was once an innocent soul. It was told by another of the First People, a man called //Kabbo, far away on the southern end of Africa at the time when /Tguikwe was a young woman living right here, two thousand miles to the north in this remote Kalahari … it was called *One Man's Story*.

//Kabbo said … I came here, when I came from my place, when I was eating a springbok which I had killed with my arrow. A black man took me, he bound my arms … I and my son, with my daughter's husband we were three, when we were bound opposite to the wagon, while the wagon stood still. They took us while we were not numerous. We went away, bound, to the Magistrate, we went to talk with him … the Magistrate talked with us, we remained with him … we remained with him …

The black men took us away to the jail at night. We put our legs into the stocks … another white man laid another wood upon our legs … we slept while our legs were in the stocks. The day broke while our legs were in the stocks. The Korannas came to put their legs into the stocks … they slept, while their legs were in the stocks.

The Magistrate came to take our legs out of the stocks, because he wished that we might sit comfortably, that we might eat … for it was his sheep that we were eating. While we were eating the Magistrate's sheep, the Korannas came to eat it.

We ate it, we and the Korannas, while our legs were in the stocks ...

We came to roll stones at Victoria, while we worked at the road. We lifted stones with our chests, we rolled great stones. We again worked with earth. We carried earth, while the earth was upon the handbarrow ... we loaded the wagon with earth ... we pushed it. We were pushing the wagon's wheels, we were pushing ... we poured down the earth, we pushed it back. We again loaded it, we and the Korannas. Other Korannas were pushing the handbarrow. Other 'people' (Bushmen) were with the Korannas; they were also carrying earth while the earth was upon the handbarrow ...

We again had our arms bound to the wagon chain, we walked along while we were fastened to the wagon chain ... as we came to Beaufort while the sun was hot. They (our arms) were set free in the road ... we got tobacco from the Magistrate ... we smoked, going along, (using) sheep's bones (as pipes). We came into Beaufort jail. The rain fell upon us while we were in Beaufort jail ...

Early the next morning our arms were made fast, we were bound. We splashed into the water ... passing through the water in the river bed. We walked upon the road, as we followed the wagon, while the wagon went first. We walked, following the wagon, until we, being bound, came to the Breakwater. On the way, we ate sheep as we came to the Breakwater ...

A white man took us to meet the train at night. I have said to thee that the train is nice. I sat nicely in the train. We two sat in it, I and a black man. The black man asked me, 'Where dost thou come from?' I said to the black man, 'My place is the Bitterpits.' The train ran, bringing us to the Cape. We came into the Cape prison house when we were tired, we and the Korannas, we lay down to sleep at noon ...

When you read this, you see that the difference in consciousness between this stream of humanity and ourselves is almost incomprehensible, the innocence inexplicable to the modern mind. This is one man's story, and he was a pure-blood Bushman ... his Soul constituted in such a way that he was incapable of malice, incapable of reflecting anything but his truth. When we think about these times in history, we must not postulate endlessly about who was right or wrong, for we were not there ... we must rather give thought to the terrible wrongs that all humans still allow in ignorance.

VOICES ACROSS THE SAND

As I lie alone to sleep I think of many things ... of many human voices raised to the heavens, where, indeed, the shape of our world is revealed through the angels to the whole cosmos ... and we should think hard of what is revealed.

I remember a time in history only four years ago, when, for a short while, I was visiting with the //Xo/xei and Jung/uasee people in Tsumkwe, Namibia. It was a still morning and there were fifty or so people sitting under a great Baobab tree ... waiting ... weighted with an anxiety softly spoken ... voices weaving through the air between them ... the sound of something changing. These were the last of the Bushman people in that region with any cultural integrity left in their lives, and on that day a man from the government was coming to see them, to speak of a very important matter ... and so they had come to listen.

Before he came, the 'important' government man had instructed the local game ranger to shoot a nice fat kudu for the people to eat ... as if he owned the kudu! It seemed that he had forgotten that the kudu belonged to the people who were waiting for his visit. And, of course, he was late in coming ... but the people waited, for it is in their nature to be considerate of others.

He arrived shortly after midday in a black BMW, and when he climbed out of the vehicle, we saw, irony of ironies, that he was wearing cowboy boots and a white Stetson-type hat, and he had come to negotiate a land treaty with the original inhabitants of the land.

How dare any of us speak of ownership of Africa when the first owners themselves do not? They make no claim for that which belongs to itself, for that which belongs to God. I remember thinking how utterly bizarre it was ... like being in a time warp and watching history repeat itself ... the endless cycles of appropriation of light by darkness, and the light somehow always finding a way to shine through again ... for such is the indomitable nature of the human Spirit. But still the cycles continue ... and whether the lie was being told to a Lakota Sioux Indian somewhere in the Black Hills in America, an Aboriginal hunter in the Australian Outback, or to the last wild Bushman in the Kalahari Desert ... the lie was always the same.

The government man was an Afrikaner, and I remember his name. He had an assistant, a Bushman who had given up the old ways and gone to live in the city. Someone said that he had been whipped for stealing on a farm where he had worked, and it was then that he had gone to work for the government because he could speak Afrikaans. In my heart I empathised, for he, too, was just another victim ... another Soul out of time.

And so the meeting began. The government man stood with his boots and his cowboy hat to make his speech to the Bushmen. The Bushmen thought it strange that a man should need to stand and talk when all the people were sitting. What the government wanted was that all of the Bushmen from this region should move into an area of land so small that it would be completely inadequate for their needs. The politician said that they would be taken care of and that they would be given food by the government, and so they would no longer have need of the large tract of land on which they had hunted and gathered for so long.

Are these same words not repeatedly spoken and recorded on the dark pages of human history ... the face of greed deceiving the lives of the innocent?

We spoke among ourselves, but what could I say from a position of historical experience that would influence the minds of these people? How could I tell them what was to come? What could I say that would stop this deception? I was talking to a people who have no suspicion, no malice ... they could not think that such wrongdoing was possible, that such evil could be deliberate. In the end, I could do nothing ... I could only share my experience in words but not my experience itself. I was only to be a witness.

And the meeting continued ...

The kudu meat was handed around so that the decision could be made on full bellies ... for such was the plan ... to feed them and make them happy. And in their innocence, the Bushmen saw only the kindness that was offered. They thought that the government man must be a kind man, because he had given them meat to eat, and so to reciprocate the kindness, they said there would be no harm in telling him that he could have the land.

The Bushmen say that no one owns the land ... for it belongs to God. And so if it would make the government man happy, then they would say that he could have the land ... and they would put their mark on the piece of paper that he was asking them to sign. They could not read the paper anyway; yes ... they could read the earth and the cosmos in so many ways, and they could teach us many things ... but they could not read this paper. It was as if they knew that this day would come and that they would have no choice. And so they signed the paper on that day, and that was the beginning of their end. In just a few short years, many of that community had become alcoholics, prostitutes and utterly heartbroken humans.

This sickening deception has played itself out a hundred times in many lands, and every time the result is the same. The lower human nature triumphs over the higher human nature and innocence is defeated. I wonder when it will ever be different? How many times in the evolution of humanity must the same lies be repeated before we come to understand the nature of truth and goodness?

I remember that day in Tsumkwe ... it was the passing of a death sentence. Fifty little people under a big tree in the Kalahari ... an event symbolising something enormous for all of humanity ... and the world did not notice.

I slept with sadness that night.

In the morning I looked with new eyes at my world, embraced in the circle of small grass shelters, each holding the morning sun in its shape ... and the people as they were in the beginning ... lithe forms moulded into the landscape of endless grasses, trees and animals, so utterly at one with creation ... as if they had been there forever.

And for such a long time they have been, for there is no other population group that shows such consistency of evidence both spiritual and physical. It is said that the Bushmen carry the strands of a cellular memory that goes back over a hundred thousand years, to a time when all peoples on the earth were of common ancestry ... the Adams and the Eves of humankind. In which way this is true I need not say, for our modern perception is more veiled than we know, and there is much that will be revealed, much that we will come to know in the coming times. Standing now at such a critical juncture in human evolution, we must be reminded that we share the blood and the memory of these First People, and of all of humanity before us. We must feel our way back into that early time of the mysteries and before, through the story songs to the first words, through all the remembered wisdom ... for that was the time of our beginning, and our knowledge of the past will be our strength into the future, and so it is written.

BACKWARDS AND FORWARDS IN TIME

I must now tell of what became of the people from Namibia and Angola who were made to give their land away ...

Before, and at that time, there was a long and senseless war between the 'terrorist' forces of Swapo fighting out of Angola, and the South African military – each side thinking that the other was an evil force, but in reality, all just confused humans in various stages of evolution. Remarkable too, that Cuba versus America had somehow gotten transposed and choreographed into the middle of this African political opportunity ... greed was the enemy, with Cuba used as the decoy.

And the Bushmen of Angola and South West Africa ... the /Xhun and the Khwe, and the //Kung and the Jung/uasee? Never in their long history had they ever known of war such as this, an idea foreign to their nature. They had no allegiance to either side, no false ideology to sustain, nor could they understand the idea of national borders and ownership of land, for if the land belonged to anyone, then surely it belonged to those who came first ... the Bushmen?

Even so, they were lured and conscripted into the military as trackers and otherwise expendable bodies, with no particular idea of what they were to fight for, nor any idea of right or wrong within the foolishness of this modern idiom, and no inclination to choose. They were 31 Battalion and 203 Battalion, and against the fundamental spiritual premise of their existence on earth they were persuaded to regard the 'other' as 'the enemy'. If they sided with the Angolans and Swapo, they would be slaughtered by the South Africans, and if they sided with the South Africans they would be slaughtered by the Swapo forces. Caught in the crossfire ... they were the real victims.

When the war ended, it was Swapo who formed the governments of Namibia and Angola. The South Africans went back to South Africa, and the CIA, who probably started the war anyway, went back to their dark place of greed and materialism ... America was now the new owner of the enormous Angolan oil reserves ... and, of course, there was also the matter of diamonds ... all paid for with the lives of innocents.

It was then decided, by whom no one is quite sure, that if the Bushmen returned to where they had been before the war they would be persecuted by Swapo for having 'picked' the wrong side. So, in 1990, the /Xhun and the Khwe of Angola, who had been coerced into this mindless political game, were moved out of their own country to a place called Schmidtsdrift in the Northern Cape of South Africa … an environment bleak and far from home. Ten thousand human souls thrown together in a way unlike anything they had known before … living in rows and rows of cold canvas tents. The entire fabric of their lives destroyed … family units torn apart, with parents left behind to live out their days in the old way, but now without the support of their children, who had fought the war and were now forced to move to another country where there was nothing … absolutely nothing with any empathy for the Soul of the Bushman.

Schmidtsdrift was a dark and hard place … many bitter winters in a tent in the Northern Cape … no electricity, no fuel wood, no sewerage system for ten thousand people with not enough space, no hunting and gathering to supplement the monotonous ration of mealie pap … and when you ask them, they tell you it was a bad time, they tell you that the old people died first … and the children … because of the coldness.

It is incomprehensible that a war is fought between two foreign forces, one white and one black – a fight for an absurd ideology, and the ownership of land and resources that they have misappropriated in the first place. And when this clash of ignorant fools comes to an end they each go back to where they came from, and the only authentic land owner is moved, like a war criminal, to a no-man's-land where he lives out his days with nothing for his children save the stories of how it once was for the old people in a far off place which they called home … //Gau//gae … and it was a warm place before the 'others' came.

And no, it is not that we more purposeful people should go back to where we came from, or give it all back to the Bushmen, for history does not unfold in that way. But surely … surely we could do more than we have done? I despair despair despair at the sickness in the human soul, which causes allows condones and justifies this same endless atrocity throughout our history. What grave absence of consciousness is this?

Sixteen long years later, and half of the Schmidtsdrift people have been

21

moved to a township called Platfontein ... small square houses with cold cement floors.

And twenty years later? A Bushman died today ... just one more.

And the funeral in Platfontein is a sad, confused gathering of little people caught in the disparity of a time that is not theirs. They have lost so many of their own in this land far from home, with no history and no threads to bind the memories. Some drink their confusion away, and others argue around the conflicting ideologies of the church which has come to invade their lives even in death. Think of an institution that appropriates the idea of God, packaging and selling it back to a spiritually disenfranchised humanity at a premium, which serves the ends of big business. Much of religion, in today's limited sense and form, is preordained to separate humans from their own spiritual nature ... prejudiced belief systems ingratiating their way into vulnerable human communities, each religion suffering from the illusion that it has the answer to a question it can no longer even formulate.

And the Bushmen? ... A people who have lived within the spiritual embrace of the Great God since the beginning must now suffer these confused purveyors of spiritual bankruptcy ... as if organised religion, in its current state of politicised obsolescence, could say what happens to a man's Soul and Spirit when he dies? It is small wonder that we modern humans know so little of the mystery of life after death, a knowledge embedded in our Soul memory for the last two thousand years ... but this, too, shall change.

There is some arguing around the coffin ... some of the old people want to look upon the face of the dead man before he is put into the earth. In the old days they would all have seen his face and been able to wish his Spirit well on the journey to the Spiritual world ... but today he is in a coffin, wrapped in plastic ... crinkly white plastic ... and the church people, in the name of expedience, say that only the man's immediate family can look upon his face ... and the old people ask ... are we not all his family? ... must we not all see his face?
I look upon his face in the coffin and see only the agony of an ignoble death.

It is the fourth day since the man has died, and his Soul already stands on the threshold of the Spirit world. 'I pray for you, little brother whom I never knew before today, and I ask that your ancestors and angel guide you safely to the Great God from whence you came.'

His widow sits in a small anguished heap against the wall … her eyes filled with pain … tears … beseeching, and she asks for nothing but empathy in truth. I sit with her on the floor, trying to absorb her trembling little body into some brief comfort. And then we follow the coffin with bare feet softly on the red earth … a stream of humans wanting to remember the life of a Bushman who goes to a common graveyard … a square hole lined up with many other square holes dug into the earth, for many people have died in this place.

Overcast sky … at the graveyard we stand … three generations, confused. The old ones … pure in blood and Soul, know that this is not the way in which a man should be buried … they see that the man's head faces the wrong way in the grave, to the north, and not to the east so that his departing Soul can rise to the realm of Spirit with the morning sun to meet the stars … and the moon is not hollow at this time, so how can it help to carry the dead one away? They know, too, that the church songs sung in foreign tongue do not reach the ears of the departing spirit … and what of the songs of the /Xhun and the Khwe … their own songs … do the people sing no more?

Silently knowing, the old ones stand, holding what vigil they can. Women's voices cry their sadness into the coming rain, and when they grieve too much, someone gently takes them a little way from the graveside, for their sadness must not cause the departing spirit to wish to return. Their grief must become a gratitude for the Spirit journey that continues beyond the threshold of death … their grief must give thanks for that which makes the invisible visible, thus binding the world of Spirit to the world of men … and then we who remain behind are remembered by our ancestors, just as we remember them.

Others around the grave now speak out their memories of the one who has died and passed on ... and just when it seems that there can be no redemption in this death, there comes the sound ... *ghrrrrrrrrrh* ... coming from somewhere among the group of old people who stand in silence at the foot of the grave ... not all hear this sound ... it is like the voice of /Tgooma the Gemsbok and it resonates as if from another realm ... and again ... *ghrrrrrrrrh* ... and from this I know that all is well, for the old ones sanctify and hold the space in a sacred way, in the way that they have always known ... for certain sounds will arise out of the dead when they depart the earthly realm, and the old people still pay attention to these things ... *ghrrrrrrrrrh* ... *ghrrrrrrrrrh* ... four times in my body I hear the sound of /Tgooma, and it is well. The earth will take the body as it must today, and the Soul Spirit ever onwards.

When we leave the grave we wash our hands in water so that we can loosen the memories that would hold back the departing Spirit ... and in this way we know that the day is done.

... and so it was in Platfontein.

The wind does thus when we die ... our own
wind blows, for we who are human beings we
possess wind, we make clouds when we die ...

the wind does thus when we die ... the wind
makes dust because it intends to blow away
our footprints with which we had walked about ...

the wind does thus when we die ... for our
footprints which the wind intends to blow away,
would otherwise lie plainly visible ...

and the thing would seem as if we still lived ...
therefore the wind intends to blow, taking
our footprints away.

Our older brother Dia!kwain of the Cape Bushmen was the one who first told this story of the wind when we die, and I tell it now, because I was in Platfontein ... and we must know that we are not apart from one another, we people, for the wind comes to blow all our footprints away ... the same wind comes for all of us.

Here in Kgoatwe in the Kalahari we still have our old life, and so, finished with my thoughts, I seek out the other men. They are sitting around a small fire behind /Nedu khu kwe's shelter, mending their weapons and doing all sorts of home-day things. Tgoo is softening a duiker skin, //Guasa ... it is a female skin and his wife Geutwe will use it for a new apron. Tso/tgomaa pulls a nice stick away from the edge of the fire, and while it is still warm he bends it this way and that way until it is as straight as can be. When he is finished it will be a good bow for shooting. Gening/u, the healing man, says that he and Tso/tgomaa were hunting out beyond the grassy plains to the west of the shelters today, and they shot their arrows at /Tehma the Wildebeest ... 'Perhaps we were lucky ... who can say ... tomorrow we will take our spears and see.' No expectations, no disappointments.

/Nedu khu kwe says that he is going hunting tomorrow and that he is short of arrows ... he asks one of Tso/tgomaa. If a /Gwi hunter shoots an animal with an arrow that he has borrowed from another man, then the animal will, in fact, belong to that other man, and it is he who must decide who should divide the meat. The owner of the animal would then let the shooter divide the meat, thereby ensuring that the shooter and his family get a fair share. It is a good way of keeping the balance, and so, as one person gives to another, then at some time in the future the other will return the gift. No one will ever be left to go hungry, and this is the way of the /Gwikwe ... a system of reciprocal obligation that ensures interdependency between individuals in the band, which in turn ensures the survival of the group as a whole.

Voices of the women ... 'I feel like sleeping while I build this shelter.'
... 'And me ... I also wish to sleep.'
    'Get out ... a new house is always nice, and not for you to play in ... get

out!' says Geutwe to the children, as the women pack grass onto the pole framework of a new shelter. To keep the rain out, they start at the bottom and pack each new layer of grass above the one below, slowly working their way to the top.

'The grass is smelling very nice even though it is old,' … says //Gama … 'It is because it caught the dew last night.'

And Geutwe: 'It smells so nice that if you lie in the shelter you will think you are lying next to a nice young man … then the smell of the young man's armpits and the smell of the nice grass will mix together and be nice.'

… clean earth … clean air … far from the dirt of cities and the doings of modern humanity … out here, everything is still clean … leaves, grass and sand … body odours never offensive … everything as it should be.

'Thatch all the holes in the shelter so we don't see through it,' says /Gaiekwe, the hunter's wife.

And //Gama: 'We are finished on our side.'

And Geutwe: 'And we have finished cleaning the inside … we have done it well.'

N/aueema the moon grows big … the night is warm. We sit, each family around its little fire, nine shelters including my own. I remember when we made the first fire under the Old Man's Tree, and the coals from that fire were given to each family to go and be fire in front of each shelter … and so all the fires are one fire, one spirit. And just as the smoke from our fires rises up into the substance that envelopes the earth, we know that we are one with the world.

Gentle voices thread people together and the sand is silver-soft with moonlight, and everything part of the wind … cosmic breath, which gently breathes us in and out of ourselves. And we small people, we sit beneath this giant sky … the moon and the stars they see us and we see them, and the earth cradles us from below. It is all so gentle … so absolute … and so are we.

THE OLD WAY

In the morning I go north with Tso/tgomaa and Gening/u to the place where they wounded the two wildebeest. We pick up and follow the blood spoor ... it is arduous, thirsty work and Tso/tgomaa, ever resourceful, finds a little water in a hollow tree, left by the rains that passed three moons ago. He sucks the water up by joining together two hollow reeds, which he carries in his hunting bag ... not enough to share, but for one man a small blessing. These drinking sticks are both rare and precious.

The sand beneath our feet tells us that the animals have not walked far from the place where they were shot ... the poison on the arrows has done its work and the tracks are slow and without direction. We run both animals down near Kgoatwe pan before the sun is too many hours old.

Hunters are only as efficient as the weapons that their resources allow them, and in this place there are no alternatives ... we hunt with the arrow and kill with the spear. The more primitive the weapon, the more functional the body must be, and in order to live the /Gwikwe must kill ... and this is the only reality. I follow Gening/u, stalking silently towards the first wildebeest ... it snorts and runs ... we chase ... hard running, sand hot under our feet ... one, two miles, and legs tearing on the bush as we pass through ... we have no choice now ... we cannot choose our path, for now we follow /Tehma ... predators, we close in for the kill. I crouch behind Gening/u, his back shining sweat powerful, and I watch as he throws with absolute focussed intent ... his entire body and being inside the spear ... and *thuk*! ... his spear goes between the ribs and into the heart ... /Tehma will run no more.

We hear breaking branches and animal snorting not far away, and run to where Tso/tgomaa has brought the second wildebeest to ground. He stands with half his spear shattered and broken ... the other half protruding from the animal's chest. Snorting froth and blood it turns this way and that until it dislodges the now useless weapon. I run in fast and throw ... too high ... through the back of the neck above the shoulders, and there it stays bent almost at right angles as the wildebeest crashes sideways through the bush ... two spears lost and now the animal must be brought down with the only remaining spear. Snorting, blood spraying, /Tehma falls onto his side with Gening/u's spear in its chest ... but the animal is not ready to die, and Gening/u, nimble and certain, darts in between the flailing hooves, and grabbing the end of his weapon he pushes it deep into the heart of the struggling wildebeest that would stand one more time ... a powerful spirit that endures until the last ... and then it is over. Yes ... today we triumph, but it is not always this way.

We stand in the silence of departing spirits ... paying our respects to the spirit of the dead animals ... and to //Gamahma, the God of all humans, we give thanks.

It is not often that the hunters return with such news ... two large animals ... enough for everyone. Two moons have passed since the rainy season, and this is a lucky time for the people of Kgoatwe ... the people of the Great Sand Face. It is not far, and even the old lady, /Tguikwe, comes to help with the carrying of meat back to the shelters. 'My old feet are tired of the hot sand,' she says. 'One of the young men must cut me a new pair of sandals from Khordze /Tehma, the wildebeest skin.' ... And so it will be done.

On the way back to the shelters we pass a herd of springbok on the edge of the pan ... their eyes are sharp and a hunter does not easily get close to !Gaima the Springbok ... and so we walk ... I think of /Tehma the Wildebeest, and tell myself to remember how a man should throw his spear ... not with mind and arm, but with his whole heart ... with his whole heart.

I will learn.

The day is spent eating ... everyone gorging themselves to fullness. Anything not eaten is cut into strips and hung, and although the sun causes the meat to rot as fast as it dries, it remains palatable, and will keep hunger at bay for a week or more. Some thick pieces of skin from the back of the wildebeest are slow-roasted in hot ash. These are kept for the lean times, for the dry season, which always comes. Such is the way of life on earth that we, in our physical form, are always challenged to survive … for how does the spirit grow but through struggle, resolution and understanding.

On full bellies we smoke the last of our supply of leaf tobacco. Bone pipes are cut from the foreleg of //Guama the Duiker, the sides of each pipe delicately engraved and pleasing to the eye. Together we sit warm in the day, our words accompanied by the soft sucking sound of lips taking rare and simple pleasure. Sharing breath … smoking in this way from mouth to mouth … bone pipes pass from hand to hand and I ponder the cultures of privilege and possession.

Dowgwi has just returned from a gathering trip with some of the other women. She squats in the entrance of her shelter and tips a large heap of spiked, dark green leaves onto the sand … these are the leaves of a plant called !Goie, and she will use them to make string. She pulls the leaves between her leather sandal and her digging stick, and in this way strips the non-edible flesh from the fibrous insides. Her husband /Nedu khu kwe uses a gemsbok horn … it is the fibre they want, and before they become too dry these fibres are rolled and twisted into a string which is also called !Goie. To make it pretty, the string is blackened with a mixture of charcoal and urine.

I see that she has also collected a bundle of the 'grass which can be thrown like a spear' – a strong thick grass called //Gae khu //gaa, and from this grass, together with the string, she will make a new sifting mat. The women use these mats to separate sand and ash from the food they roast in the coals. In everything the /Gwikwe do their communal spirit is always reinforced, and so as Dowgwi begins to make her new sifting mat, the other women, Geutwe, //Gama and /Gaiekwe, decide that they, too, need new sifting mats … doing anything together is always preferable to doing it alone.

My eyes follow the line of !Goie trailing from Dowgwi's hands and over her legs to where it threads through her toes and comes to a sizeable ball of string. /Nedu khu kwe says that he would like to use some of this string to weave into a thicker rope to make a snare for catching small antelope like duiker and steenbok. He tells me that the bulbs of this !Goie plant are eaten by the wildebeest. Nothing lives for nothing ... there is no wasting of what is given by the earth, for that would be to dishonour the sacrifice. It is in our simple doings and observances that we nourish the Soul of the world, so that we, in turn, have life.

In the late afternoon I walk away from the shelters towards the north and into the early autumn wind ... soft and cool it carries the scent of the desert. I check two of the snares I had laid for guinea fowl ... one is still set, the other is sprung but empty ... guinea fowls are crafty birds. They lay their eggs during the rains, and now – with the breeding season finished – they gather and move in large flocks. There is a flock of about thirty birds that sometimes roosts in the trees around where I stand, so I know that it is just a matter of time before I catch one. Carefully I reset the snare in the way that I have been taught ... burying the rope noose just under the sand and leaves, I take melon and cucumber seeds from my skin bag to sprinkle as bait around and on top of the small stick-trigger. If the trigger is touched or pecked on, it will release the long stick-trigger that holds the rope noose which, on a lucky day, will catch the bird around the neck. It is during the next four moons of autumn and winter that the meat of the guinea fowl will be clean and free of the worms that sometimes infest this bird in the hot summer months.

I collect some moulted feathers for a game called Szanie that the boys like to play ... with a longer stick, they flick a small stick with a dung ball tied to one end and a feather on the other, as high as they can.

Back at the shelters ... *whiek*! ... and ... *whiek*! ... the Szanie shoots up and floats down like a circling vulture hurrying to land, but just before it touches the earth they catch it on the end of a thin flexible stick and flick it up again ... *whiek*! ... and again it circles and weaves its descent ... and then, caught once more, shoots skywards again. The men find it hard to resist joining in this game, and soon it becomes a shrieking, howling, running free-for-all of boys and men. Watching the ingenious whirlybirds floating and circling like vultures, or scarabs, I think of how dung beetles with a target in sight look so like alien space capsules on an observation flight to planet earth ... but upon landing and setting about their earthly duties, they transform instantly into a form so magnificently prehistoric ... ancient creature of an old old earth.

The great sun sets.

♩ ooh eah oh yeeah ooh ... ooh eh oh eah yeeah ♩ ... a song as old as the grass itself and the first autumn evening, it is //Gae khu //gaa ... one of the oldest forms of all traditional music. Three women singing soft harmony ... each holding a bunch of thick grass in one hand ... shaking and brushing the melody, and striking the rhythm against the other palm.

/Tguikwe, my old mother, has told me that this was the first music of the people of the early race. She says they sang with the grass in the time before there was metal for Denku, and before /Tehnu, the bow harp, and all the other instruments. There was always grass ... //Gae khu //gaa ... 'the grass which can be thrown like a spear' ... ♩ ooh eah oh yeeah ooh ... ooh eh oh eah yeeah ♩ ... and as the last birds settle into their favourite sleeping trees I see the delicate bow of the moon just above the western horizon. Between the setting sun and the evening star it stands up on its end like a taut hunting bow ... for that's what the moon does in April in the Kalahari Desert. It is as if the moon would shoot the sun to sleep, and the streak of evening sun-ray, which joins the sun to the moon, is the path along which the arrows would fly. And N/aueema the moon says, 'Go //Gammsa, go ... you must sleep, for it is my time now,' ... and so the sun goes to sleep. But the moon is close to the western horizon itself, and soon follows the sun to sleep ... leaving only the stars to put light into our dark autumn sky. In the silent whisperings of the stars I hear my name ... it is Paul and softly it is spoken ... for the stars they say Tsau, they say Tsau, and in the tongue of the early race Tsau is Man ... and so the stars say Man ... they whisper what we are ... each human, as we draw our first breath at birth, imprinted by a positioning of planets and a constellation of stars that bespeaks our own nature ... and so we are written in the stars. Our destiny is laid down in this way, and it then becomes ours to see, or not to see. In the time before birth, we ourselves, in conference with the spirit world, lay our own path down before us, and then we come to walk that path, or to stray as we choose ... to remember, or to forget.

/Han‖kass'o, an older brother of ours, tells it this way:
The stars take your heart
for the stars are not a little hungry for you
the stars exchange your heart for a star's heart
the stars take your heart and feed you a star's heart
then you will never be hungry again

because the stars are saying 'tsau! tsau!' ('man! man!')
and the bushmen say the stars curse the eyes of the springbok
the stars say 'tsau!' they say 'tsau! tsau!'
they curse the eyes of the springbok
I grew up listening to the stars
the stars saying 'tsau!' and 'tsau!'

it is always summer when you hear the stars say 'man'!

In this parable, /Han‖kass'o bears testimony to the immutable relationship that men have with the stars and the heavenly bodies, and we humans on earth are thus reminded that we are bound to a greater order.

♫ oh eh oh eh yeeah !! ... oh eh oh yeeah eh ♫ ... and the music takes us into the night ... and there is another story of the moon in April.

N/aueema the Moon is a male and a hunter, and at this time of new moon he

begins to hunt for the Hartebeest to feed his hungry family. As the Moon comes to
fullness he shoots and skins the Hartebeest, and then slowly he pulls the skin over
himself like a cloak until you can no longer see his light ... and this is the time of
'new moon'. But the Sun is the wife of the Moon, and she pulls away the darkness
of the skin cloak until, once again, her husband comes to be revealed as the full
moon. And the Moon then pulls the cloak back over himself, and the Sun then
pulls the cloak away until the Moon just shows that first sliver of light ... the
bow in the sky ... the empty belly moon, and again at this time his children
ask him to hunt the Hartebeest, for they are hungry ... and so he hunts as he
comes to fullness, and cloaks himself once more with the skin of the Hartebeest.
But always the Sun comes to pull away the cloak of darkness until she reveals her
husband shining in his full Moon splendour.

And it goes this way ... moon and sun ... husband and wife in constant
cycles of closing and opening ... and I see that the truth of this great
phenomenon lies in the changing, in the time and space between darkness
and light. In this story, the metaphor reflects the cycle of the moon ... of
coming towards light and fullness in the waxing moon, successful hunt, full
moon, full belly, feasting ... and then inwards digesting and resting into
the darkening of the waning moon, and sleeping in the darkness of the new
moon. Always the breathing in and the breathing out of life, always the
language of a living cosmos expressed in the stories of these people.

Sitting around our fires we hear a cicada in the nearby bush. 'Aiee!' shouts
Gening/u. 'Autumn has come, people! ... It is a favourite time ... do you
hear that cicada?' The people agree that autumn is a favourite time.

The Great Sand Face turns from green to gold and brown, and a full moon
has passed since the women came with the last of the sweet berries. Even the
//Annsa melons are scarce and slightly bitter now ... they have disappeared
from their normal collecting places much earlier this year ... perhaps
because of last year's drought. There are no more cucumbers, and for the next
six moons or so we will eat only the more bland and bitter tubers and bulbs,
mostly /Gaa ... and even Bie roots when the /Gaa are finished.

Nature arranged in subtle perfection holds me in awe, everything impeccably timed and placed to facilitate the survival of all the earth's creatures. During and after the summer rains the primary elemental forces at work are water and earth, and these two forces working together in nature produce the sweet tastes. Sweet in the form of natural sugars, nectars, berries and plant oils. 'Sweetness' also in the carbohydrates and animal fats that are more abundant at this time. In the natural cycle, summer is appropriately the time of contentment, of tissue building, both physical and spiritual, in preparation for the more difficult times.

As the hot, dry autumn unfolds, the elemental forces at work are ether and air, and these two forces working together bring about the increasing astringency in the taste of veld foods. This astringency assists with the toning and tightening of body tissue, encouraging the drying and purifying of bodily secretions in preparation for the time of less, the winter, when fire and earth will become the primary elemental forces at work.

And later still, when the hot spring and summer approaches, the forces at work will be air and earth. And in this dry desperate time before the rains, the bitterness in the plant food increases. The bitter tastes further encourage the tightening and purifying of body tissues, and in small amounts they reduce the bodily secretions. The inherent cooling properties in the bitter foods are vital for survival through the hot dry season. And then once again, the water comes to earth.

By understanding, and living with these subtle relationships between the physical body and the elemental forces, we strengthen and balance ourselves, and these /Gwikwe people, living as close to nature as they do, instinctively respond in the right way at the right time. It is this way through all the cycles of the earth, and one can endlessly explore the detail and alchemy of these natural processes, the principle of which remains constantly impeccable ... but that is another story.

I remember two years ago and before, when women returned to the shelters with their gathering bags full, each carrying close to her own body weight ... always then, there were Kwhootse, Kalahari truffles, and plenty of /Tgara ... juicy, crisp and delicate sweet. For the last two seasons there have been no truffles at all ... it is because of the rain not coming. And when the women do find /Tgara bulbs these days, they are too few to bring back, and they eat what they find while they are gathering. It is their privilege for they are the gatherers, and so they eat some of the choice sweet bulbs to refresh themselves on their long journeys, just as we hunters sometimes eat the liver and the kidneys of the animals we kill before we return to the shelters. However, being mothers, they always return to the shelters before dark, and they always bring back something choice for the smaller children who stayed behind.

AND THE CHILDREN

The day begins. Dzero-O comes to my fire ... his old body moves slowly this morning. He greets me: 'Tsamkwa /tge?' which means 'are your eyes nicely open?' I say, 'Yes, my eyes are nicely open, but my body still sleeps.' He tells me that when men become old like us their bones sleep for a while after their eyes have opened. It is the winter ... he is ninety-five and I am thirty-two, and the cold mornings, as always, are slow. People take time to visit, to sit together and talk, perhaps about yesterday's hunt, or whatever hopes they have for the day ahead.

We watch the little ones, Seka and //Nale/twago, who, having only recently mastered the art of walking, feel compelled to try out their balancing skills. They play on top of Magu while he sleeps in the morning sun ... they stand on his head, they walk and fall all over him, and their little voices crow with the delight of discovery of cause and effect whenever he grunts in response to their existence. Otherwise he just sleeps, for this is a lazy day.

With children the /Gwikwe have endless patience ... a child is to be indulged, not endured, and no child is ever excluded from the company of adults. For a /Gwi child, living within a group of families like ourselves is like having six sets of parents and as many brothers and sisters as any one child could want. So they just play from one shelter to the next, drawing off this never-ending source of human sustenance and comfort.

And the older ones – with boisterous voices and the bravado so typical of adolescents – would-be hunters Geamm and ⁄Qua⁄tgara head out and away from the shelters with the younger boys in tow. They speak more loudly than is necessary, for they are 'hunters', and the adults should take note that the hunters depart. We smile silently … nothing changes. My eyes follow the so familiar straight backs and lean young bodies as they fade into the bush followed by their own determined voices …

Geamm: 'I am a devil of a shooter, today I am hunting.'

⁄Qua⁄tgara: '⁄Tgooma the Gemsbok will fall today, and we will be eating plenty of meat.' And so it goes, and so they go.

Silence descends and the smile lingers. Woe betide any careless creature on the sand face today, I wonder that the entire mouse and lizard population of the Kalahari has not been wiped out. These /Gwikwe boys relate to hunting just as soon as they can walk, and by the age of six or seven are already accurate shooters, effectively making and using their own small bows and arrows. They hunt within a radius of about two miles around our shelters, and their prey is anything that moves. I think of their names, Geamm, 'little tortoise', and ⁄Qua⁄tgara, which translates into 'wanting sweet roots' … and so together they go hunting … 'little tortoise wanting sweet roots' … 'little tortoise wanting sweet roots' …

Dzero-O acknowledges the warmth we have shared at my fire. I watch his old, bent legs recede across the sand and I see the distance he has walked through his long life. His memories become my memories and I know of the Great Sand Face, and I know, too, that I love this old man. /Tehsa the Fire, the force that makes gentle and sanctifies the space between people, envelops me, and I dream for a while longer. I dream of knowledge that has receded in the face of ignorance, but which lies dormant and waiting in wild and sacred places for each of us … for each of you who seek to know … and you must go into these places and open yourself in a way that you have not done before, and what is yours will come to you. For this manner of communion in nature is the process by which we are bound in Spirit to all life, that which stands in service and sacrifice to humanity. Such is the human moral obligation to the whole living world.

//Gammsa the Sun has now warmed the cold sand face, and I see two of the women, Geutwe and /Gaiekwe, leaving with the sun on their backs, going west, probably towards Gantam//nau for the last of the sour berries. They say they know of a small patch of berries out near one of our winter hunting camps, which always ripen a month or so after the usual time ... I feel the sweet-sour taste in my mouth. They must hurry though, for the browsing antelope seek out the same leaves and berries at this time.

The older girls, Khaba and Abeh, will spend the day looking after the younger children, learning to fulfil the roles that they one day must as women and mothers ... their time for gathering and providing will come when it does.

I decide to spend the morning with the boys, and so follow to where we last heard their voices and then pick up their spoor in the sand. There are no secrets out here, the earth holds the memory of everything, of all the creatures that move upon it. One must only learn to see. I see them before they see me ... they are caught up in the spirit of the day, and so I follow and watch for a while ... lithe young bodies already synchronised into the desert rhythm ... urgent voices and bold intentions. A Bushman boy does not dream outside of his reality. When he grows up he will be a hunter, and he hopes, if for anything, to be a great hunter like his father. And they are so much like their fathers in all of their mannerisms ... Kuramatso, quick, volatile and explosive like his father Gening/u, the doctor – and Geamm, the little tortoise, who moves with a fluid confidence, unassuming and certain like his own father Tso/tgomaa, the hunter. They move quickly, silently, and the intensity with which they kill is as pure and definite as when we men kill a wounded gemsbok.

A thrown stick brings a Kalahari scrub robin to ground, and they stop to make a fire. *Tsk!* ... *tsk!* ... the bird's mate scolds vainly from a nearby bush until it, too, falls prey to the same missile ... and now there is food. Kuramatso darts away into the bush and returns with two sticks, one soft one hard, and proudly states that they will soon have a fire. Geamm produces a knife and cuts four flat planes onto the end of the hard male wood. They use the soft dry tinder from inside the nest to attract the spark from the deftly twirled fire sticks, and smouldering ash soon becomes flame surrounded by the boundless exuberance of boys living in freedom. They roast the birds on the coals and share the small meal among themselves.

My heart smiles at the uninhibited joy they express in exchange for the gift of life, delighting in the animated relationship they have with the world around them ... immersed in everything, secure in their own identities, they share one and the same reality ... unlike the children of modern civilisation who are presented with so many conflicting alternatives. It is so much simpler this way ... but for how much longer? I see the shadow of their future before it comes.

After a while they see me and we laugh together. I amble along in tow of their hunt, aware only of a strange nostalgia in my gut. It is almost as if everything that I see today, as on so many other days, is already something of the past. Do they know that they may never hunt the eland and the gemsbok about which they dream and shout today? Somewhere in my Soul I have been where they are. I know how their lives will change and of the pain that lies ahead, and that is my burden ... the knowing ... and they ... innocent rhythm moving across the sand ... I wish it could somehow be different. There is nothing to say, life will run its course as it has since the first awakening ... autumn runs into winter, and spring remains the eternal hope.

The voices continue ... 'There, under that //Xane bush ... that's Pelo's big giraffe there ... shoot it with an arrow ... I shot it, but my arrow went past ... what kind of bows are these that we are using? ... my arrow has broken ... give this boy another arrow, we have broken his ... '

'It has eaten my bow,' says Kuramatso when he misses. With six or seven arrows having found their mark, one very dead mouse looks decidedly more like a porcupine. Shrieking and whooping their victory, with the mouse brandished aloft on the end of Geamm's arrow, they race off in a new direction, to where /Damegu says he saw another very fat mouse just the other day ... again the voices trail behind and I, following, gather up the meanings like treasures left hanging in the air ... 'Pelo is at the back, we are running away from him' ... 'I am running very fast, you are just galloping' ... and the voices fade into the golden grass, redolent, rich with the wonder of life.

I return to the shelters and my fire, to sit and carve bushman images out of wood. Today is such a day for dreaming ... and sounds ... they drift around, inside and outside my head, across the sand between the shelters, wood on wood, scrapers on skin from behind Tso/tgomaa's shelter ... scraping and whistling, the blades stay sharp and we live! Geutwe's crowing laughter echoes gently through everything, that laugh we know so well, and which secures us to ourselves and to each other ... all these sounds. Little //Nale/twago's voice gurgling in her chest as she challenges the newest obstacle in her life. She is two years old and today she dances in a circle, stomping her little feet onto the Great Sand Face ... it is her idea of a healing dance, the rhythm and the harmony beautiful, instinctive. Dancing or hunting, both part of the same integrated whole which /Gwikwe children relate to from birth.

Denku music lifts and falls through the space between us ... somewhere a voice raised in anger, just for a moment, the women laugh and I see visions of distance and time, of forty thousand years in Seman/ua's eyes and all of us who live here in this Kgoatwe place with everything and each other, which we know so well even as it changes.

Some days are longer than others, and today the sun hangs, suspended in the middle of the sky ... just as their fathers would, the boys return to the shelters with the spoils of their hunt ... something to show the women and the girls. At this stage of their lives, success is still something to brag about, failure easily forgotten. Later in life their survival may depend on the difference. I remember when we killed //Ahmahma the Red Hartebeest only three miles from the shelters. Geamm and /Qua/tgara had come to help with the carrying of meat saying, 'We are old hunters who can walk any distance and never get tired.' So be it.

The smaller children, Seka, //Nale/twago and /Nana run excited circles around their older brothers, little hands insistently prodding and touching all the while. They must know about these things ... the age-old process of sensory education shows in their instinctive response to learn everything of their environment ... to grow and survive. /Nana, the oldest of the three ... a shy and sensitive little girl ... she is not strong. //Nale/twago, the second oldest, whose quest for life is powerful and vigorous, an energy that won't be tamed. And Seka, the youngest, the little bull, filled with a gentleness and concern for all things, and a strength that lies in tenacity and endurance. His present disadvantage in age puts him always two steps behind the others, but in the end it is not time that is important ... but life.

Aware of my eyes he turns away from his present endeavours, plods his little body across the sand towards me and stops a little way away. I say, 'Habe ... come,' and he walks with his shy little smile and plonks himself into my lap and the shyness disappears. He sits for awhile ... we both take what we need of each other and then he squirms off my lap and plods off towards some new attraction. Such is his day, continuously browsing from one source of sustenance to another.

His feeling stays with me and I know that I am home, and the dreaming continues ... my heart says ... listen carefully to the voices of your children, for everything lives in their laughter.

THE EARLY RACE

I hear Kamageh talking from somewhere behind the shelters … flowing guttural sounds punctuated with strong clicks. The people should know that he is going to check the snares, and so he talks more loudly than he needs to. I decide to follow him, my body now tired of dreaming and wanting to feel like a hunter again … I know that he wants the company. Kamageh is an old man who no longer hunts nor sets his own snares, but by checking snares for the other men and helping with the cutting and carrying of meat on most of the hunts, he ensures his keep in the band.

We walk west, away from the shelters towards that so familiar orange ball of late afternoon sun. A few words pass between us and then we walk silently, his right hand signalling every so often the spoor he recognises in the sand … three red hartebeest passed to the north, a duiker, a kudu bull gone west … but all a week or more old … nothing fresh, no big meat.

The excitement builds as we near the snares, that familiar hope that neither one of us voices. Perhaps we will be lucky today. The first snare is empty, it is /Gowsi's snare … and the second, the third … nothing. We walk west again and south, circling slowly back towards the shelters … only two more snares, both belonging to Tgoo. Tgoo is the snare man … often lucky. I have watched him laying snares and have learned from him, carefully and slowly … he is a man who says little but feeds his family well. Again we draw closer and the excitement grows … less sure now … only two more snares … something? … Yes! … /Gaema the Steenbok is caught and we run forward … it must die before fear lends it the strength to break from the snare. The !Goie rope holds fast … bleating … legs thrashing … horns and hooves are formidable weapons. A hunter must be sure, certain … no mistakes. Kamageh raises his stick and in that last moment of life /Gaema lies still in fear, pretending death … *thwack*! … *thwack*! … twice, and then it is over … food … Kamageh grunts … I watch. I am caught somewhere between the passion of my own living and the pain of another creature dying for that reason … but that's the way it is.

There is no emotion in death itself, and to presume otherwise would be to invent an unnecessary lie. There is empathy, but no sympathy or compassion for a wounded or dying animal ... it is a simple necessity to kill, and the cry of a dying animal only observes the triumph of the hunter ... a full belly means that we live. All creatures have the same chance of survival on the Great Sand Face, and no one begrudges victory or mourns death ... it is understood.

Kamageh folds the dead animal's back legs together, and then the front legs ... like a food parcel that can be conveniently carried, he hoists it across his shoulders and we follow our feet towards the shelters, I behind and he in front. The last snare is empty ... no matter. Kamageh with the steenbok on his back like a banner. He, who more than any of the others, is still so absolutely primitive in his ways, as if he were a throwback from the early race, the ancestors of today's Bushmen. And so we walk, an ancient hunter and his prey followed by another ancient hunter ... there is no gap between us, just a short stretch of sand with one feeling. Looking from behind, a man sometimes sees many things that he misses when looking backwards ... and so we walk, and the cry of the steenbok, like that of a child, hangs frozen in the space between our hearts and the world.

Our backs, already straight, become straighter as we walk in among the people and the shelters, the air fills with happy words ... tonight we eat! Some men and children gather behind Gening/u's shelter near the roasting pit, where freshly cut leaves and grass are laid down for the skinning.

Green, brown and blood, the last rays of evening sun cut through everything and the steenbok, binding all together in the eternal timeless ritual of life. The day would end, but not for us, for a fire burns in the roasting pit.

The girls soon tire of men's talk, and drift away to the smaller fires in front of the shelters and women's business to pass the time. Skinning and roasting is a man's work, and it will be a long while before the meat is ready for eating.

Tgoo is the owner of the animal ... he cuts the foreleg and says, 'The front legs of /Gaema are always thin ... only eland have big front legs ... shorten yourself (squat down) and hold,' ... and he asks, 'Why doesn't a male duiker get caught so that we men can drink fat?'

I think of how these people imbue all creatures with their own self-determination and will ... it comes from the clear comprehension that everything that lives on this earth is connected to soul in one way or another ... so instead of asking 'Why did you not catch a duiker?' a man will ask 'Why does a duiker not get caught?' ... thereby acknowledging that the duiker, too, has some control over the event of its own existence and its own death. These people do not give to the notion of having dominion and control over all creatures and all life ... 'dominion over' and 'relationship with' are two different things. They respond instinctively to the patterns and cycles that govern all the laws of life ... inadvertently aware of the relationships of cause, effect and consequence.

Gening/u says, 'Male steenbok and kudu both have penises with the foreskin back, and that's why they are so thin.' Dzero-O, the old man, says that //Gamahma the Great God has made it so that all the male animals are thin from chasing the female animals, who become fat and pregnant. One of the boys laughs shyly, and Gening/u says, 'Why are you hiding yourself and laughing? We men are always laughing.' And then he laughs from the belly, rich and strong as only a free man can laugh.

Tgoo says, 'The women staying here have plenty of food ... now we must kill young ones so that we can drink lots of fat.'

Gening/u says to /Gowsi, 'When you killed that male kudu, the females were fat and strong so they managed to run away, you should have left that devil of a thin male kudu and chased the fat females.'

/Gowsi says, 'Next time I will take my spear with me so that I can quickly kill the thin male and then chase the fat females.'

Gening/u says , 'You should have left that //Gama and just killed the females.'

... they laugh.

I see that the fire burns down ... the coals will soon be ready for roasting. The talk continues. 'Hit the horns off ... now turn it so we can take off the skin ... the hooves are always sharp.' Gening/u tells the boys, 'Go and pull some grass and then lay it down and put the intestines on it, they must be cleaned.'

The boys: 'Haa! This is the shit! ... Aah! These are male intestines ... let us milk them, we are men.' (The /Gwikwe differentiate between male and female intestines within the same animal ... the male intestines are the ones with the runny excrement in them, and those with the hard excrement in them are the female intestines.) They willingly clean the entrails so that they can roast them and eat their skin.

Kuramatso complains to his father about his young brother, 'Father, he does not want to share the intestines, he wants to eat them alone.'

'No,' says Gening/u. 'You must not say so ... you must share with all the children, you must all eat together.' Participating in this way, the boys learn at a very early age about skinning, and about the anatomy of the animals they will one day hunt.

'Muuuaah,' ... says Gening/u and everyone howls with laughter. 'Muuuaah' is a joke that we men all understand ... and in this instance he is teasing the boys by saying that this 'muuuaah' noise is the noise that their !Annsa (penis) will make when the foreskin is being pulled back, just like the steenbok's. The boys laugh the loudest, they always do ... it is good for them when they share a joke with the men. A joke like this would never be told in the presence of women ... it is simply a way of sharing the common reality of male anatomy ... so that each boy in relation to his own physical explorations knows that he is part of a male circle of understanding and safety ... there can be no shame and no confusion.

The steenbok skin is pegged out to dry, after which it will be scraped until it is thin enough to be softened for other use. The men make their hunting bags and loin cloths from steenbok skin, while the slightly larger skin from the duiker is used to make the front and back aprons worn by the women.

At last all is ready. /Gaema is lowered into the roasting pit and covered with hot coals, and we drift away to our fires ... our own and each other's.

Although tired from the day, we cannot sleep with the smell of roasting meat wafting on the wind-breath between the shelters … little fire-red groups of people in gentle anticipation of a meal … we humans of the Great Sand Face … the last people of Kgoatwe. Eight small fires in front of the shelters and the old man's fire in the middle … nine small fires that burn like one … /Tehsa, around whom we gather to cook our food and keep warm at night, whose light provides shelter in the darkness.

The ash and bone heaps scraped into a pile outside each shelter tell the story of our lives, and the size of the ash and bone heaps says that we people have lived in this Kgoatwe place for many moons. It was two years ago that we first came to this place … it seems like such a long time ago, almost another life …

We were four men and we had travelled for some days already, looking for a place that felt right … good veld food, plenty of animal signs in the sand … a place where they could feed their families and continue in their way … a place where we could live away from the ever-encroaching alternative of civilisation. For me it was the hope that they would stay away as far as possible from the life that I had left behind … neither dream would last forever. I remember that day.

And now, this is home … //Gau//gae … with the smell of roasting steenbok and the cold breath of night air, which every while blows colder and reminds us that we live … gemsbok skins drawn close around golden-brown bodies in the firelight … eyes that shine … voices low and sweet like wind … all joy and harshness interspersed, there is no difference, only the changing … like the smell of fire and the hope for water. Sounds in the air like one breath and the breathing of our bodies on the earth … voices and music carry the meaning of why we are here.

The fires burn and Seman!ua sings, his beautiful voice filled with the ancient soul of the First People … an aching sound that carries far across the desert face and into the memories of our deepest hearts.

Later we eat well-roasted steenbok and one by one we go off to sleep with our full bellies and our dreams ... dreams of nothing, which forget themselves in the morning because they are only dreams, and we still live here in Kgoatwe.

We awaken after the cold of the morning has passed and the day is already half lazy, people sitting around in small comfortable groups, picking the memories of last night's steenbok from their teeth. The after-images of a good event imbue this day with an optimism we all share ... today is a lucky day.

/Gaa roots roast in the coals of Dowgwi's fire, and the men fix their weapons ... it is always this way between hunts. Some arrowheads are bent from impact on bone, and must be straightened. A man does not like to hunt with less than four arrows in his quiver bag ... metal is a valuable asset and great care is taken to retrieve those arrows that miss their mark. The bushman hunting arrow, //Auusa, is a frail shaft of reed or other light wood, made up of five different parts but structured into two main sections. The longer back shaft breaks off when a wounded animal runs through the bush, leaving behind the shorter front section, which carries the poison. The function of the arrow is not to kill on impact, but simply to carry the poison into the animal. The longer back section of the arrow is usually found along the spoor when the hunters follow for the kill.

The hunting bow is about a metre long, with a bowstring rolled from the sinews of the upper back and neck of large antelope such as wildebeest, gemsbok and kudu. If the bowstring is made from gemsbok sinews, then it is /Tgooma the Gemsbok who will call more loudly to the arrows of the hunter, and when the bowstring is made from wildebeest, the arrows will more easily find their way to /Tehma. In olden times, before the use of metal, the arrows would be tipped with different animal bone and because of this they would call differently to the animals ... but that was in the olden time.

The arrows are carried in a bark quiver made from the root of an acacia tree. When heated, the bark separates from the root-core, which is then pushed out ... the ends of this hollow bark tube are then capped with the wet skin of a large antelope, which dries and shrinks onto the bark, and so the quiver is formed. The quiver, containing the arrows and fire sticks, a digging stick, a knife, snare ropes, the hunting bow and the spear, are all carried in a whole duiker or steenbok skin that hangs easily over the shoulder. A hunter must be prepared, his weapons strong and true, for in this world there is no substitute for lost opportunity.

/Gwikwe men have a respectful relationship with their weapons ... they handle them with a deference that implies that the weapon has its own life force. They comprehend the energetic nature of the weapon in relation to their own energy, knowing that their forces are channelled through the weapon, and that a man's feeling must always be true. In all human endeavours the underlying intent is always manifest, whether sooner or later ... what you think will come to be.

Gening/u is making a new handle for his scraper, and for this he uses the wood of the Hook thorn, the /Nooni tree. Last night he had asked Tgoo for the skin of the steenbok which we roasted. 'My son, ⱡQua/tgara, is becoming a man now, and so he must wear a man's clothing. If I have this /Gaema skin I can make a ⱡTaema for the boy, and then teach him how to hunt like a man.' Tgoo had given him the skin, for a boy must always be encouraged on his journey into manhood.

The younger /Gwi boys wear only a small covering skin in the front which they tie with a string around the waist. When they reach the age of twelve or thirteen and their testicles 'drop', they will begin to look at women with different eyes ... they will see them no longer as 'mothers' but as 'women'. This new awareness is noticed by the men who have those same feelings in themselves, and they know then that the time has come to acknowledge the growth of a boy into a man.

ⱡQua/tgara's friend Geamm has already seen the skin that his father Tso/tgomaa the hunter has put aside for him. He and his friend ⱡQua/tgara are equal in growth. They brag that 'mothers' are only for small boys, and that soon they will both be wearing men's clothing ... so be it ... the journey is long. A boy's passage into manhood is less formal than when a girl goes through puberty. For a boy it is a gradual growth, a slower 'coming into his body', and so a less eventful journey. From time spent helping with the cutting and skinning of animals, and from conversations among the men, he learns to understand the working of the male body. From his observations in the wild he has learned that seed becomes fruit. I remember as a boy, that I was excited by my growth and the changes in my body ... never fearful, but secretly proud.

For a girl it is a more powerful personal experience, bleeding from the centre of her body ... life-blood going out of her for the first time. If not held by the knowledge of older women, this could be a fearful time in her life. The understanding is further reinforced through the ritual of a puberty dance, an acknowledgement of the collective female spirit, and therein lies great comfort.

/Tguikwe the old lady chooses gatherings like this to talk – she rambles on about nothing and everything ... about the past, the present and the future as if it were all now, and perhaps it is all now ... the memory, the deed and the hope. No one really listens, but we are all here, and today she basks in that security. Her grandson, Seka, is scratching his fat little legs with the upper jawbone of a porcupine that he found on one of the bone heaps ... the old lady watches him, and her ramblings then take the form of a porcupine story ... a mood comes over her and she does a pantomime to show us just how a porcupine feeds. The porcupine says, 'Which shall I eat? ... Which shall I now eat? Shall I eat the /Gaa or the Nn!oduu root?' ... And so it goes on and the porcupine shuffles around undecidedly. Now everyone is listening and laughing as the old lady prances around the shelters like an ostrich saying, 'Olden-day ostriches ... olden-day ostriches ... oee ... ooee ... oooh ... olden-day ostriches,' ... she looks more like an ostrich than even a real ostrich does.

Three of the little ones, Seka, //Nale/twago and /Nana stomp around in her wake, shrieking and gurgling their own rendition of /Geruma the Ostrich, and /Tguikwe's wrinkled old body fills with feeling and energy as she struts ahead of the ragged little procession that wends its way around the shelters ... our hearts and our laughter. She is so beautiful, she is so old.

After telling me once or twice in the last few days that she has lost one of the earrings I had made for her, and showing me with much sadness the empty hole in her ear, I had taken the hint and made a replacement. A little breathless now from playing 'porcupine' and 'ostrich' she comes and sits her old body down next to mine. I show her the new earring and she crows her pleasure. She will probably lose it before too long ... but never mind, for today she is my mother. The other women sitting around examine it, all the while exclaiming how happy and pretty they would be if they, too, could have such nice earrings to wear, and I know with smiling resignation that before long I will oblige ... I will make many earrings.

As I thread the earring through /Tguikwe's old ear she tells the women how pleased she is, and then she goes on to remind me and everyone else that I am her son ... and that's why I always do these nice things for her. For /Tguikwe this little ritual ensures that what she says will come true. Although she will never say so, she does need to be taken care of. We sit holding one another, and her old gnarled hand rubs across my belly ... then she rubs her own wrinkled belly and says, 'See people! ... See how me and Paul touch one another ... we are just the same and we have the same blood, because Paul comes out of this old belly here.' The gnarled old hand rubs across the wrinkled old belly, and then she rubs me again to show that our flesh is one and the same. Her voice crows her pleasure and my pleasure, because I feel proud that these people are my family and this old woman is my mother, and all the people agree. This little ritual always brings the same feeling to us all, it helps us to remind ourselves that we are here in this Kgoatwe place together, and that we are all still equal.

Midday comes and old Dzero-O returns to the shelters ... each time I see him I think of the miles. He always comes so silently, with his walk as sure as it must always have been, for almost a hundred years now. And when I look at him, this old, absolute human creature, I know how it was on the sand face a long time ago when the world was clean, and there was only one way of life. It was in the time before the black man, the time before the white man ... it was the time of the Bushman.

He walks to the Old Man's Tree and his whole body seems to sigh as he comes to rest next to his fire. Dzero-O never comes empty-handed, and today his hunting bag is stuffed with bark from the roots of a sweet berry bush, which he will use for the colouring of skins. The root bark of this Kalahari taaibos is full of tannin, and the dark outer surface of the bark is scraped into a mixture of Bie juice and urine, and then painted onto the already cured and softened skin to make it a lovely rich red-brown colour.

The day passes comfortably ... talking and laughing as the shadows grow longer. //Gammsa the great, silent Sun has lost her fat and goes to the western horizon more quickly every day. I see the great star called //Xau Yede, which shines on the other side of the sky in early June when the cold first begins. It is Venus, both morning star and evening star, whose ray invokes the love and brotherhood between men on earth. Geutwe says that this star comes to take all the bad luck away ... but the winter will still be hard.

IN THE LIGHT OF THE DAY

In the morning I sit with Gening/u and Seman!ua in my shelter and we talk of a hunt three moons ago, and of /Tgooma the Gemsbok ... a remarkable antelope so well adapted to the heat in this waterless environment.

Body temperatures in the summer can rise so high that overheated blood will cause damage to the animal's brain cells, and so, to facilitate its survival, the gemsbok's breathing anatomy has undergone an important adaptation. Before passing through the brain the blood is cooled by circulating through an extensive network of capillaries in the animal's nasal passages, thus protecting its sensitive brain from excess heat.

In all the Kingdoms of Nature there is constant expression of the synergy between all forms of life ... every life force and form in perpetual support of the principle of sustainability, for nothing survives outside of this active principle.

Another remarkable adaptation here in the Kalahari, is in the hydroscopic grass species. These grasses contain only a very small percentage of water during the heat of the day, but then, by absorbing atmospheric moisture at night, they miraculously rehydrate to hold as much as fifty per cent fluid. This adaptation by the plant kingdom for the good of the animal kingdom makes it possible for many desert antelope to live completely independent of water, and /Tgooma the Gemsbok is one of the many who graze during the cool hours of darkness.

//Annsa melons, gemsbok cucumbers and several surface plants, along with the many plants with underground storage organs or tubers for moisture, together make the Kalahari Desert less precarious an environment than is generally believed. And if anything, it is the lack of surface water that is the primary reason for the fortuitous isolation of the last wild Bushmen. But that, too, is changing ... the greed for minerals and other resources that translate into material wealth continues to attract the attentions of that soulless part of modern humanity which destroys without creating, which takes without giving ... that aspect of modern humanity that denies the world of Spirit, unthinkingly feeding that dark force, which inexorably pushes life to the brink of extinction in the name of greed and power.

Hard words these, but how can we stop the destruction? Only when we come to the understanding that there is no way forward but through the realm of Spirit, and begin to rebuild that which we have destroyed both inside and outside of ourselves ... only in this way can we re-enliven the dying earth. We modern humans have exploited every resource available to us for so long and in every possible way ... a way of life that apparently secures our position of tenure and control. For so long have we misused the earth and all that lives upon it, and yes, in so doing we have accumulated more wonderful and varied wealth than ever before in our known history. We have surrounded ourselves with unparalleled cultural abundance … and yet, deep within the human Soul, that feeling of emptiness persists, and with it the insecurity that compels us to the futile chasing of illusions, of rainbows we have no hope of catching. How, in deed, do we lift to heaven that which has fallen to earth?

Seman!ua pushes his hands into his armpits, which he says are burning, and the burning tells him that the hunters who went out this morning have been lucky, and they will soon return to the shelters. He is a gentle and deeply sensitive young man, his eyes always brimming with words that do not come easily from his mouth. We talk a little more and then Seman!ua says that he, too, feels the urge to hunt … and so he leaves.

This thing of presentiment, or the tapping of forces as the people call it, is a very real thing. It is no magic or super-consciousness of being, only a very real contact with yourself and your surroundings … a reading of your own life-body and the life-body of the earth.

Gening/u and I sit in silence for a while. Time passes, and we hear quiet voices behind /Nedu khu kwe's shelter … the other hunters have returned. The voice of Tso/tgomaa says, 'When next I am in the valley, I will go to the licking places and dig up some poison to share with you.'

And the voice of /Nedu says, 'Long ago I used to shoot fat gemsbok, but I don't know what has gone wrong these days … when we pass through the licking places I will show you where I once saw a very fat gemsbok.'

Early this morning both he and Tso/tgomaa had gone from the shelters before the rising of the sun. /Nedu went north to where the valley begins going eastwards from Kgoatwe pan, and Tso/tgomaa hunted further to the east, around the licking places where some of the larger antelope look for salt in the small pans at the bottom end of the same valley. It is because of the salt that the water holds in the sand for many moons, and that is why the much-favoured Kanna plant grows only in this valley.

Both men have returned, and now each one sits alone ... each man still inside the memory of his own hunt and the feelings that begin somewhere in the belly and then move up and out through his body like a web of energy that links him to everything and to the animal who carries the poison from his arrow. The hunter cultivates and holds this sympathetic relationship with the animal ... after wounding an animal he returns to the shelters to be alone, just the hunter and the hunted, and the line of energy, which separates them and joins them together all in the same feeling ... and in this way they are bound together in time-space.

They face the same alternatives in their quest for survival on the Great Sand Face ... one must kill to live and the other must die so that the one can live, and that which lies between them is the paradox that separates life and death until the moment they come together. Both victor and vanquished know there is no real difference between life and death, only a moment they share. And when the moment has passed and the hunter returns, he carries those feelings within himself, and only those who have known that feeling will see how it is with the hunters when they return from the hunt. They sit quietly for there is nothing to say ... the way they sit and the tiredness in their bodies are enough. Written in their eyes is the story of heat and miles and life and death ... it is not a new story.

The poison on their arrows works slowly, and sometimes it takes as long as twenty-four hours before a large antelope is sufficiently weakened for the hunters to run it down. Tso/tgomaa and /Nedu khu kwe will remain aloof from the people tonight ... they will not share in any feasting or games, neither will they play with their children, nor sleep with their wives. If a hunter indulges himself at a time like this, by bragging or otherwise, he will weaken himself, and as he weakens his quarry becomes stronger. He must maintain his psychic link with the wounded animal, so that in the morning, when they take up the blood spoor, they will find the animal weak and close to the place where it was shot ... and as they draw nearer, hunter and the hunted, the line between them becomes stronger, and both man and animal feel it in the same way as it pulls them closer and closer still, drawing them into that single moment in which only one of them can be lucky.

The old man Dzero-O says that a hunter must leave the //Annsa melons and the /Gaa roots alone while hunting, 'A man must keep the dryness in himself, and then the animal too will be thirsty ... and if a hunter eats //Annsa melon then the strength from the melon will go into the animal and the poison will surely lose its strength, and the animal will run far while the hunters become weaker ... and the people will not eat.' A man with a full belly does not hunt like a man with hunger. And he says, 'A man must not eat the meat of a springbok when he has shot his arrow into another animal, lest the wounded animal takes on the manner of the springbok and walks far during the night, for the springbok walks far in the night, and when the sun rises it will be in a different place from the place where the hunter first found it.'

Dia!kwain of the /Xam Bushmen said that when we show respect to the game, we act in this manner ... because we wish that the game may die ... for the game would not die if we did not show respect to it.

If a hunter shoots an animal and is asked about it, he will never reply in the affirmative ... he will not presume success before the kill. He will only say, 'Men, I think I have wounded an animal, I am not sure ... perhaps if we go tomorrow and follow the spoor we may find the animal ... and if we kill it ... then we are lucky,' ... no expectations ... no prejudice. This spoken philosophy is a way of softening any possible disappointment, for it is not always that we are lucky. So today, no one talks about the hunt ... it is not yet finished.

The women sense by their men's behaviour whether or not they have succeeded in wounding an animal, and today the feeling in their bodies causes them to sing and then to dance ... //Annsa yeeah, the melon dance. It is just a feeling, for no one knows of tomorrow ... but today the women dance. The

/Gwikwe call all dances and songs 'yeeah', which literally means 'step', and this dance, //Annsa yeeah, or the melon dance, is one of the oldest traditional women's games. The first song is called the honey song … Dauginii. The women say that it is Geutwe's song because she is the one who first sang it, before showing the others how to sing the song too.

The story goes … that when Geutwe was a little girl of five, which was in the 1920s, there was a young hunter who one day went to take honey from a bees' nest. This young man was proud and so he did not wait for the right time to take honey. On the day that he went to the bees they were making honey, and so they became angry and stung him all over. When he came back to the people they could see that his face was all swollen up, and because he looked so funny they laughed at him and made up a song to tease him … and so that is how this story came to be 'the honey song'. A man should have his eyes nicely open when he takes honey from the bees, for we all live on the earth … the animals too. We have all walked far, we have all known hunger and thirst, and we all share equally in God's gifts.

The /Gwikwe will tease anyone who has been the victim of a not-too-serious misfortune. This, for them, is a way of making light of something that might otherwise be taken too seriously … a way of sharing and keeping all things equal, thereby re-ensuring the harmony and stability of the whole band. To be reminded thus of the broader perspective is all it ever takes to maintain the balance in all of our lives.

They finish Dauginii, the honey song … clapping and dancing … the familiar sound of happy woman laughter, draws us together … and so it is that in the sharing of a story, of a day, we are drawn closer to one another, and 'one another' becomes 'ourselves' and all things are then equal, because today is just such a day …

… and then begins a song called /Gede, which is a very old traditional song for melon dancing. The women say that this is the original melon dance song, sung by the olden-day women. /Gede is another /Gwikwe word for

//Xann, or melon ... it is a word from the old language.

In this dance the women move in a circle, clapping and singing ... whoever holds the melon does her own improvised dance step and then throws the melon backwards over her shoulder, under her arm, or between her legs to the woman behind, who must catch it. Whoever drops the melon suffers the laughter and teasing of the other dancers ... and so it goes, each woman in turn doing her own dance interpretation of the story being sung, while the others clap and sing their accompaniment. In the dry season, when there are no melons, they will dance with a nice round tuber ... for always the women will dance.

I see that //Gama does not dance the melon dance with the other women today, she busies herself with small things around her shelter ... sweeping the ash from last night's fire onto the ash heap, to the side but in front of the entrance. She and her husband /Gowsi had talked long into last night ... for it seems that there is some unhappiness between them, and we could hear their voices in the deepening darkness.

But for now, the women dance ... human forms moving, talking, laughing ... and I see only beauty expressed in freedom.

Some songs are favourites, and these they sing for much longer than others, but whenever one of the women suggests a new song, they all, out of courtesy, give it a try ... and then if the singing falters after a short while because it is not such a good song, they begin with a new one. There is such energy today and the women sing many songs. They sing // //Gam // //ade – the flying ant song, and they sing /Outsi/noro – back-of-the-head feathers ... about a bird with feathers on the back of its head, which calls early in the morning. It is an old /Gwikwe song ... the song of the crested barbet. They sing the eland song, /Tede kham, and this too is an old song. The word /Tede comes from the ancient tongue, it is the word for eland ... the greatest of the antelopes. Today the word used for eland is Geuma for the male, and Geusa for the female ... and on this day the stories and the songs go on and on.

I sit and watch beneath clouds in the sky like giant beings forming our thoughts and our world, and my smile feels to me like the first smile that ever came to a man's lips ... and from moments like this I know that somehow I will always know these moments ... and the smile will not fade.

I feel the red Sun, //Gammsa, as she sits on the horizon and paints her last warmth onto the side of my naked body and on my face and onto the Great Sand Face ... and she paints the bodies of the women who dance golden-red ... dancing and prancing ... lithe dusky creatures who live and share the earth.

... and the women sing a new song, and they dance the melon dance and they dance the melon dance and the red sun goes down and then it is gone.

The Great Sand Face would sleep.

At the time of the red morning sky we follow Tso/tgomaa to the place where he wounded the animal ... I walk behind, still carrying the night and my dreams in my head ... this land does strange and powerful things to people. The last week has been one of pain for me, so many things from within have been wrenched to the surface and exposed to me and all around me ... memories from my deepest Soul. Gening/u says that I have been crying in my sleep, and sometimes roaring like a lion. I feel so strange ... memories of an ancient Self ... my Soul through many lives ... but in this strangeness I grow stronger.

We are five men, for /Gowsi does not hunt with us today ... he says he has no luck after last night and the disagreement with his wife, //Gama. The animal we hunt has weakened through the night, and before long we find and take up the blood spoor ... it is /Tehsa the Wildebeest, and we see from the sand that she is slow ... undecided ... for the poison boils in her blood. She has not walked far, and the sand is still cool under our feet when we find her, alone and angry ... she sees us and runs ... we chase ... running ... one ... two miles, fast ... our hearts drumming like wildebeest hooves on the dry Kalahari earth ... we pass the herd ... they startle and run ... not many animals ... like the fingers on a man's two hands.

Gone are the olden days when great herds of wildebeest ran like waves of grass over the Great Sand Face ... gone ... gone ... and /Tehsa ... now she has no more strength ... she stops and turns to face the hunter ... we hold our spears ... today we eat. And in this dying there is no sadness, no ending, for the forces that give rise to the form ordain in each creature its purpose and symbiosis with all other life ... and in every dying there is a living.

Tso/tgomaa makes the first cut on the knee for the passing of the animal Soulspirit. We drink from the body fluid of the animal, squeezing liquid from the undigested grass in the stomach ... rich and green-yellow, it brings strength into our tired limbs. He throws the gallbladder onto the sand, saying with uplifted tongue that we should always hunt like this and be lucky. This is a respect ritual, which every /Gwi hunter calls to the elemental beings and the Soul of the dead animal when he makes a kill ... '/Tehsa ... you must die for us, you must always die like this ... we must be lucky like this all the time, killing you and eating you so that we can be fat ... you must die from our arrows and our spears ... that is how you must die.' This old observance stems from the time when humans understood the inner workings of the body, they knew that what was thrown out with the gall bladder was everything unwanted by the animal body, everything that was not to be consumed by the human.

Kamageh goes back to the shelters and returns with the some of the women ... they will help to carry the meat. It is unthinkable for /Gwikwe to eat alone, and back at the shelters the meat is fairly distributed so that even the less fortunate hunters and their families receive meat from the hunt. Everything is used ... the bones for marrow, the intestines for roasting, the horns for work implements, and the skin for clothing, sandals or thongs.
From this time on, life will become more difficult. Already the plant foods are scarce ... the melons will soon be bitter and the berries no more. The

large antelope are no longer as plentiful as they once were … the big herds
of yesteryear have gone. Winter comes … and the dryness.

THE SOFTENING OF THE SUN

The days drift past like a string of memories … the moon becomes hollow,
the south wind finds the strength to return and the nights become cold, and
we who are sometimes so much smaller than the wind, we stay in our shelters
in the mornings, around our fires, until //Gammsa the Sun has begun to
warm ⁄Guam/tge, the cold sand face.

From inside my shelter I watch Dzero-O under the Old Man's Tree … he
whiles away the cold hours playing /Ehnuma at his fire, and the melody
hangs softly in our hearts, as gentle and infinite as his Soul.

Our shelters face inwards in a rough circle, and in the centre of our lives is
the old man, who, simply by the integrity of his relationship with himself,
the earth and the cosmos, sanctifies the space between and around us, and
our lives. I watch his contentment, and wish that it could one day be mine,
for I know that I look upon the most human of beings I shall ever have the
honour of knowing … and if anyone epitomises the fundamental nature of
the First People, then it is this man … Dzero-O.

I think of how there were once other men, old hunters living on the southern
tip of Africa, who told their stories to a man called Wilhelm Bleek … while
at that same time a young hunter called Dzero-O was walking here on the
Great Sand Face two thousand miles to the north, and today, here among
us, he still gives living context to those old stories. I am in awe of this bigger
picture, and the knowledge that the past lives always in the present … joined
by our memories and stories.

Aiee! … these people of the Great Sand Face … born of the earth, they
live on the earth … they laugh, they dance, they eat and sleep on the earth.

Always the contact with one common reality ... ⧸Guam⧸tge ... and if this is where I come from ... then this is where I wish to be.

Today is a lazy day. We sit around working skins, fixing weapons, talking, eating and smoking. Tgoo roasts and eats a small tortoise he picked up on yesterday's hunt. The shell he will use to make a spoon for his wife Geutwe, for she has asked for a spoon. Seman⧸ua plays softly on his thumb piano and the sun stands in the middle of the sky.

The sun crosses the sky ... I go with Tgoo, Seman⧸ua and Kamageh to check the snares. We find a steenbok still living in one of Tso⧸tgomaa's snares ... Kamageh clubs it once ... twice ... and then silence ... the cry for life always cuts and echoes in my heart. He takes it back to the shelters while Tgoo, Seman⧸ua and I continue.

In the late afternoon we see something caught in one of Tgoo's snares and run with excitement ... it is a young hartebeest bull ... already dead. We skin the animal, sometimes talking and laughing softly, but mostly quiet with our thoughts. Tgoo and his son Seman⧸ua are both shy by nature and say little in words. Seman⧸ua has a stutter, and I tell him that I, too, had difficulty speaking when I was a child ... and so I understand his silence. There are days that his eyes are filled with words, and I remind myself to watch, to listen to the silence and remember how it was those countless times when I could not speak my words into the world.

We take the meat back to the shelters, and the people eat well.

Just a few days later they find an ostrich caught in one of their snares ... ostrich meat is a favourite, and everyone talks of ⧸Geruma. There is a small disagreement over a favourite portion of the meat, but this is quickly masked by raucous laughter as ⧸Tokwa struts across the sand like an angry ostrich, perfectly mimicking the actions of a real ostrich. These people are so apt at caricaturing ... anything that moves is fair game.

The boys play one of their own games called Ostrich versus Steenbok. The game is a challenge between two individuals, or between individuals in opposing teams, and consists of fast movements of strike and feint with sleight of voice and hand. It is played until there is only one survivor. This leads to their favourite game, Steenbok versus the Spear ... an age-old challenge between the hunter and the hunted ... strike ... reflex and focus ... pull ... strike ... feint ... strike! strike! ... to the untrained eye, a fast confusion of movements and expletive sound effects imitating the sounds and actions of the animals emulated in the challenge ... and they continue thus, inside their controlled cacophony of energy until Geamm, the little tortoise, emerges as the victor, but also the victim of a raging thirst ... the consequence of youthful enthusiasm in a dry season.

Night falls and the cold draws us back into ourselves, to that place where we consider the flame within.

EYES NICELY OPEN

It is a long walk and we leave before the dawning of the day ... Tso/tgomaa the hunter takes Gening/u, myself and Kamageh to where he saw a bees' nest during the past summer. He says he had followed the voice of 'the bird who asks for the help of man', and now she waits for his return. And he has waited until now to rob the nest to give the bees a chance to build up a good supply of honey for the winter. We go northwards towards Kgoatwe, ever drawn by our anticipation ... until the smell of warm honey, redolent in the morning sunlight, pulls us closer to the honey tree ... a smell as wonderful as the first taste of pleasure. I am enchanted at how smell seems to hang in pockets in the air ... following slow air currents like threads of colour, each with its own meaning and message ... weaving its way into questing nostrils breathing each scent-filled memory into the back brain, which says instantly that this is one thing and that is another.

The /Gwikwe believe that a man with sharp eyes does not get stung, and so we take no precaution against the thousands of bees. By 'sharp eyes' they do not mean having good eyesight, but rather to have eyes that are open, that are able to see and know what they are looking at ... for there is, indeed, a right time to take honey from the bees. And so, chopping an entrance hole into the trunk of the tree just below the nest, we stand enveloped in a huge cloud of bees, mesmerised into calmness by the hum of thousands upon thousands of wings beating in unison, perhaps forty thousand bees in all. To stand thus, safely inside the swarm, one must be as if in a trance, a softer state of consciousness ... held in faith and knowledge of the Soul of living creatures and the laws of nature.

A soft *trrrrr* ... and another, reminds us that a certain sharp-billed honeyguide waits in the tree shadows, and it is she who asks that we open the bees' nest.

The synchronised force expressed by forty thousand bees compels one to a state of absolute reverence, and in this way we are held within the group-Soul of the whole hive ... the collective bee mind, which, if given cause, can change in an instant. And when this 'mind' changes it is not that one bee becomes angry and then tells the other bees, who all become angry in turn ... it is the whole collective Bee-Soul, which responds in the same way in the same moment ... one unified mind that holds and directs the mood of the hive. In this condition we humans are set apart from the animal kingdom, for we each have our own individual Soul and mind, and so each our own choosing with its own set of consequences.

Inside the hollowed trunk the honeycombs hang in deliberate alignment with the earth's magnetic field, a multitude of beautiful hexagonal cells reflecting a design impulse nothing short of miraculous. Each cell constructed for queen, drone or worker ... the type or gender determined solely by the feeding or withholding of pollen-rich honey at critical times in the development of the young bee larva in the cell. And none but this hexagonal shape could so effectively support the enormous weight of honey in the combs, while at the same time maximising the available space within the tree trunk ... this six-angled form that grows out of the earth as quartz crystal ... a geometric blueprint repeating itself through many of nature's forms.

And the simple fact of honey, produced from the life-effort of this singular insect, is a wonder of wonders ... to think that the honey that fills a man's two hands comes from a thousand bees flying as much as ten thousand miles to collect the offering of nectar and pollen from a million flowers or more. One can only stand in awe of the host of small lives given to this sacrifice, and offer thanks for this nectar of gods and humans since the time of Beginning.

It is a good time to rob the nest, for the honey is still fat at this time. We take as much as we can for the other people and for the women, but leave enough for the bees to survive the rest of the winter. The little honeyguide now flutters into the open nest for her share of larvae and comb ... there is enough, and she has waited. It is a wonderful relationship between man and bird ... this little flying creature who so insistently leads the hunter to the bees and then sits politely, with no more than the occasional *trrrrr*'d reminder that she waits. It will be a sad day indeed when there are no more free men to open wild bee nests, and no one to hear the voice of the honeyguide. And yes, it is true that a man with sharp eyes does not get stung ... and the honey song, Dauginii, which the women sing, says that there is a line between the deep respect that comes with knowledge and the arrogance of foolish pride ... and just as we take honey today, so must a man do all things ... utterly committed to the task, with respect for the other life, and the relationship of faith that it entails.

We return to the shelters and I give generously of my share to /Tguikwe, my old mother, and the rare sweetness paints a joyous smile on her wrinkled face. It is an old proverb which says that 'honey to the body is as wisdom to the soul'.

As with all things, she becomes older with each passing moon. 'My eyes are fading, I am an old woman,' she says. She spends more and more time in her own shelter, in silence with her dreams and her fire ... now close to eighty-five years old ... she is proud and will not become a burden to the people. It is good that we /Gwikwe live with the old ones ... a reminder that none of us is above the laws of nature.

In the dark sky before morning I look out from my sleep, and there she sits, tending her memories and the small fire in the entrance of her shelter ... the flame still burns. I see the sickle moon with no belly rising alongside the planet of Jupiter, which shines the impulse of wisdom into the world of humans. I ask that the flame in my soul reach ever upwards to spirit.

OLDEN-DAY OSTRICHES

Because old people require little sleep, it is /Gwikwe tradition that the old bachelors sleep in the open, surrounded by the other shelters, from where they can best keep watch at night. The tree, situated in the middle of the circle of shelters, under which Dzero-O sleeps, is now called the Old Man's Tree. /Tguikwe says that Dzero-O is at least ten years older than she ... she remembers him as a young hunter when she was still a small girl ... and now he sits, all of ninety-five years old, this fine old man who carries his miles in wisdom. He no longer participates in the longer and more rigorous hunts with the young men, but still remains useful to the band in so many other ways.

I greet him quietly as I approach his fire, 'Tsamkwa /tge? ... Are your eyes nicely open ?' I ask. 'Kiri kwa /tge,' he replies, my eyes are nicely open.

The sand face warms a little, and he tells me that today he digs for poison ... the poison grub //Ua chorooma, which /Gwi hunters have used to poison their arrows for as long as they can remember ... and so we go. I walk behind him, towards the northeast and into the rising sun ... there is no hurry ... it is a day for learning. He talks of many things, gently and easily ... he shows me the spoor of //Guama the male duiker, shy and elusive. He talks of the animal's character and habits, and all this he reads in the sand. He shows me how //Guama changes his mood and the pattern of his walk when there is another male duiker in his territory ... the spoor becomes deeper and the animal takes shorter steps.

And then he stops and rubs the back of his right shoulder. '/Nee, Paul, look, /Geruma ... do you see, do you see the ostrich?' He points into the distance ahead and I see nothing ... I look, and still I see nothing.

I say to Dzero-O, 'We have not seen the ostriches for six moons now, not since they finished the sweet berries and left none for the people.'

And he says, 'Look, Paul, look with long eyes, and you will see a big male ostrich running away from the morning sun, across that patch of open sand under a Giraffe thorn tree with a curved trunk ... look nicely and you will see.' I look but I see no ostrich and I see no such tree.

He says, 'Habe ... come, I will show you.' And so then we walk for three hours in a straight line towards where the old man sees /Geruma ... we walk for twelve miles, and there in the sand, just three hours old, lies the spoor of a big male ostrich ... and it was running, just as Dzero-O said ... away from the morning sun, across a patch of open sand and under a Giraffe thorn tree with a curve in the trunk.

He stands quietly, waiting for me to finish with my thinking. Again he rubs the back of his right shoulder, and tells me how he could feel the ostrich itching in his body ... how he could feel it was running ... and then he could see where it was. The ancient clairvoyance is still strong in this old man, and he is able to read the feelings in his body as pictures, and then bring them to cognition. He says how he feels each animal in its own way in a different part of his body, and that, when I have been away, he feels me returning in the palm of his left hand, and so he always knows when I am coming. I think that nothing in my life has given me a greater sense of belonging than this simple revelation.

All life is, indeed, interconnected to the extent that any displacement of energy caused through thought, word or deed has a ripple effect into the surrounding life-body of the earth, and this impulse is felt in one way or another by all living creatures, either less or more consciously. And that is the way in which the old man sees the ostrich.

I begin to comprehend the depth of his relationship with the earth ... an intimate companionship without boundaries ... communion on a level as profound as life itself ... a sharing of common truth that I begin to comprehend. All the animal forms ... the gemsbok, the lion and the ostrich echo thus within ourselves as human types, and in this correspondence we open a whole world of understanding in ourselves in Nature. And this is how it always was with the First People, in the time when there was only one language that was spoken by all of God's creatures, a language still heard and spoken by some of the old people, and I, coming from a place ahead in time, know that this language has already been forgotten. I resolve to search for the wisdom to somehow be a bridge between this simple truth and the place from which I come ... the place of forgetting. In this world, there is a universal language ... a language of absolutes, and if ever we pray for anything, let us pray that we remember.

When Dzero-O was a boy, back in the 1880s, there lived a man called //Kabbo on the southern edge of Africa, and this man //Kabbo told the same story of how the language of the Soul speaks through the body of the Bushman.

The bushman's letters are in their bodies ... they speak, they move, they make their bodies move. A man is altogether still when he feels that his body is tapping. A dream speaks falsely, it is a thing which deceives. The presentiment is that which speaks the truth.

The bushman, when an ostrich is coming and is scratching the back of its neck with its foot, feels the tapping in the lower part of the back of his own neck; at the same place where the ostrich is scratching.

The springbok, when coming, scratches itself with its horns, and with its foot, then the bushman feels the tapping. He feels a tapping at his ribs; he says to his children, 'The springbok seem to be coming, for I feel the black hair on the sides of the springbok.'

This tapping is like the beating of the heart in different places in the body. The beatings tell those who understand them which way they are not to go, and which arrow they had better not use.

They inform people where they can find the person of whom they are in search ... which way they must go to seek him successfully.

When a woman who has gone away is returning to the house, the man who is sitting there, feels on his shoulders the thong with which the woman's child is slung over her shoulders ... he feels the sensation there.

//Kabbo explained that the soft beatings in their bodies, here described, are the Bushman's 'letters', and they resemble the letters which take a message or an account of what happens in another place.

Some miles later Dzero-O sits on his heels to examine the spoor of /Gaesa, a female steenbok. He says that the animal's stomach is tight and so she walks with a strange, stiff movement. Her droppings will be constipated and held together ... not loose as they should be. We follow the steenbok for a short while before Dzero-O says, 'Come, Paul ... let us dig for poison.' He kneels at the base of a small, nondescript, spiky bush and begins to dig.

I ask, 'Why this bush?' and he shows me the beetle droppings in the sand, each just the size of a grain of sand ... I see. The //Ua beetle, after eating the leaves of this bush, soon after the rainy season, burrows down under the earth's surface where it forms a small mud cocoon, or Choroo, into which the beetle lays an egg ... the egg hatches to larva, and in the stomach cavity of this larva breeds a bacteria that is the poison. It is only this bush, the African myrrh (*Commiphora africana*), that is eaten by the Diamphidia beetle ... no other bush and no other beetle.

Of the sand beneath the bush he asks, 'Can I see this poison so that I can dig it out ... why does it not come out ... am I not going to shoot in the future?' Gently he digs until he finds the cocoons, each the size of a small fingernail. He holds them in the palm of his left hand, and says that the poison is 'hot' ... he feels and sees the life force emanating from the cocoons. Everything that lives has its own energetic impulse seen in light-colour and felt in heat-coolness, which indicates its characteristics and inclinations ... is it food, is it medicine, or is it poison? Each plant has its own voice, and to read or tap from this residual source of knowledge is simply to immerse oneself in the space that lies between all that is visible, into that realm that holds the memory of all life since the beginning ... the realm that holds the spiritual energetic residue of every mineral, plant, animal and human, of every thought and word and deed ... the collective memory of all that ever was and is. To read this is the process of presentiment, of clairvoyance, and more or less conscious, we humans have in us the means to this end, or this beginning.

I ask him how the old people first knew where to find this poison, and he says that they always knew ... from the time when the people could hear the earth speak, they always knew ... when they first dug out this //Ua choorooma they could see that it was 'red' and so they knew that it was poison. In that earlier time of atavistic clairvoyance the memory was carried in blood, and so the memory of great-grandfathers was passed through the fathers and to the sons in the blood, through generation after generation. And when a man says that he knows because his grandfather knew before him, then he speaks a truth, for he carries in his blood the unconscious memory of his father's fathers.

We modern humans are no longer connected to our forebears in this way, we do not inherit the memory and knowledge of our forefathers ... our way of coming to knowledge is through our own seeking and doing, and by conscious choice.

I know that if I am to understand the invisible in the way that these people do, I must seek not in my world of intellect, but in their world of imagination ... and there I will find the way to read the wisdom of the world ... the language of which is embedded, spoken into the inner being of man ... it is ours to know.

And in the sand circling closely around the bush is the spoor of the female steenbok ... she, too, has stopped here, to eat of the small pinkish-red berry-like fruits. Just a handful of these will warm and loosen her stomach says Dzero-O.

In this one small nondescript bush so much of the circle of life ... a poison to harm and a fruit to heal ... and more ... he scrapes some of the gum and resin that exudes from the bark into a small piece of skin that he folds and places carefully into his bag. This, he says, he will give to the women to mix with their perfume, which they keep in small tortoise shells in their shelters. While walking he collects some of the bark of the Hook thorn. The sap will be mixed with the poison grub into a paste for use on the hunting arrows.

I follow the old man in silence, awestruck by what this earth is for all of us ... the absolute truth of it. And if we ask what truth is, then surely it is not only that which we know ... for that which we do not know is also true. We walk in the constant reminder that every living thing has purpose ... all in complete symbiosis ... all things unified. Who, indeed, can deny the immaculate structuring of life through all the kingdoms of nature ... and who can deny the Creator?

From whence come the voices, which tell a man that one plant is poison and another is the antidote? This knowledge has not come about from random foraging through the ages, it derives from a source of wisdom that is both real and absolute. So what ignorance makes us modern humans believe that we cannot know and share in this wisdom? What dark force lures us away from our true nature? The answers to many questions are ours for the asking.

What forces of nature so wonderfully interpenetrate all that we see, hear, touch and smell ... what is it that so obviously lives in the invisible? These are the Elemental beings, the Nature Spirits, and by extending our reverence and awe into the realm of nature we give life to these Spirits ... of Fire, Air,

Earth and Water. It is our veneration that redeems their very existence and purpose on this earth, and which, in days gone by, evoked their support in our lives. When one fears or denies the existence of these Spirit Beings one becomes prone to a retribution in this life or the next ... but manifest it will, this retribution, for our foolishness does not go unnoticed.

It is for us, now, to come to the truth of that which will assist humanity on the path of evolution, to know the nature of the power that governs our world. Forces of spirit and earth give rise to forests, jungles, oceans and deserts ... everything that humanity could ever want, and all this as sacrament to the evolving human Soul. And on our path of slow learning, what terrible things we do in the name of greed and power. What is it that will bring us to choose our way in wisdom? How much more darkness before we see the light of life? And these children of the First People ... what do they hold in trust for us? One by one, we sever the last threads of hope and memory ... soon there will be nothing left.

We talk of many things on the journey back to the shelters, but more than anything from this old man I learn in stillness to see into the vast invisible world around me, and in my breath to embrace the air that holds soft and alive our planet ... the substance of life within which we all live and are joined one to the other to all ... coming to know the nature of myself, and my place in the symbiosis between the physical and the spiritual ... my purpose between heaven and earth.

I walk with small feet behind a man whose purity of soul draws me like a golden thread.

A LONG STORY

//Gammsa the Sun goes to rest and we gather in circles around fires. In any /Gwikwe place there are several fires constantly burning inside or in front of each shelter, and frequently a communal fire. During the day the women sit around the fire while they cook, talk and watch the children, and at night the men sit, to talk of the hunt, of animals, of friends and relatives in other places. Fire for warmth and fire for light, for dancing and the telling of stories ... so many stories ... by word to pass on through countless generations the unwritten literature of all the Bushman peoples.

It has been too often assumed by modern humanity that only what was written could be true. Spoken words, the stories and legends passed from generation to generation, were thought only to be quaint folk- and fairy tales ... as if they could not contain the truth. This was and is a thoughtless perception of world history, for the oral traditions that record the human journey do remain faithful to the truth when told from person to person, passed from mind to mind. The fundamental facts remain consistent through countless generations, and even between widely divergent cultures on opposite sides of the earth, who were witness to the same great events in human history ... the stories of a living cosmos ... the Genesis mythology, the rising of early humanity, the time of Eden and the fall. Stories of global conflagrations, of ice and floods ... stories of great cataclysms causing the suffering of humankind through years of cold and darkness before emerging back into the light are many, and they are consistently expressed in the race memories of peoples right across the earth.

These stories unfold from far back in the mists of time, and so in the retelling, the geography might sometimes shift, the name of the deity may change and even the time of the event, but never the primary facts. The core facts of these stories always hold true, the same human observations of natural history unfolding are reinforced over and over again ... telling of a decline in spiritual morality among the races of men, which evoked the punishment of the gods in the form of great natural catastrophes ... they recall the battles between gods and demons, dragons and serpents, the records of those who perished and those who survived ... and they tell the story of we who stand here now. There was a time when humanity participated in these stories ... now, we barely remember them.

Stories ... there are small stories that hold the memories of an individual or a group, told for the simple pleasure of remembering a shared past. There are big stories that hold the memory of a people, of their time and place in history. And there are archetypal stories that are recalled and recounted for all of humanity, carried in wisdom by few for the many ... these are the stories that transcend the boundaries of culture and time, and which convey a truth common to all humanity.

Some stories are told over many years, teachings from one who knows to one who is coming to know, and each time they meet, initiate and pupil, what must be heard is told. There is no hurrying this process, each wisdom is imparted in its own time. The mouth will not speak before the ears can hear ... and with the core meaning often veiled in metaphor, it becomes imperative that the one who listens enters into the life of the story itself, that he becomes the story, and the story becomes his own ... this profound attitude compels the complete understanding of what is being told.

These stories continue through history and time, and by their very nature they cannot be told 'out of truth' ... they are told and remembered in absolute truthfulness, for they are not someone's opinion of an event or a truth, and neither are they told from individual prejudice and memory ... they are the stories of life that speak the wisdom of the world from the beginning of time ... the threads that bind past to present to future.

Eyes filled with light, Gening/u, the healing man, tells the story of /Tehsa ... of how the first people came to have fire. It was in the time before time ... the time before the fall from innocence, when the 'gods' and 'beings' of the spiritual world had much to do with the lives of men on earth.

When the animals were people
It was in the time when all things were of one voice, in the time of the early race

when animals were as people and the people were still as animals, and they ate their meat and all of their food raw.

Ostrich was then a man, and he was called by the name of ‖Gamah, the lesser god … and he was like the devil personified, for it was he who had fire and would not share it with the people.

The Greater God ‖Gamah was a man with two wives, and his children were the Sun and the Moon, and it was he who one day followed Ostrich's spoor across the Great Sand Face to the place where all the ostriches would go to cook their food. Man found Ostrich cooking his food in that place, and he wondered how he could take the fire from Ostrich and give it to the people. He saw that whenever Ostrich left his fire, he would keep the burning coals under his arm.

The Man remembered some tall sweet berry bushes that he knew of, which were full of fruit, and with this thought he decided that he would go to Ostrich the next day.

Before he went, he asked his wives to collect many of those thorns which the people called !Ou bea !aba … the devil's claw, and he asked them to spread those thorns over a certain place on the sand face. And then he went to Ostrich and told him of the sweet berry bushes that were laden with fruit, and asked if he would come and pull down the tall branches so that they could share the ripe berries on the top.

Ostrich agreed and followed Man to that place, and as he stretched up his arms to take hold of the top branches the man snatched the burning coals and ran away. Running … running … as Ostrich chased after him, Man jumped over the patch of thorns that had been spread by his wives … but Ostrich did not know to jump over the thorns, and so got caught in the devil's claws.

When Man got back to his wives he found them already busy roasting VKhaa, cucumbers in the hot coals, and this was because the fire had spread to all the people in the same moment that he had taken it from Ostrich.

The next day Ostrich came to Man, and asked him to give back the fire, but Man refused and said, 'You must go now and altogether become an ostrich, and lay eggs in the sand so that I can come and take your eggs and roast them to eat' ... and from that day onwards Ostrich was altogether an ostrich and no longer a man ... and the people who were People, had fire.

It is /Tehsa ... spirits of the fire who remember every story that was ever told in the light of flame ... for it is this warmth, which holds the human heart ... holds the human heart.

ANIMAL TO HUMAN

The metaphor in this story is utterly, utterly profound ... I perceive this to be the most important of stories ... our 'first human' story. The people of the early race did not have the wide-awake consciousness of modern humanity, theirs was still a dreaming consciousness, and the coming of fire is the metaphor for the coming of light into the human Soul, the birth of Spirit.

The story tells of a transformation of consciousness in humanity, from a dreaming to a more wakeful state of being ... it tells of the time when early humanity, by choice, and for all of us, began the journey to Light, to 'God consciousness' in Self. In man is both good and evil. We hold within us the choice of opposites: the Greater God, or the lesser god – the light, or the darkness. We humans do not learn by default, we learn only through our own experience in this world, through conflict and pain, by constantly traversing the age-old disparity between our higher and lower natures.

In this story, the metaphor for //Gamah the Ostrich, in his selfishness, is the lower human nature ... the lesser god. And the metaphor for //Gamah the Man, who would share in the Light, is the higher human nature ... the Greater God. The conflict between these two aspects of our Being is the seemingly eternal human condition. And coming to fire, to light, is the first overcoming of the lower nature, the animal nature in man, an important understanding of our evolving human nature.

It is the customary defence of the intellect that anything we modern humans no longer understand we relegate to the realms of 'belief' and 'myth'. To comprehend the truth embedded in mythology we must track back into the primal wisdom of that time. The banishing of animals from the human kingdom is a core element in many stories from many cultures, and the fact is that the First People do recall how it was when humans were still more 'animal like'.

To enable the human being to evolve, to come to completion, the animal nature needed to be extricated from the human by an act of cosmic will, so that humans could develop further in the way that they have ... so that we could become fully human.

From a spiritual perspective one can see that animals, and especially the higher animals, are leached out of the human as a part from the whole, and that many of these animals reflect aspects of the full human nature. When you gaze into the countenance of one of the great apes, like chimpanzee or orang-utan, you see the 'almost human' ... the 'fallen human'. There seems an unconscious sadness reflected in the eyes of the great apes, the longing for what almost became ... in these creature forms you can see the last of the animal nature that was leached out of the human, so that we could come to fullness. And if you look anew at your fellow humans today, you will see among them those who reflect the residues and characteristics of the animal nature ... some who are as cunning as the jackal, and some as brave as the lion ... those with the countenance of the eagle and those with the strength of the bull ... and still so many as foolish as the jackass! I know that I must look with care at the animal soul to see those aspects of my own nature reflected in the animal, and the animal nature reflected in my own Being. I must know my own Soul, and so understand the nature of that in myself as human, which must be filled with Spirit.

So, from the realm of spirit the animals are descended from the human … they are the physical form of the animal nature that was purged out of the human, and they reflect much of that 'early human' residue. This fact of evolution is repeated over and over again in First People stories, a clear and simple observation that in the story of human evolution the animals are descended from man, and that man is not ascended from the animal. Physically it appears that man ascends from the animal, but spiritually it is the animal that descends from man. In nature and in truth, the greater does not arise from the lesser, the lesser derives from the greater … the part from the whole.

It is simply a question of how we see the earth. Do we see it as a physical object, subject only to physical laws that explain only half of it and so hardly make sense, or do we see the earth as a physical-spiritual Being, which completes all the senses and so makes complete sense.

In terms of creation, 'spirit' is not dissolved matter, spirit does not come about through the dissolution of matter. It would be correct to observe that matter, as frozen energy, is condensed out of spirit, and that the spiritual thus gives rise to the physical … the forces give rise to the form.

The process of physical evolution is exactly the process described by natural science … if you look at evolution from a purely physical perspective then it appears from the outside that any physical form builds upon the one before it. However, if you extrapolate from the perspective that matter is condensed energy, it follows that the physical arises out of, or is condensed from out of, the spiritual. This perspective does not take away from the physical theory of evolution … it simply makes it understandable without contradiction, it brings the missing half to modern humanity's materialistic view of life.

The Bushmen refer to themselves as the First People, and they speak of those who came before them as the early race, who, in their nature and spirit still lived as kin with the animals, in the time before they could stand fully upright, before they could rise out of the animal horizontal … before they were imbued with the forces of Spirit, or the I that would later enable the first humans to stand 'out' of gravity, upright between heaven and earth. In many of their stories the animals are banished from the human kingdom, cast out to go and be animals and no longer in humans ... and these stories ... are true ...

It was /Han∤kass'o of the /Xam Bushmen who told of *The woman who was a sister to the vultures*

The vultures formerly made their elder sister of a person ... a woman was the one of whom they made their elder sister ... the woman was a person of the early race ... they lived with her.

They, when their elder sister's husband, who was a man of the early race, brought home a springbok, they ate up the springbok. And their elder sister's husband cursed them ... he scolded at them.

He again, he went and killed a springbok ... he brought the springbok home, slung upon his back. They again, they came and ate up the springbok. Their elder sister's husband scolded them, and they moved away, they sat down.

Their elder sister singed the springbok's skin, she boiled the springbok's skin. Their elder sister was giving to them pieces of the skin, and they were swallowing them down. Their elder sister's husband scolded them, because they again, they ate with their elder sister of the springbok's skin, when they had just eaten the body of the springbok, they again, they ate with their elder sister of the springbok's skin.

Therefore, on the morrow, their elder sister's husband said that his wife must go with him ... she should altogether eat on the hunting ground, for the Vultures, his younger sisters-in-law, were in the habit of eating up the springbok. Therefore, the wife should go with him. Then, the wife went with him.

Therefore they, when their elder sister had gone, they went out of the house, and they conspired together about it. They said, this other one said, 'Thou shalt ascend, and then thou must come to tell us what the place seems to be like.' And a little girl said, 'Little sister shall be the one to try, and then she must tell us.' And then a Vulture who was a little Vulture girl, she arose, she ascended.

They sat ... they were awaiting the time at which their younger sister should descend. Then their younger sister descended from above out of the sky, she came and sat in the midst of them. And they exclaimed, 'Ah! What is the place like?' And their younger sister said, 'Our elder sister who is here shall ascend, that she may look, for the place seems as if we should perceive a thing when we are above there.'

Then, her elder sister who was a grown-up girl, she arose, she ascended, she went, disappearing in the sky. She descended from above, she sat in the midst of the other people (vultures). And the other people said, 'What is the place like?' And she said, 'There is nothing the matter with the place for the place is clear. The place is very beautiful, for I do behold the whole place ... the stems of the trees, I do behold them ... the place seems as if we should perceive a springbok, if a springbok were lying under a tree ... for the place is very beautiful.'

Then they altogether arose, all of them, they while they felt that they altogether became vultures, ascended into the sky. They felt that they were people while they wished that their elder sister should eat, for their elder sister's husband scolded them.

Thereafter, they used, when they espied their elder sister's husband coming, they ate in great haste. They said, 'Ye must eat! Ye must eat! Ye must eat in great haste! For that accursed man who comes yonder, he could not endure us.' And they finished the springbok, they flew away, flew heavily away, they thus, they yonder alighted, while their elder sister's husband came to pick up the bones.

They, when they perceived a springbok, they descended, and their elder sister perceived them, their elder sister followed them up. They ate, they ate, they were looking around ... they said, 'Ye must eat ... ye should look around ... ye shall leave some meat for elder sister ... ye shall leave for elder sister the undercut,

78

when ye see that elder sister is the one who comes.'

And they perceived their elder sister coming, they exclaimed, 'Elder sister really seems to be coming yonder, ye must leave the meat which is in the springbok's skin.' And, they left it. And, when they beheld that their elder sister drew near to them, they went away, they went in all directions.

Their elder sister said, 'Fie! How can ye act in this manner towards me? As if I had been the one who scolded you!' And their elder sister came up to the springbok, she took up the springbok, she returned home ... while the Vultures went forward while they felt that they altogether became vultures, they went to fly about, while they sought for another springbok which they intended again to eat.

There are other stories, about the origin of death and the knowledge of good and evil ... *The Hares Katten-ttu-u* by Dia!kwain, tells of how the hare was cursed because he did not believe the moon when the moon told him that his mother was not altogether dead, and that she would again return alive. And because he doubted the word of the moon, the moon became angry and the hare was cursed to be mortal, and all humans along with him 'that we should now altogether die when we die'.

And the Moon said, 'They who are men, they shall altogether dying go away, when they die. For, he was not willing to agree with me, when I told him about it, that he should not cry for his mother ... for his mother would again live ... he said to me that his mother would not again living return. Therefore, he shall altogether become a hare. And the people, they shall altogether die. For, he was the one who said that his mother would not again living return. I, the Moon, said to him about it, that the people should also be like me; that which I do; that I, when I am dead, I again living return. He contradicted me, when I had told him about it.'

This story records the banishing of humanity from Eden through a surrendering of faith ... man's tasting of the tree of knowledge and the consequence, his forfeiting of the tree of life and his descent to physical mortality. This story is a living observance of the changing nature of the 'falling' human ... that we forget our journey through cycles of reincarnation.

//Kabbo told a story of how the sun was thrown into the sky ... of how the sun and the moon, as living beings, were once a part of the earth, and that their separating from the earth pre-dates the time of the early race.

How the sun was thrown into the sky
The men of the early race were those who first inhabited the earth. Therefore, their children were those who worked with the sun. Therefore, the people who later inhabited their country, are those who say that the children worked, making the sun to ascend, while they felt that their mothers had agreed together that they should throw up, for them, the sun ... that the sun might warm the earth for them ... that they might feel the sun's warmth ... that they might be able to sit in the sun.

When the first Bushmen had passed away, the Flat Bushmen inhabited their ground. Therefore, the Flat Bushmen taught their children about the stories of the Early Race.

The Sun had been a man, he talked, they all talked, also the other one, the Moon. Therefore, they used to live upon the earth while they felt that they spoke. They do not talk, now that they live in the sky.

Of consideration here is the recounting of a primordial cosmic event by an ancient race ... that these three bodies were once joined as a single form, and that first the sun, and then the moon, separated from the earth.

It is good to consider that the sun, moon and earth were all formed around the same time ... according to modern science it was 4,6 billion years ago ... and that the volume of the moon equals that of the Pacific Basin, and that all of the minerals found in the moon's rocks are found also on the earth. It is not so much a question of whether or not this cosmic event took place, it is more the given timeline that must be reconsidered. Over many millennia the moon's gravity has affected the speed of the earth's rotation ... long ago it was much faster and earth days were much shorter, and so, by inference, our whole assumed evolutionary time frame becomes questionable. When the moon first coalesced or formed as a separate celestial body, it was only 14,000 miles from earth ... now it is more than 280,000 miles away. One must also consider changes in the earth's oscillation, or the background base frequency by which the world's clocks are set, to see that time was not always what it is now.

Imagine a moon that looked three times larger from earth than it does today, and the living relationship between early humans and this great heavenly body. Out of primal memory, people of the early race perceived the separating of the sun and moon from the earth as a prelude to the fall of humanity, a prelude to the tasting of the tree of knowledge and the human descent into matter and mortality ... denied the tree of life and separated from Eden after tasting the tree of knowledge – of good and evil.

And also in the separating of the sun and the moon from the earth there began the outer cycles of the sun and moon, the physical cycles by which we now measure our time and our mortality. Within the cycle of this current great sidereal year, determined by the movement of the heavens and the precession of the equinoxes, this separation from the world of 'spirit', this fall of humanity, would have begun around ten thousand years ago ... spiritually preordained so that the first 'people' could begin the journey from light through darkness towards light, the start of the human quest to gain mastery over matter.

This same 'story' is recorded and repeated over and over again ... it is part of the observed record of the evolution of humankind by those who were there at that time, and this is an absolutely vital observation to knowing our own place in the world, for only when we understand the evolution of spirit will we understand the evolution of form.

Science, by its own mandate, can only observe and describe the physical empirical, and from that limited perspective these facts put forward might seem absurd. But we must remember that we once thought the earth was flat, and that we beheaded those who said it was round. And what more evidence do we require than the endlessly repeated observation of the first peoples and our own common sense!

We modern humans have become unpractised at the language of metaphor, hence our antipathy for the truth embedded in many ancient stories. The metaphor lies as a veil between the perception and the understanding of archetypal wisdom, and as such, in the current epoch, is the untravelled bridge between the physical and spiritual realms. The metaphor serves also as a predetermined cosmic coding system, compelling humanity to lift the veil and so come consciously to knowledge ... coming to the full comprehension of truth in every age or epoch gives birth to that which is right in the succeeding age. And in looking forward one must try to see the truth of man that existed before the fall, the divine archetypal image of man ... and in this to consider the choice that now lies before us.

FIRE IN OUR HEART

The fire in my body makes me dream of a time long ago, some say it was a million and more years ago in our distant past, when our only knowledge of fire was in the sun ... the first giver of life. If anything had been God for us at this time in our early evolution, then it was the Sun-god. For it was the sun who killed the demons of the dark, it was the sun who warmed our frozen bodies after a cold night, it was the sun who gave us the light by which we lived our life on earth ... it was the sun ... the Creator ... our then-God.

In my 'warmed' blood I know how it was in that dawning of time when we early humans first made fire, it was in that moment of recreation of the sun that we became co-creator ... in that moment was born our first glimmering awareness of the forces of creation and life. The sun had always been the giver of life, and now we humans could make the sun, we too could give light and life. In that first making of fire we gave birth and breath to the primal idea of co-creator and Self ... the first inadvertent awakening of human consciousness. In that first enormous act of co-creation we became aware of something greater than ourselves ... the whispered beginnings of a God-consciousness on earth as it is in heaven.

So, in the light of the first fire we extended ourselves through the universe and to the heart of the sun itself, and in our acknowledgement of this relationship we extended the idea of ourselves from earth to infinity in the greater cosmos ... this is the way it is in a qualitatively expanding universe, our idea of God always just beyond the outer reach of human perception. And this was the first primitive perception of the feeling of God in a sleeping humanity ... a thought-feeling, which even now lies just beyond the furthest boundary of human consciousness.

Even the /Gwikwe's daily greeting holds the question asked of the dreaming consciousness ... 'Tsamkwa /tge?' ... Are your eyes nicely open? ... Have you come to full wakefulness?

We humans stand always at the cutting edge of consciousness on earth, and with that commission comes a responsibility. It is the nature of our spiritual relationship with the universe that fuels the process of earth evolution ... and when our participation in that process stops, then life on earth as we know it will end ... for the heavenly dream of earth can not continue without the earthly dreamer, and this is the interrelated nature of all.

It is almost deliberately naïve that science has so endlessly postulated on the idea of an expanding universe ... it fails to concede that one cannot measure a qualitative phenomenon through quantitative perception. So when, from our physical perspective, we try to explore the process of a living spiritual universe, then of course we fail.

The idea of a universe continually expanding at an incomprehensible speed is, indeed, a daunting one. So daunting, in fact, that by design it completely despiritualises humanity. For what are we but less than nothing if the universe we are trying to understand expands in perpetuity at a speed we cannot even comprehend? To catch up to our own understanding is therefore utterly impossible!

Perhaps this theory is designed by our own lower nature to make it so, designed to keep us always smaller than our universe and so smaller than our Spirit Self. What semiconscious collaboration between our science and religion perpetuates this bigotry? What inadvertent reluctance in human consciousness causes us to hold on to theories like this, almost as if we fear the knowledge that would set us free?

Like all living beings, the universe breathes in and it breathes out ... and we who live in this epoch in time are part of a great out-breath ... but this too will change.

Even our use of language disables our desire for knowledge, our choice of words often binding us into redundant patterns of non-knowing, as if through some innate fear we seek only to consolidate the old, over and over again. But then something in the human spirit compels this repetitive process until at last we penetrate the veil and our redundancy stares us in the face, and only then do we seek in ourselves the vocabulary to create and use those words and ask those questions which open the way for what lies beyond.

In the penetrating of the veil we change the state of the human Soul. From an expanded consciousness we will comprehend the true nature of our existence outside of earth time and space and within the greater cosmos ... and so our journey continues, through one epoch and dimension to the next.

I sit alone into the night, held by fire and flame and the forces that bind one thing to the other ... I think of the day ... of /Geruma and the old man, and I see how the ostrich, simply by the unconscious projecting of its energy through action, communicates its doings through the ether ... and I see how Dzero-O, simply by his sensitivity to the processes of life, is able to perceive and interpret this movement of energy through the ether ... through his body to recognise this 'feeling' as that of /Geruma the male Ostrich. It is no magic this, it is the language of the universe, and one must learn to listen and then to speak ... for in this understanding of the invisible world lies the only certainty that each one of us can make a difference.

And thus, in the light of fire, I feel the echoes of our story, and come to know the meaning of our long soul-journey through time.

TALKING BONES

When the morning sun rises I see that Dzero-O prepares poison for his arrows ... it is a careful process this. He breaks open the small mud cocoons and removes the larvae, which he rolls and pummels between his finger tips to soften the insides ... and carefully squeezes the //ua, or poison, onto a bone placed next to the fire to keep it warm and liquid. He chews the bark of the /Nooni tree and mixes its juice with the poison ... this strengthens the poison and helps it to bind onto the shaft just behind the arrowhead. This section of the shaft is also wound with sinew and covered with gum from acacia trees, both Camel thorn and Hook thorn, which further helps affix the poison onto the shaft.

The poison itself is a protein of considerable strength, and shot into the rump or anywhere into the body will kill a large animal like a wildebeest or gemsbok within sixteen hours.

Dzero-O says, 'When I was shooting a gemsbok the other day the arrow-stick did not go where I was pointing it ... it went down under the gemsbok ... /Auudze (arrows) are not listening to old men.'

The children keep away from a man when he works with poison ... it is the only area within Bushman culture that is strictly taboo for them ... like hunting it is men's work, and the men have an old relationship with the poison. Contrary to common belief, there is an antidote for bushman poison ... but that is a story for another day.

Gening/u throws the bones to see if we will have a favourable hunt ... the bones say that we will not hunt well today, but that there will soon be meat for the people. We hunt anyway, for today is just such a day ... Gening/u, Magu, /Gowsi and I. We walk for about fifteen miles in a large circle on the western side of the shelters and see nothing, only spoor. I watch and learn as they read the sand ... everything, every movement of all the creatures that live upon the Great Sand Face. I envy the depth of their relationship with the earth, and I determine that I, too, shall have such a closeness with the earth and with all of life ... both inside and outside of myself.

Using gum or /Nauu as bait, /Gowsi sets a snare for a civet whose movements he has tracked for some days now. The civet has a scent gland near the anus from which it excretes a musky substance, and we observe closely the scent marks left on various bushes in the animal's territory ... markers that serve to stake out the routes used during its nightly ramblings, but which also show /Gowsi the best place to set his snare. Magu lays a snare for a grey duiker that has regularly travelled a certain path. He and I walk in front and, passing a sour berry bush, are startled by a loud rustle ... it is a non-poisonous snake twined in the branches. The snake is called Juaneeh and is believed to be a sign of luck ... if you kill the snake then the good luck comes into you, and if you do not, then you will have bad luck. /Gowsi kills the snake and I skin it ... I like snake skin. Looking carefully at the skin, I see that every single scale has a basic hexagonal shape, just like each perfectly constructed cell in a beehive ... a design that serves both for maximum strength in motion and for structural strength in stillness ... a symmetrical form weaving its impeccable wisdom in perfect synergy through all forms and lives.

Slowly we make our way back to the shelters ... empty handed but for the snake skin, and there we find that the other hunters have been lucky. Tgoo, the snare man, Kamageh and /Nedu khu kwe have brought two duiker and a steenbok from their snares ... it is just as the snake said it would be.

N/aueema the Moon is full tonight ... and the meat is welcome. The children make a fire under the Old Man's Tree, and there the women gather ... laughing and clapping and clapping until slowly they sing the men into dancing ... /Nabehsa yeeah ... we dance the giraffe dance, and I see that Gening/u, the healing man, is the first to dance.

He dances the circle ... sand, feet and fire ... each time pausing behind Dowgwi who sits with her head down ... she knows and he knows, and I recall that she has been very quiet during this last week. He places his trembling hands on her shoulders and draws the heaviness from her body, the simple act of acknowledgement reminding us that we all have a place here which we call home, and that we have each other. The heaviness lifts from Dowgwi's body, and so too from all of us ... a soft smile as the song returns. It is in these moments that I am drawn into the revelation of simple miracles.

I learn to dance, and in this dance today I come to understand /Nabehsa ... the tall one with the soft eyes ... energy and healing, and somewhere in the middle of the night the women finish the dancing with the dove song ... and Dowgwi sleeps, soft wings in the darkness.

EARTHGIFT

In the morning Geutwe announces the departure of the women with her usual crowing laughter ... she calls to me that I should walk with them to offer protection from the lions while they gather veld food. Ggamm the lion is always the excuse offered when anyone feels in need of company on a long walk, or equally when someone wishes to avoid having to go on an unpleasant journey. The /Gwikwe, both men and women, have no real fear of lions. When encountered, they will treat the lion with a confident, almost comical contempt. To //Gama she says, 'When you walk around you must take Seka with you ... I would ... 'when a child is old enough to go around you must carry him with you.'

Shadows glide gold upon the sand as the women walk behind Geutwe, one behind the other towards the southwest and the last of the sour berries already blackened by the winter sun … straight backs and soft voices fade into the morning grass. I follow, thinking about the lion.

These /Gwi women are extremely able plant ecologists … an old knowledge carried in the blood. They examine and appreciate plants in the minutest detail, and then turn this intimate knowledge to their own practical ends. They know which plants can be eaten and which cannot, and where and when in the band territory each species can be found. Today they will gather in the place called Gantam//nau, always the last place to hold good food before the month of the dry moon.

Most plant foods are seasonal … !Oba, /Tgara, /Gaa, Bie, !Nauu … some of the seventy-odd species of edible plants that grow in this part of the Kalahari and are gathered and eaten by the /Gwikwe. At this time it is unlikely that they will find much more than /Gaa and Bie roots, and these with the bitterness already creeping in.

Tshk! … *tshk*! … *tshk*! … digging sticks in dry sand … gifts from the earth. From his vantage point on his mother's back, little Seka observes and learns the secrets of the Great Sand Face. Already he begins to know the difference between edible and non-edible plants, and his learning comes only through experience. If his mother finds anything sweet and juicy like /Tgara, it will be his pleasure … for such is the privilege of innocence. Just as each tree or plant grows and flowers in its own right season, so too does the human soul incarnate and flower when the cosmic conditions are right for its life, its growth and development.

Tshk! … *tshk*! … *tshk*! … *tshk*! … the digging stick reveals a sprawling patch of !Oba, a small, spiky, succulent plant whose fleshy stems will quench our thirst. The stout underground stems will be baked in hot ashes and shared at the shelters.

Geutwe uncovers a nest of ants which have a rather salty taste and a somewhat savage bite. She stuns the ants with her flat hands … smacking … scurrying and biting … the pain of the bites she blows away with noisy huffs and puffs. The other women laugh, but not too loudly, for they know the stinging price that must be paid. After stunning the ants she wraps them in a bunch of grass, tied with the bark of a sweet berry bush, and tucks the bundle into her already bulging carry bag. They will add flavour to roasting meat.

These Kalahari sands yield an abundance and variety of food for those who know how and where to find it. It is, acre for acre, probably the world's most prolific underground larder, and yet there are many who have perished from hunger and thirst on this relentless sand face … dying simply for want of knowledge … for failing to remember.

I marvel at the eyes that can see one small dried tendril of creeper woven discreetly into the stems of a bush, and know that it tells of a succulent root beneath the surface … these smallest of signs, each revealing what the earth holds in store for eyes that see. I know that my purpose here is to learn what I can, to awaken that ancient knowledge that sleeps within the place of memory in my body … wisdom of the world written in the immeasurable space between all that is measurable. I, too, was once a child on my mother's back as she walked, old feet on the earth seeking food so that we First People might eat and live … I remember that time … my own beginning.

And then the long walk with tired backs, and the sun touching the edge of the earth by the time we return to the shelters … each woman carrying as much as the earth has given. Geutwe says that the lions did not bother them today because I was there to protect them, and I think with a soft smile of how I love the simple charm of /Gwi humour, and of all that is said in kindness when the sun sets.

Krggggggggk … krggggk … whee wheeeeeu! … a cold morning dawns with the sound of scrapers and shrill whistling onto blades and the night dream becomes the daydream. Khordze /Tehsa … it is the skin of the female wildebeest we killed in the beginning of winter, and now that the cold has come Tso/tgomaa wishes to clean and soften the skin to be a cloak for his wife, /Gaiekwe.

This man Tso/tgomaa, quiet and shy in the company of people, but as a hunter incomparable ... he has three sons, the youngest of which, ⁄Gaie, begins to take his first steps, and his wife, /Gaiekwe, is content and happy with her man who says very little but provides more than most.

Krgggk ... krggk ... wheeee! ... whe ... whe ... wheeeeeu! ... strong hands scrape warmth and comfort into the skin for the mother of his children. In preparation, he had left the skin open to catch the night dew to make it soft and wet for the scrapers. The /Gwikwe believe that whistling onto the blade of the scraper helps to keep its edge sharp. And so they scrape the inside layers from the skin, he and Gening/u together ... all the while whistling ... scraping and whistling onto the blades ... and when the skin is thin enough they will soften it with a mixture of urine and some of the brain from a duiker caught in the snares a few days ago. The scrapings from the inside of the skin are saved to be cooked with melons and eaten.

It is only the skin from the female wildebeest and gemsbok that can be used for making a cloak. The skin from male animals is too thick to cure. If not eaten in the dry season, it will be made into sandals, or cut into strips for the making of thong. Thong like this can be used for making a net to carry heavy loads of meat from the hunt, or for melons and roots on long gathering trips.

Skin scraping is a male communal task, and so it becomes a time for talking and joking. The men also do most of the sewing, using sinew thread and metal awls. Dzero-O says that in the olden days these awls were made from the leg bones of large antelope ... and so were the arrowheads that we use for hunting. Gening/u says with uplifted tongue, 'Red hartebeest and blue wildebeest ... I swear by my father, were gathered together ... they were so many ... *!Olaa* (smoothly)!' He shouts because the scraper is indeed scraping smoothly.

And then to Tso/tgomaa: 'Mind, your moochi is coming off, or we will all see your balls.' He laughs loudly and shouts, 'Ama ggouu … cut it!' And teasing, 'You should have left this skin in the dew last night so it could be nice and soft … aiee aiee aiee aiee aieee! What kind of scraper is this, that makes the skin cry?' … as the water comes off from the collected dew … and then: 'No! Tso/tgomaa, you are not sharpening properly … you are only taking off the top part of the skin … you must sharpen your scraper nicely like me … *heea*! *heea*! *heea*! *heea*! … No! Geamm's father … you must whistle hard and sharpen it nicely.'

This is followed by prolonged whistling and loud laughter … and then: 'This scraper that stands out like a penis should be made short.' He means that the blade should be sunk deeper into the handle.

Another voice: 'An old man was chopping a big tortoise with that scraper … *wheeu*! … *wheeu*! … *wheeu*! … Kneel down and scrape hard! Don't let the wind blow the scrapings away … the women have gone for melons, and when they return we can make a nice meal with them … *hah*! … *ah hah*! … *ah hah*! … A scraper that makes this noise is blunt!' This is followed by lots of sharpening, whistling and laughter. The scraping becomes a game and our talk remembers the day of the hunt and honours the animal whose spirit has passed … it is in this awareness that we sanctify our trespass in a world sometimes cruel and harsh.

WINTER MOON

The power of life sits under the cold sand, held and nurtured by the will of winter. We sleep longer these mornings, our bones cold on the Kalahari earth and slow to awaken.

Game is now scarce and we hunters must walk a long way before we pick up the spoor of the gemsbok, which Tso/tgomaa wounded yesterday.

About twenty-five miles from the shelters, and the grass is dry and brittle like our feet on the hard sand face. I walk in awe of these First People, hunters and gatherers of Africa ... I comprehend now the incredible effort of the hunt which depends on the will of the body and a free flowing spirit. These /Gwikwe men are hunters in the true sense of the word, theirs is not the pleasure or pain of a high-powered rifle at two hundred metres, and the illusion of the word 'hunter'. They have the limbs and the heart of the true hunter ... they know of the pain of endurance ... they know how to wait inside of time itself while the sun burns and the animal stands ready to flee ... they know how to pause and then to move with the rustling of leaves in a small breeze ... they know to move softly when a bird in flight moves the energy away from a suspicious animal ... they know how to lie like the lizard on the sand and to move only as much as one inch in an hour ... they know all these things and more, for they are hunters, and they hunt so that they can live and their people can eat.

We modern men, who exercise the gift of power through the misuse thereof ... I wish that we could all walk this path of learning as we go forward. How long before we learn that there is no other reason to take life but to give life?

The blood spoor on the sand ... with real hunger as a motive it follows that a wounded animal seldom, if ever, escapes a Bushman hunter. Their ability to search for, to find and to follow the faintest of signs in such vast and difficult terrain, is unparalleled. It is more than the following of footprints in sand, more than broken grass and blood spots, more than just physical signs ... it is to listen with your fingertips and look with your feet ... it is a feeling in the body that calls to the animal's life-body, and you follow these feelings in yourself as much as you follow the animal ... and in this way, predator and prey, you come together in sacrifice and redemption.

We walk long through the day on dry earth quietened by the winter until at last ... a male gemsbok stands. Tso/tgomaa stalks to throw the fatal spear before the animal flees ... but not yet, it turns and runs with tired legs ... for the last time. After twenty-four hours the poison has done its work ... /Tgooma the Gemsbok is weak and the hunters close in for the kill.

Injury suffered out here can have serious repercussions, and so we take no brave or unnecessary risks when killing an animal ... there is nothing to prove ... everything is only a matter of time. The first throw ... Tso/tgomaa's spear hangs stuck between the gemsbok's ribs ... Gening/u diverts the animal's attention while he darts in to remove his weapon for another throw. A wounded gemsbok is remarkably fast at close quarters, with lethal horns quite capable of killing a lion. I run forward with arm drawn back and my focus on the heart ... through the ribs and into the heart ... /Tgooma the Gemsbok watches my spear fly through the space between us, and then with a deft flick of his head he catches my spear and flicks it cartwheeling away into some bushes. Gening/u throws the final spear, and then it is finished ... all creatures, man and animal, face the same alternative in their quest for survival ... it is life on this Great Sand Face.

We quench our thirst by squeezing liquid from the stomach contents of the dead gemsbok ... it is the only way. After resting for a short while we begin with the cutting and skinning ... and we eat the choice portions of meat, the liver and the kidneys, and the udder when the animal is female. Gening/u drinks from the pocket of fluid between the skin and the flesh ... crystal clean fluid ... anything to replenish the liquid in our dry bodies. I drink too, the smell of flesh warm in my nostrils ... it is to the simple needs of my body that I respond with the instinct that keeps me alive. I no longer think or consider the alternatives of another life, I have gone beyond the boundaries of that existence. I no longer live in my head ... I simply drink. There is no water in this thirstland, and the rains, if they come, are still far away.

We cut the meat into strips to hang and dry, and by the next day the weight is sufficiently reduced for us to begin our long walk back to the shelters and the comfort of home fires. The smell of gemsbok meat on burning coals pulls my thoughts back through the day and the hunt. A hunter tracks with all of his senses, and the sense of smell is never to be underestimated. You best smell through your nose with your mouth open, so as to taste that which you smell. In this way you bring more information to the Jacobson's organ, and then process this information in the limbic system and the reptilian back-brain ... for it is there, somewhere in the back-brain, that one holds the blueprint of all those ancient odour-linked memories, and the nature of the animal form you hunt.

Many are the odours and fragrances that permeate our lives ... I remember the smells of people long after I have forgotten the way they looked and felt. It is as if the information held in the remembered smell is more absolute than that processed through the other senses.

/Geruma ... filled with the spirit of our lives we dance the ostrich dance that night, a celebration of male victory. In this dance the men set each other up as protagonists in a challenge situation ... the hunters and the hunted ... eh! ... eh! ... /Gerumahh ... eh! eh! ... lithe bodies, powerful and lean on the desert sand, dance, leap, growling in the belly, for today we have returned successful from the hunt. The women clap and sing ... voices high and resonant ... sharp staccato claps, which punctuate and startle. A remarkable harmonic combination that awakens the memories in blood and muscle in an ancient acknowledgement the body well remembers.

Orange sun cuts through dust, crouching hunters, thrusting, twisting, turning in pretended battle ... the age-old companionship of predator and prey, and the great Sun Being threads its last rays through our lives ... my belly contracts and the fire within compels me to dance, and we dance ... eh! eh! /Gerumahhhh ... the burning breath that explodes from the solar plexus is so intense that we dance only in short expressive bursts before diverting our energy into earth-binding joyous laughter. In this wild and wonderful evening we dance the animal soul and the sun to sleep ... but even in the night the sun lives on through the moon which has no light of its own, but reflects in the darkness the light of the sun and the whole firmament, and we dance until the moon hangs like a fat melon in the sky above ... silvering the sand and our souls.

I lie awestruck … in utter reverence for the immaculate arrangement between sun, moon and earth, and all the heavenly bodies moving in time and space, and for each perfectly choreographed step in the great dance of the heavens. And I ask that while my body sleeps, the night take my spirit into those far celestial realms, that in the new day I may return with some of that which I did not know when I closed my eyes to sleep.

BLOOD MEMORY

The morning is light, and a sense of contentment pervades our world … full bellies, and no pressing need to hunt or gather food.

The bone and ash heaps outside the shelters have grown large, and the people go further and further for firewood each day. On days like this, some of the women gather and bring large bundles of hardwood from afar … those around the shelters watch in silent appreciation as //Gama comes in with a stack of wood easily as heavy as herself. I marvel at the pure animal strength and the power of will in her small and beautiful body.

I recall a delightful description of negative space given by Dia!kwain of the /Xam Bushmen when talking of the bone and ash heaps. He said: *They put down the bones opposite to the entrance of the shelter … the place which the shelter's mouth faces, and they call it 'the shelter face's opposite' … and they go and they pour down the bones at it … therefore they call it the heap of meat bones, and they put the bones nicely aside, while they do not throw them about.*

I see that here among the /Gwikwe it is important that the bones, no matter who has eaten from them, are poured down in front of the shelter of the man who hunted the animal … in this way the hunter and the prey remain joined together in respect.

Geutwe uses the time to play /Ehnusa, a traditional women's instrument. A sinew string is plucked on a bent reed to produce the notes, and the tone changes and echoes with the shape of her lips and cheeks over the end of the bow. Soft like a wind it weaves its way gently through the shadows between the shelters and another day would pass … but all is not well.

//Gama's husband, /Gowsi, is angry … for a long time now he has been unlucky with his hunting. It was eight long moons ago that he chased and ran down the kudu bull … I remember well because I was given a choice portion of the liver. Since that time nothing has fallen to his arrows and nothing comes to his snares, and with each passing moon he becomes more angry with himself. It is important for a man to be able to feel the hunter in himself, and so to feed his family. His wife, //Gama, has had an abortion by the older women … she says that life has become difficult. /Gowsi will not help her to look after their three young children, so how could she bring a fourth one into the world at a bad time like this? Their unhappiness is causing some tension within the band, so Geutwe says that the whole family should be tattooed, to bring them luck. She has gathered the various roots and plants that are required for this ritual … some that will cleanse and some that will bring strength and luck.

Because it is neither kind nor considerate to speak openly of the abortion, the people say to each other that the reason for the tattooing is because //Nale/twago, the youngest daughter, has been weaned from her mother … the white spots that she had in her mouth have gone, and always when these spots go the whole family must be tattooed. It is enough to know the real reason for this ritual, there is no need to speak of it. Again, I acknowledge the fineness of these people … everything considered for the greater good of all.

Geutwe says that the juice from the fresh leaves of the Kanna plant will help little //Nale/twago to sleep while she is weaned from her mother's breasts. This is the plant *Sceletium tortuosum*, which they say grows only in one place in this central Kalahari, and that is at !Omchoro, the place of dead locusts, where the animals go to lick the salt in winter. She wonders out loud if anyone has some of this plant to share. But the gifts of nature are small in the winter and no one answers, for they know that she talks only to ease the tension and to say that there is no blame.

Geutwe, Dowgwi and !Tokwa gather themselves inside the shelter of the unhappy family ... it is always the older women who do the ritual cutting. /Gowsi and //Gama wash themselves with a mixture of ground melon seeds and juice from Bie root ... this takes away the 'old dirt' from the past that has brought sickness. The children are washed in the same way.

Geutwe sharpens a small flat piece of iron called //Ie-gosa, for a cutting blade, and says, 'This is how the old people did it ... and we are doing it in the same way as the old people.' This blade may only be used for the cutting of hair and for tattooing.

Dowgwi holds her hand like a hollow tube, and blows onto various parts of their bodies and heads ... blowing off the old dirty air, she makes place for new clean air. *Tshk* ... *tshk* ... small surface cuts into the skin make the blood flow and cleanse. /Gowsi is cut on the upper arms to make him lucky when he sets his snares. //Gama is cut above and between the eyes, and this will help her to see clearly and to be lucky. I see that these small cuts are directly on the sixth chakra, above and between the eyes, and understand that the physical action with the accompanying intent will indeed help her to see more clearly ... more clairvoyantly.

Through the letting of blood, memory is released, and energy patterns are broken or transformed. Through the transformation of blood we strengthen the relationship between our inner world and the outer world, between the physical world and the spiritual world. And it is the strength of this relationship that specifically enhances our ability to function and survive in any environment.

After the parents, the oldest daughter, /Nau//tge, is cut ... and then /Oie/tge, the boy. Finally it is little //Nale/twago's turn, and she really does have her doubts about all this and screws up her little face in anticipation of the blade. For a child perhaps an anxious moment, but on the whole it is a happy and positive event. The three older women speak constantly and softly in warm tones. They laugh gently and often, for reassurance of both parents and children … it is a time of healing.

The cuts on the forehead will bring them luck in a general sense. The cuts on their bodies prevent them from getting thin … instead they will become nice and fat. With their forefingers the old women mix the blood from one person to another. Mixing the blood brings the family close together and will also make them fat … even from eating a small thing. ǃNanǃte seeds are ground and mixed with a root called Peetsa … eating this again makes them fat, and charcoal added to this mixture is wiped into the small cuts to stop the bleeding. In this way the tattooing serves both to heal and to decorate, staying on the body as a constant reminder of the value of the day and of the lessons learned. If someone were to die, then all the families must tattoo themselves to bring back the good luck … and until then, the hunters will shoot nothing.

Dowgwi blows the ground ǃNanǃte seeds onto various parts of their bodies. The 'old dirt' is gone, and then she blows new strong clean air onto the family … and so it is done.

ǀGowsi says that if a man sits for too long in one place he begins to dream, and so he stands and leaves the shelter, his friends and family … and he leaves with a brave heart.

THAT WE LIVE

ǀGowsi's luck as a hunter did change … the day after the tattooing of his family he finds the fresh spoor of an antbear recently gone to ground just a short distance from the shelters. The men check all the surrounding holes to make sure that ǃAuusa does not escape, and Tsoǀtgomaa begins digging out the hole in which they think the animal is hiding. There is great anticipation, and anxiousness …they must be lucky today. Antbear is good meat … it will be fat, and the people need fat.

'Let us dig down on that side,' says Kamageh.

'She is digging deeper and throwing sand out,' says Gening/u, 'She might throw the rope snare out with the sand.'

'No, it is still on her,' says Tso/tgomaa.

It is not long before Tso/tgomaa spears the animal inside the hole and we drag it out. He cuts the skin with the edge of his spear, and we see that it was, indeed, a good time to find it, for the winter is not old, and the antbear still carries much fat. We stand in a moment of stillness for this gentle creature with soft night energy … we acknowledge the spirit that moves in all things, just as our mouths water in anticipation of the feast to come.

With a snare rope made of /Goie, the dead animal is secured to a pole. Gening/u and Kamageh hoist it onto their shoulders and carry it back to the shelters, while the other men go further to check the snares before returning to feast.

I follow the antbear towards the shelters. The people see us coming and run to meet the pole bearers shouting and laughing … /Auusa … Antbear! … Aiee! … there is huge excitement. This is something special, for there are no taboos on antbear and everyone will eat! The women lift their back aprons, expressing their joy with an impromptu melon dance around the tree in which the antbear is hung. They bare their buttocks whenever comparing their state of health and fatness. This is their way of saying, 'See … we will no longer be thin, we will now become fat and beautiful.'

The antbear is a strange subterranean creature … a powerful spirit animal, solitary and beautiful. It forages around through most of the night, relying almost entirely on its remarkable senses of smell and hearing to find its way around its home territory and to locate its food … exclusively ants and termites.

The old man Dzero-O helps Gening/u with the skinning today. He is the father of /Gowsi and has asked for the claws of the antbear ... he says that there is something that he would use them for. They are willingly assisted by the younger children, who have never eaten such a creature before, and are greatly excited by the idea. Behind the shelters, a large bed of coals is prepared for the roasting of the whole animal ... slow and reverent we will eat. /Gowsi roasts the skin of the antbear on a fire in front of his own shelter, and hungry mouths water in anticipation of the coming crackling feast.

Night falls and the waning moon bears witness to our joy.

In the days that follow, /Gowsi hunts with renewed energy and spends much more time looking out for his young children. And around the fire he tells a story of how !Auuma the Antbear will escape the hunter who is not careful and quick ... It was one night on a faraway hunt, and the winter moon was full bellied. A young leopard had caught an antbear away from the safety of its burrow and had tried to take hold of the antbear's neck, but the antbear would tuck its head in between its front legs and kick its powerful back legs so hard that it would roll right over and knock the young leopard off its back. Each time the antbear would get back on its feet the leopard would try again, but after rolling in this way many times, and each time sending the leopard sprawling, the antbear had gotten safely back to its burrow and the young leopard had slunk off with much to consider ... and in the same way the young hunters must know that !Auuma is a powerful 'medicine' animal, and the claws of the antbear can take a man to many secrets hidden in the dark.

The sickle moon with empty belly hangs in the night sky, and when morning comes Tso/tgomaa finds lion spoor just a short distance from the shelters. We see from the sand that Ggamm was watching us in the night, and like the moon he has no food in his belly.

We sleep again in the darkness, and the following morning we see that Ggamm has returned ... for two nights now the same lion has watched us sleeping from the same place. The hunters say that when a lion watches our shelters for two nights in the same way, we can be sure that he sees the people as a food thing, and that he will come to eat our flesh on the third night.

This is sometimes the way of old lions who no longer hunt as they once could; or solitary nomads ... young males without pride or territory, who are not able to kill large or dangerous prey by themselves ... an insecure existence compels them to take whatever they can get. In the olden days before the fences, these nomads would follow behind the great herds of wildebeest migrating across the Kalahari, but these moving herds are no more, and the nomads now find themselves trespassing in occupied territory for long periods of time, where they must adapt or perish. The spoor tells us that this is an old male.

Says Tso/tgomaa, 'We must follow Ggamm and talk to him in our way, so that he will know that the people have seen him and will not have him come into our shelters.'

And so we follow the spoor, five hunters, for two or three miles to where the lion sleeps the day away in the shade, for such is his way. We smell his musky scent sprayed with urine onto grass tufts, and we see where he has made his territorial marks in the sand, two parallel grooves scraped out with the hind paws.

We speak loudly with uplifted tongue and walk with big feet, for we are not hunting today, we are marking our own territory. Ggamm hears us coming and gives way ... we follow behind his fresh spoor with the wind at our backs.

The men say, 'He must know that we follow after him, and he must smell and hear that we are People ... that this Kgoatwe place is our place and we have our children. He must go to another place that is not near ... he must not have bad ways and must not come again into our place, for we are men who do not fear the lion.'

We chase after him in this manner for a further five or six miles, talking loudly and leaving our strength on the sand until we know that he has heard our voice ... for we are the people of the Great Sand Face, and the lion too, is reflected in our human countenance.

When we turn back to the shelters we know that Ggamm will not return ... if he follows our spoor he will smell our strength on the grass and the sand, and he will know that we are angry. In the light of the sun we show him our power so that in the light of the moon he will remember.

There is talk in the night. The people have decided to stay in Kgoatwe ... the hunters say that there is no more food in the other areas of the band's territory, so why move? We have our snares here in Kgoatwe, and our shelters. The south wind is still cold, and the women will patch the shelters with new grass to keep the cold wind out ... and so it is.

In the morning the women come with grass, and listening to their talk makes me think of the other day ... they are saying that //Gama is not allowed to patch her own shelter, because she is still unclean after taking a human life when she aborted her unborn child. Together, the older women will do the work, only on the sides though, because when the rains do come they must fall through the roof. //Gama and her family must get wet ... they must be washed by the first rains. If this does not happen, then the rains will not come and bad luck will come to all the people ... and this is the way everything in all of our lives must be resolved.

For me, perhaps this is the time to talk of it ... it was a still day ... I had overheard some of the older women speaking behind Se/twago's shelter ... Geutwe, Dowgwi and Se/twago were sitting close around //Gama who was lying quietly under a gemsbok skin. I sensed that this was women's business and had ventured no closer than a man should.

There was a feeling of austerity about the women, which was something I had not experienced before, and so I had watched from a little distance and waited for a more appropriate time to ask.

//Gama was washed and naked under the skin blanket, and Geutwe massaged a medicine mixture in a circular motion onto her sixth chakra, above and between the eyes, and then the same onto her lower belly, the second chakra, just below the navel. Dowgwi and Se/twago sat one on either side of //Gama, and were crooning softly all the while ... a peculiar harmonic overtone ... unfamiliar to the ear ... translike and soothing.

A short while later, Geutwe had carefully removed from under the blanket a bundle of soft, absorbent cotton-like plants. These she had wrapped into a bundle inside her cloak, and walked into the grass, away from the shelters, to bury the bundle. When she returned, //Gama had emerged from under the blanket and, with the other women, gone about her daily business ... and that was all. It had looked like a small thing but felt like a big thing ... nothing was spoken, and the day had remained silent.

When I asked of this later, I learned that the older women had induced //Gama to miscarry ... through circumstances it was necessary, and so it had been done. And at the end of that day, when /Gowsi had returned from the hunt empty handed, he had said nothing that anyone could hear ... but he and his wife //Gama were talking softly, with anger and unhappiness. We left them to their business until the next day when Geutwe said that the whole family should be tattooed ... and so it was then that a healing had been done.

It had all seemed so simple on the day, but now I see how carefully these people hold the threads of thought and accountability ... how each event must unfold until it is done. All memories, good and bad, are held in a person's life-body or ether-body by the forces of water, and so, washed by the first rains, these memories will be transformed, and life will once more be as it should for //Gama's family. All that we do has consequence, and this must be remembered as we go through our days ... each thread held thoughtfully until the cloth is fully woven.

For now, the winter holds and the dry season is yet to come. The fires burn long into the night, and the sounds of Denku, the thumb piano, say everything ... and Seman/ua, his beautiful haunting voice piercing the still blackness, brings light to darkness and the warmth of ancient memories to my silent heart.

THE SPIDER'S MESSAGE

One moon passes and a cold morning finds us in a hunting camp two sleeps away from the shelters. It is before the dawning of the day. We have hunted to the edge of the band's territory, in a place called Gantam//nau ... and the people need meat. We have walked perhaps eighty kilometres on the trail of the tall one, called /Nabehsa, but the spoor is always older than we who come too late with tired legs ... scratched, aching, stiff.

The sun is still below the edge of the earth, and the men sleep around the ashes of last night's fire ... their only protection from the biting wind is //Aauuma, a blanket made from gemsbok skin. I awaken to the soft movements of the old man as he blows last night's embers back to life. I roll out of my skin blanket and there sits beneath me an extremely poisonous spider ... Kiam/ah, half dazed from the weight of my blanket, or my body. The spider drags itself sluggishly towards me and I move carefully away ... for the people have said that when this spider bites you, you die! Finding a stick, I pin the spider to the ground ... later we will use it to poison our arrows.

Dzero-O reacts as if I had been bitten by the spider ... he reaches into his hunting bag and pulls out a dried vegetable of sorts which he says he will use to treat the bite. I tell him that I have not been bitten, and he puts the antidote back into his bag. When I ask him what he would use to kill the spider's poison, and he does not answer, I say to him that today is the day I should be told what the antidote to Bushman poison is, and that is why the spider has come. The other men have woken by now and have listened to our conversation ... no one objects to my reasoning and the old man says softly,

'Yes, it is so ... today I will tell you this /Gwikwe secret.'

And so it is on this day that I come to be the one person outside of this tribe of people to share in that ancient knowledge. I ask the old man why it is such a strong secret, and he says it is because of the strength of the poison ... I understand his meaning ... powerful forces require powerful relationships, and so I honour the day. To the world of natural science, which has often asked me to reveal this information, I have only said, 'Some things must remain sacred ... and if for the right reasons you wish to know, then go and walk as a Bushman ... and what is yours will come to you.' Suffice it to say that there is an antidote to the poison that all Bushman hunters use on their arrows ... it is derived from a vegetable substance and is carried in the quiver bags of most old /Gwi hunters. The older the substance the more effective it becomes, and its source remains a well-kept secret.

When one considers the structure of the universe, it is obvious that for every poison there is an antidote ... for every force there is an opposite, the cosmic ebb and flow of tides, of darkness and light ... of truth and deception. This principle of opposites in balance reflects through the entire universe and through all the kingdoms of Nature, from the physical through to the realm of Spirit. It is the principle by which all things on every level of life are interrelated in wholeness, and this is how it always was for the First People. This is their source of knowledge and means of survival ... their only access, through a reverence for the Soul of the earth.

Tso/tgomaa puts the dead spider into a grass bundle in his hunting bag ... and then we walk. For three days now we have been tracking giraffe, !Nabehsa, but the spoor is old. This Gantam//nau place is where giraffe can be found around the time of the last winter moon ... it is here that !Nabehsa looks for the last edible leaves on the Camel thorn tree, and perhaps with his long neck he can reach the one or two dry seed pods that still hang in the topmost branches. The veld around is dry and brittle and there is nothing for the animals to eat. It is the same everywhere ... a surreal, hollow landscape imploded on itself in waiting, and we, an integral part of all the cycles of the earth. All life forces, all power held and nurtured inside the earth through the winter … strengthened and waiting for the time of spring-birth.

As if from a distance … I see five ancient hunters joined by wind and dust, tracking across an immeasurably vast sand face, and these are the visions I will never forget. Primordial pictures of humans immersed in an ancient journey, which continues and still continues … and nothing has changed except the integrity of our relationship with the earth.

Our earth mother is so very old … she has borne and buried so many sons and daughters, and yet we seek no council with her. We modern humans have wandered far from the Divine cycle, and today in our bastions of civilisation we live in fear, surrounded by the price we have paid. We foolishly believe that our proprietary position is one of safety and strength, but alas, this illusion may be our final undoing … for there are indeed dark forces that prey upon doors opened in foolishness.

The hunt is a hard one and we have not been lucky … what the earth offers at this time is not enough to maintain our strength … the miles are long and a great tiredness fills our bodies with slow and aching muscle. It is not that we feel we should have any more or any less, for we accept that these are the patterns of life … that we have what we have, and that all is measured by the grace of our doing. The physical adaptation and endless enduring of all creatures in this brutal dry-season Kalahari is never short of remarkable, and one asks what for? Why is it so imperative that we survive in this way … that we continue? In the end, it is Spirit that compels us to continue through all cycles of time and life, from coherence to chaos and through our own free will back to coherence … the choice on earth lies always with us, and in these difficult times we learn many things.

From his hunting bag Gening/u pulls the gift … a small twist of dried Kanna, carefully wrapped in grass. He and /Nedu khu kwe had collected what little they could of this plant when they went to the licking places to dig for poison for their arrows. While still fresh, the leaves and stalks of the

Kanna plant are twisted and dried together, and then kept for such days as these when the distance travelled is not a little distance. If twisted really tightly, the plant will ferment a little before drying and then it will both intoxicate and quench the thirst.

We each take only a pinch of the dried leaves and stalks, which we chew and hold in our mouths much as one would any homeopathic medicine. Like all medicinal plants, Kanna has powerful and specific life forces, and before long a feeling of gentle wellbeing comes into our bodies and we find that we have the will to continue our long journey. The feeling is as if one is no longer contained only in the physical, but expanded through the physical body into the etheric or life-body that permeates and holds the physical, and so in becoming more, we have more to draw from.

The perceived boundary between the physical and the super-sensible is both the illusion and burden of modern humanity, for our ability to endure comes not only from strength of muscle, but also from the forces that flow through the muscle. What are we in the physical sense but forces of nature in different stages of refinement and capacity? And so, in this way, we draw the strength that enables us to continue without hunger and thirst. Mile upon endless mile through heat and dust we run across the Great Sand Face ... and this is how the Bushmen have always used the Kanna plant.

With any plant medicine you must understand the plant itself, the nature of the forces within the plant, how they can best serve your being, and how in each different circumstance these forces will affect you. These are not random forces placed on the earth for our simple hedonistic or ignorant pleasure, they are part of an impeccable design that facilitates life and wellbeing in the highest sense. There is much to consider when one thinks of the distinct nature of any medicinal or poisonous plant, for every poisonous plant, if used correctly, is a form of medicine. And therein lies the choice for healing or sickness. Our alchemic relationship with this knowledge is an ancient act of consecration in itself ... the transforming of poison to medicine through knowledge, and it is within this relationship that we redeem the offerings of the plant kingdom. And so when you use any of the traditional psychotropic plants like Kanna or Hoodia, the joy lies not in any feeling of senseless intoxication, but in the understanding and respectful sharing of the forces of nature.

It is always astonishing that in this vast Kalahari, if one plant is needed for whatever purpose, then there is someone who will know exactly where to find it. It is as if there is an enormous database written somewhere into the collective memory of these people, a sharing of every botanical experience, from their forefathers, through time. I decide that I will never take this Kanna plant, nor Hoodia, nor any other sacred plant out of the Kalahari and into that world, which will find some way of appropriating what has been sacred to the First People since the beginning of their time. There are many things that must remain secret until we humans have overcome the impulse of greed and learned to measure our wealth in a different way. For what use is a system of healing that measures itself not by the number of souls healed and made whole, but only by numbered money?

The sun is close to the middle of the sky and in single file we cross Gantam//nau ... the wind hard and dry. Tgoo stoops to lift a medium-sized tortoise from its purposeful endeavours and puts it into his hunting bag ... again, I see that familiar hexagonal shape giving strength to structure in the tortoise shell. Tso/tgomaa squats in the middle of a place from which we can see for many miles and tips out the contents of his bark quiver ... a hard male stick as long as his forearm and as thick as his little finger, and a soft female stick half that length and as thick as his thumb ... with these he will make fire. Between his feet he holds the female stick on a dry bark catcher. He and Gening/u take turns ... hands rubbing, twirling the male stick until the friction produces a smouldering wood dust that trickles down onto the bark catcher, from where the hot embers are carefully tipped onto fine, dry grass and blown gently into flame.

The pure alchemy manifest in this simple process always astounds me. In the history of humankind, this must surely have been the defining creative moment ... the spark, the fire ... and light for eternity. And it was never an accident ... what divine impulse causes a seemingly primitive mind to devise a process so simple yet complex ... the exact alchemy that would lead to the recreation of fire? Of Light?

/Tehsa the fire that we make today is necessary ... it must burn out the old grass to make way for new grass, so that the animals can return to this place and the hunters can be lucky. The strong wind will take this fire through many hundreds of square miles. It will burn fast and will do little damage to the life in its path, and when the spring comes, and the new grass, this will be a good place for hunting.

We stand in the darkness that night, Dzero-O and I, looking out over the burnt and blackened plain ... each bush with the tips of its glowing branches like so many lights of buildings in a big city. He turns to me and says, 'This looks like *Oooohga/noo – white people's country – the place I have visited in my dreams.'

We will sleep one more night cold and hungry, but filled with life and our place on the path. When men are together on the hunt they are joined by a common spirit, and things shared are often secret ... things that only men can know. Brothers with tired eyes, we sit close around the warmth and safety of our fire as late as our weariness allows, and then together we sleep, one beside the other. Tonight we sleep close to the light in the darkness ... and our dream continues, for we are always a part of the changing.

In the morning we sit for a while, our bodies reluctant to begin the day too soon ... our carry bags are empty and our tiredness is deep. The animals have gone from this place and the old people have said it is so. The sand face to the west and south is for many miles burnt and blackened from the hand of /Tehsa ... but one must not see fire as a destructive force in nature, it must be perceived as a great regulatory force, fundamental to the processes of growth and reproduction. There are many plant species that rely entirely on the coming of fire, the heat and smoke causing their seed to come to a state of preparedness, ready to germinate when the first rains beckon them to life.

On the journey back to the shelters we find and chase an aardwolf that takes refuge in an old antbear hole. We must dig it out … it is food.

A strangely evolved animal is the aardwolf, in behaviour neither dog nor cat, but somewhere between the two … and in the form of its body somewhere between its two relatives, the civets on the one side and the hyenas on the other. Unlike the hyena, the aardwolf is a shy and timid creature with weak jaws and small, peg-like teeth adapted to feeding on termites, other insects and on well-rotted carrion. It seems to favour one species of harvester termite, which forages in the open at night … how tenuous the relationships that sustain life. The aardwolf is for the most part nocturnal, and so our chance meeting is graciously taken as an offering of food from the earth.

There is no hurry, for //Geesa is trapped in a hole with no other exits … not too deep, it lies still with its rear end facing upwards. From the scent glands under its tail it emits a foul-smelling fluid in a vain effort to ward off our intrusion, and Gening/u laughs at Tso/tgomaa who lies with his body out of the line of fire while he probes down the hole with his spear. 'You must pull it out by its feet,' says Gening/u. 'But will it not bite the old people?' asks Tso/tgomaa. 'No it is nothing, it cannot bite,' chorus the two old men. 'Well then, why don't you hold it?' asks /Gowsi … 'It has gone down into this side hole,' says Dzero-O. 'It has taken the old antbear's hole and made it into its own home,' says Tso/tgomaa. 'Put the spear in and feel where it is,' says Gening/u. 'It has gone this side,' say some. 'No, it has gone that side,' say others. 'That's why I said you must put the spear in, so we can feel where it is and take it out! … It will not run, its foot is broken,' says Gening/u. 'If it jumps out who will it face? It might jump out at me!' says Kamageh 'Even if it bites a man he will not die,' says Gening/u. 'This hyena can still run away from us,' says Tso/tgomaa. 'Is it dead? … No, it is still growling.'

He manages to spear the animal while Gening/u snares its back legs with a grass rope and begins to pull it from the hole. But suddenly //Geesa comes to life and chaos ensues … fierce growling, mane raised, twisting, fighting, jaws snapping the animal will to live … and we, predators now circling and darting in for the kill … sticks whistling through the air and *thwack*! … *thwack*! … *thwack*! … this time there is no trickery … it is dead.

In silence we give thanks to the spirit of the animal, and continue our journey with the aardwolf hanging from a stick over Kamageh's shoulder … in our thanks we redeem the sacrifice. I walk behind him, observing with care the strange countenance of the animal … a leathery mask of black skin formed over the snout, a sheath of hard skin that enables the creature to use its snout like a burrowing tool when in pursuit of termites under the ground, while also protecting it from the angry bites of soldier termites … a remarkable adaptation. It is almost sad that our hunger brings us to this, but there is no other way … at least we live. The skin we will trade for leaf tobacco when next we meet some passing hunters from the distant settlement of /Xoie!om. It is a long and silent walk back to the women and children, and all we have from many miles and five days of hunting is one aardwolf and a tortoise … not much for thirty-four hungry people.

Dowgwi roasts the tortoise in a bed of hot coals, and Geutwe says that if we roast a tortoise the colour of this one, then the rains will come as they should. She tells a funny story of an old man who, one day, turned his back on the fire while he was roasting a tortoise. The old man was eating wild potatoes, //Xam, at the time and he just kept on eating, while not thinking about the tortoise. The tortoise exploded and burnt him all over his back … and so a man should never turn his back on the fire when he roasts a tortoise. No one laughs. The joke is just an attempt to hide the disappointment everyone feels.

Says Geutwe, 'I'm not laughing because my stomach is weak … if a person who is old like me laughs on an empty stomach then the air comes into me, so I must eat first and then laugh on a full stomach.' Dowgwi laughs. Within the story is a subtle passing of wisdom … the tortoise is a 'creature of the rain' that lives under the protection of the water spirits, and one must remain cognisant of this truth when roasting a tortoise … and so it is.

I see old /Tguikwe sitting alone in the entrance to her shelter, with hands stretched over a small fire, drawing strength from the flame. She has lived her life … as a child, as a mother … and now the grandmother speaks, 'My old body is tired, the hunger and the thirst have killed me … and now the winter …'

We sit in silence, listening to the wind which carries the sound of the earth which we call the Great Sand Face … today we can only sit in silence.

The worst is yet to come …

THE TALL ONE

The days move on … winter makes way for the hot dry season, and then the rains … if they will. The big game have all moved eastwards to the valley where the ground food lasts longer than elsewhere, and for now, here in Kgoatwe, we survive only on small game.

Hunters from the settlement pass by … they come from the southwest and they carry little meat on their donkeys. They say the sand has shown them old spoor, and they go back to the settlement with only enough for their own families. They have nothing to trade save a handful of tobacco for the skin of the aardwolf. It seems that the people from the settlement have forgotten the old way of sharing … perhaps it is because there are too many people forced to live in one place now, and each can only care for himself.

Gening/u says that in the settlement there is no place for the ways of the old people … in the settlement we will surely die. He squats on the sand surrounded by the shelters and the people who wait without waiting … today, again, we will throw the bones to see which way the hunters must go. We look to our weapons with new hope, for perhaps the bones will say that we should hunt this way, or that way ... who can know?

From a small skin bag he tips the bones into his hand, and holds them so that they can know him again. He looks to me ... 'Paul, ha behn/igaw?' ... he asks that I come and sit with him. I too hold the bones, for over the last two years Gening/u has been teaching me the way.

The outcome today seems more important than itself ... the bones must tell ... perhaps the anxiousness is only in me, for I have not known the face of hunger for as long as these people have. For thousands of years they have lived through the relentless dry seasons, with nothing for crying children save the comfort of a mother's love. For me it is different, for me it will end when I go away to a kinder environment with only my memories of this time. But for them it never ends ... there is last year a thousand times before and next year a thousand times again ... it always comes ... this time of struggle and hunger, and the burden of the strong is that they must survive to go on repeating themselves through this forever.

I hold the bones ... waiting ... listening for the wisdom held in my body. The bones stay long in my hand for I have not yet learned the full measure of my own faith ... there is nothing else ... only faith ... for what is ours will come to us, nothing more and nothing less. My voice calls within ... let the nature spirits of the animals show us which way to hunt ... let the gemsbok speak to me as he has done before. Will I hear the sounds of wildebeest tongue rasping on the salt at the licking places to the east? ... Will I hear the sounds of the animals stung by our arrows and the noise of hooves running towards our spears?

And then, the bones thrown up like an offering ... asking ... holding, suspended for that moment in the ether ... and then falling, spread on the sand to show what is already known ... and as they lie they tell of !Nabehma the Tall One ... far to the southwest beyond Gantam//nau, in a place called //Aiee/u ... there we will find the fresh spoor of an old bull giraffe, and also young giraffe, and eland, which we have not seen for many moons.

In my thoughts I know that it is not the bones themselves that hold the knowledge, for they reflect only what comes through the human spirit. After a time the body comes to know in itself, and the outward tools, the bones, are no longer needed to show what is seen within. The memory of the world returns to the human who seeks.

And so it is decided … in the morning we hunt … all of the men. Khaachiro says that he will stay behind to keep safe the women and children. We know that he has neither the strength nor the will to hunt at this time. //Aiee/u is a faraway place and one man must stay with the women and the children. His name 'Khaachiro' means 'the peels of the wild cucumber'. He stays.

In our sleep we nurture the will for tomorrow's long hunt, and above us in the night the starlit sky … many animal forms in the ring of stars that circles our earth, each in turn reflecting its form and character into the earth's creatures … and on the southern edge of the earth I see the giraffe star – !Nabehma!Ono the Southern Cross – reaching up to the night sky … it is called by this name because the old people have said it that way.

I awaken in the darkness long before dawn, and through the opening of my shelter facing east, I feel it before I see it, the planet Mars in the new-moon sky … unblinking orange-red … and I ask this bearer of solar fire under whose gaze I lie, 'What wisdom, what courage will you evoke in these human souls today?'

We leave before the sun shows its face … black silhouettes against the first light … walking in the silence of our thoughts with many miles between ourselves and the Tall One. And later under the sun we walk beneath the huge vault of blue sky arching above our heads … the beginning and end of our perceived world … we walk through the day, weaving like a giant songololo across the endless sand face, dreaming … nine men … each held by the strength of the others. The man in front is the pathfinder … he must choose the way, and as he tires he slips back into the middle of the line, supported then by those behind and in front of him ... an energy line that lifts and binds us, one to the other. Through the endless afternoon we run and walk and run and walk until the first night fire ... sleep-weary brothers cradled on the earth. We do not talk of !Nabehma, for the time has not yet come.

In the way of the old people who heard it from their fathers, we offer a prayer to the young moon who evokes in us a feeling of what tomorrow may bring ...

Hail Young Moon!
Young Moon! Speak to me!
Hail, hail, Young Moon! Tell me something.
When the sun rises thou must speak to me, that I may eat something.
Thou must speak to me about a little thing, that I may eat.
Hail, hail, Young Moon!

Again we rise before //Gammsa the Sun, and continue on our journey. Late morning comes and two of the men branch off on the spoor of a single eland ... it is not fresh, but who can say what the day will bring? We others follow our feelings towards the tall one who waits for our arrows and spears, through the midday sun and onwards until the shadows grow longer and we cross the spoor that is less than an hour old ... an old bull giraffe as the bones had said. Tso/tgomaa and /Nedu khu kwe are the shooters today, and so they follow the spoor with bow and arrow. We others find ourselves under a large Giraffe thorn tree where we make fire, rest and wait. We have walked and run a long distance ... perhaps seventy kilometres from our shelters.

Time passes ... Kamageh pulls a /Gaa root from the ashes and says, 'There are no melons left here in //Aiee/u and these roots are bitter ... !Ouii ... they have no fat! ... no water ... even the small ones are bad.' And he asks, 'Did we not stay here once and eat /Gaa?'

'Aiee ... it was us,' says Gening/u. 'We were staying here and eating /Gaa.'

Tlok, tlok ... tlok, tlok, tlok ... ever resourceful, old Dzero-O uses the back of his digging stick to dislodge a large chunk of gum from the tree bark. He breaks it into smaller pieces for all to share. This /Nauu is the resin exuded by various acacia trees growing in the Kalahari ... Hook thorn, Camel thorn, Sweet thorn and others. It is a good and reliable source of sustenance, and also very nutritious ... a small handful will sustain a man on a day when there is nothing else to eat. Resin ... blood of the tree, which, when fossilised over millions of years turns to amber, sometimes holding trapped in its golden core small memories from a distant time, that we humans might be reminded of how much time and life has passed before our coming ... the memory of the world is held in so many ways, in so many forms visible and invisible.

We sharpen our spears, for the skin of giraffe is very thick. It is dusk when the shooters return. They say they did not walk far before they came upon the old bull ... they managed to shoot three arrows into him ... they say he did not see them, and so he will not be far away when we follow with our spears ... tomorrow will tell. And we know that no more can be said of /Nabehma, for he will hear our talk and become stronger than the poison on the arrows, and then he will run away from us.

The night comes, soft and gentle ... there is little talk but for the whispering of stars, bright and alive. In knowing obeisance to the forces that work in the world, we hold the lines of energy between ourselves and the Tall One ... we must wait for the rising of the sun before we give chase.

In the morning we take up our spears, but not too quickly, for the poison must have time to work against the strong blood forces in the giraffe. The young hunters go first, and the two old men, Dzero-O and Kamageh, follow at their own pace, collecting what bitter melons and tubers they find along the way.

The blood spoor lies on the sand face ... the old bull has walked some distance from where he was shot, out of a small valley and onto a great flat and barren plain. We find him ... /Nabehma ... he runs long graceful strides across the sand and we give chase … one … two kilometres, and then suddenly he turns and we become the hunted. He kicks out with huge front hooves that could easily kill the man caught between them … *clach*! … *clach*! … he kicks and we run. He chases us for a kilometre and then stops exhausted, as the heat of the poison takes its toll. We turn and chase him back the way we have come … he turns and we run again … and so it goes on and on, back and forth across the barren, sun-scorched plain until neither can run any further …

I will never forget the ridiculous picture of five little hunters being chased across the desert by an enormous bull giraffe. Shrieking and whooping our exhilaration under the sky, while at the same time wishing that the giraffe would just get tired so that we could all stop running.

After two hours of chasing each other around the Kalahari !Nabehma can run no more … he stands, long legs splayed … the heat of the poison stronger than his blood. We gather our strength and make ready for the kill.

Tso/tgomaa: 'Bring the spears … the giraffe will move … come closer on that side … call him towards you.'

Thuk … thuk … two spears.

Sema!ua: 'It has a hard skin … hit it, hit it!' … *Thuk* … 'Quickly!' … *Thuk, thuk …* 'You can see it is dying, its neck is coming down.'

/Nedu khu kwe: 'Run in now and kill it … this is how we do it!' … *Thuk*! … 'Blood is pouring!'

And !Nabehma the great bull … silently he stands looking down, swaying slowly back and forth as the light fades from his eyes, now gentle … at last then, his strength gone … the Tall One falls to earth. We stand, five men in silent awe of the truth and beauty that lies before us.

This has been no ordinary hunt, it was surreal and ritualistic … a moment was chosen and given, the bones had spoken and we had seen it from afar … suspended in the universe … an understanding that everything that comes into existence must perish, that one would surrender his physical form on this day so that others could continue. A sacrifice preordained ... that blood could flow and spirit be released into the ether, and in this way we are bound together in the common purpose of life, we and the Tall One continue as two parts of the same whole.

We begin with the enormous task of skinning, and with this comes the delightful graphic simplicity of male language unencumbered by the presence of women.

Gening/u proclaims with uplifted tongue, 'Hey! This one has got big balls!' (By this he means that the animal is thin.)

Seman!ua says, 'It is fat! We will be happy when we eat it, and we will throw sticks at one another ... anyone who is angry on a day like this will just die because of the giraffe.' He laughs.

/Nedu khu kwe: 'This is a big giraffe ... the one that ran off had light brown skin ... that first one was fatter.'

Gening/u to Kamageh: 'You must not be like a jackal ... hold it tight ... for the jackal is the one who eats last.'

Kamageh: 'Was the giraffe eating melons? ... Sometimes yes, because he has come from afar ... this giraffe has come from where the old melons are ... let me take off this back meat so that I can have the bones and eat their marrow later.'

Gening/u: 'Don't cut the stomach because the shit will spray all over ... that's a male intestine, Paul (indicating the small one to me) ... that's why it has got soft shit inside it.'

'Who has taken all the fat from the intestines?' he asks.

At the roasting pit nearby ... Kamageh says, 'The meat is tough but we can still eat it ... it's because this is an old giraffe.'

Seman!ua: 'A young giraffe has passed by here with tender meat ... this old giraffe has a big skull for roasting.'

/Nedu khu kwe: 'You chew loudly ... just like an old man!'

Seman!ua: 'It is long since we had meat like this.'

Kamageh: 'I wonder how long we will be in this place.'

Later that evening Tso/tgomaa walks out of the circle of firelight to urinate into a bush, and lets out a rather melodious-sounding fart ... everyone exclaims and laughs, and he turns deadpan and asks, 'Who me? ... No one farted here ... it was a gemsbok on the other side of the bush.' His remark is followed by howls of delightful laughter.

We sleep with bellies full of meat and the night is filled with dreams ... listening to the jackal and hyena who wait for what we will leave behind.

In the morning ...
    Tso/tgomaa: 'Come, let us cut this meat ... it is not too much.'
    Kamageh: 'We have been cutting since yesterday ... why does it not get finished so we can rest and wait for those men who have gone hunting eland?'
    /Nedu khu kwe: 'Who will cut the eland meat?'
    The old man: 'Even if the animal is big, one man can do it. A big eland can have a lot of fat around its heart.'

We hang endless strips of giraffe meat in the trees around us ... a mountain of meat that dries while we feast and wait for the hunters who went after Geuma the Eland.

I run my hands over the now bare skull of the old bull ... reinforced here and there with fist-size deposits of bone, each a testament to past battles fought against rival males. Male giraffe will engage in 'necking' battles by standing braced against one another with their legs splayed, and from this position swing paralysing head blows at their opponent's body ... powerful sledgehammer blows ... like wrecking balls smashing into the flanks and belly the other male until one surrenders. The skulls of old bulls show many of these battle scars and bone protrusions ... mapping the story of their lives.

Strangest of creatures, this /Nabehma ... tallest in the world and so exaggerated in form, but with a poise and grace like no other ... and so wonderfully adapted to its ecological niche, with oddly prehensile lips and a strange extensible tongue for stripping shoots and leaves from the tallest of trees. And with a great big heart, especially adapted to channel the forces expressed in the life-blood which pumps up a twelve-foot-long neck, held and formed around twenty-four strengthened, elongated vertebrae ... no more than we humans have. Large, expressive eyes with long beautiful lashes, and eyesight unrivalled in the animal kingdom ... the whole highly developed sense of this animal designed to gaze out upon endless landscapes ... altogether an utterly beautiful creation unique to Africa.

My hands on the skull feel the two bony horns ... about ten inches long on this old bull and inclined backwards ... and between and in front of these horns is a third unpaired horn, shorter than the others and inclined forward. This extra protuberance of bone bespeaks the concentration of forces in this beautiful sense-orientated head. /Nabehma ... the Tall One ... the name giraffe is derived from the Arabic word *geraph*, meaning 'the lovely one' ... and indeed, it is so.

Voices in the afternoon ...

Seman/ua: 'Cut it off and take this piece of meat.'

/Nedu khu kwe: 'Is this the knife which you went to look for this morning?'

Seman/ua: 'Aiee!'

/Nedu khu kwe: 'Is your quiver bag all right? How can you lose your knife?'

Seman/ua: 'I was running fast and my knife fell out.' And then adds sarcastically, 'I do run in the bush sometimes ...'

Kamageh: 'I told Seman/ua to turn the giraffe towards us, but he just ran past it and then the giraffe stopped ... it was tired.'

Seman/ua laughs and /Nedu says, 'No ... you were really running ... you were really running.'

/Gowsi and Magu return before the light fades on that day ... they say that the eland they were tracking had not stopped for their arrows and they have walked far.

After four sleeps the giraffe meat is dry and light enough to carry. Together we are nine men, and with our carry bags and sinew nets packed full, we leave for the shelters and the waiting people. Our return brings jubilation, and many days of rest and talk.

Morning comes … I sit with Tso/tgomaa behind his shelter and watch as he slices off the head of Kiam!ah. Most spiders are collectively called //Goobaa, but when one stands out with obvious power, it speaks its own name … and this spider is called Kiam!ah … it is the same as the one that came to me on the hunt. The poison beetle grub becomes scarce during the dry season, and although the spiders are more difficult to find, their poison is equally effective.

'This spider is for you, Paul,' he says. 'The poison will be hot.' He pushes the broken shaft of a gemsbok femur into the sand with the socket positioned upwards, and carefully squeezes the poison drops into the bone bowl. To this he adds juice from the chewed bark of a /Nooni tree, and then pastes the mixture onto the arrow shafts just behind the arrow heads, which he bakes slowly next to his fire, not too hot … not too dry.

We sit … each with our thoughts, from time to time rotating the arrow shafts towards the heat of the coals. On the other side of the shelter his youngest son /Gaie voices his sense of victory as he learns to stand … upright at last! I marvel at the nature within the human being that causes him to stand against the forces of gravity … to stand out of the horizontal … out of the animal inclination … into the human, upright position.

The sun hangs straight above the earth and the poison cloaks the arrow shafts just as it should. Tso/tgomaa asks if I would like to shoot with one of the arrows, and I accept his courtesy.

Two moons pass from the time of !Nabehma the Tall One … the feast now only a hungry memory as winter loosens its hold on the sand face.

THE TREE OF LIFE

Gening/u cannot walk the next day. He says that he had a bad and strange dream in the night, and then he awoke in terrible pain. The long hunts have taken too much out of him, and his left leg has seized up as if from some kind of rickets disease, a form of mineral deficiency brought on by the constant and excessive demand made on the body's life forces.

I watch his wife, Se/twago, and /Gaiekwe who carefully help him out of his shelter. Each holding an arm they take him to lie on a gemsbok skin in the morning sun ... so that //Gammsa may warm his cramped-up leg and nourish the pain. The people are hushed, for this is the first time that anyone has had any form of dis-ease in a long time. The /Gwikwe have enormous resistance to pain and hardship, they are as strong and resilient as any of God's creatures, and to see such an open admission of pain is worrying for all of us.

During this time the onus falls on the women to supply the band with food, and they too must travel far beyond their normal collecting places. The only tubers offered up by the earth in the dry season are /Gaa and Bie. The Bie root is normally eaten only by animals, and sometimes it is the spoor of /Tgooma the Gemsbok, which shows the way to the few remaining tubers.

Watching as the other women walk away, Geutwe says that if we cook the Bie roots and then add the leaves of the /Gaa creeper to the juice, it will become palatable. She says that she will not gather roots on this day, for she has other work.

'Du du du du du du du du haaaa!' Sitting in the entrance to their shelter she sharpens a small, flat piece of iron called //Ie-gosa, which she will use to cut tattoo marks into her husband Tgoo ... for even his snares have brought nothing for the last few weeks. Softly she says, 'By the time we leave this Kgoatwe place the ostrich will have killed you.' She is referring to the time when Tgoo killed an ostrich and the people were not happy during the time they were eating the meat, some were arguing over their portions, and so from that time on the hunting and the snaring has been bad. Tgoo says that there is no need even to check the snares these days ... there are no animals.

So Tgoo must now be cut ... for through the letting of blood there follows a strengthening of will, and in this he will bring back his luck as a hunter. Seman!ua, their son, watches quietly as Geutwe cuts his father on the arms, chest and forehead. 'Du du du du du haaaa!'

His mother has much to say, and she continues with a soft voice, 'Ostrich must die, Eland must die ... I am short of food ... Ostrich must die, Duiker must die and //Xau Ɣede must take all the bad luck away.'

'Du du du du du du' is the sound used when calling for good luck and 'haaaa' the sound of the duiker falling dead. And so she says, 'All the animals must die, Ostrich you must die, Eland you must die, Po you must die ... you must die so that your eyes can burst when we cook you in our fires ... don't be afraid of the snares you animals ... step into them and die.'

The cuts on Tgoo's forehead resemble the black mark on a duiker's forehead ... in the centre above and between his eyes, and these will bring him luck. And Geutwe says, 'Father of my eldest son ... no one can kill the animals like him ... his first wife is crying of hunger because Tgoo is now with me. Kgoatwe belongs to Tgoo, and now I have come to Tgoo. Die ... die ... all the animals must die ... 'she' has said it, and she is crying to the people to go and take the Ostrich ... some of the people will be carrying the Ostrich and some of the people will be carrying the Po ... du du du du du aiee! ... Aiee! ... I am talking of my eldest son's father ... his first wife has heard him and now she is crying.'

The cuts on his chest and arms will make him strong when pulling his hunting bow, and will ensure that he does not miss when shooting ... and Geutwe says, 'It is your land this ... it is your place ... does Kgoatwe hate you?'

Tgoo presses the ends of his hunting bow into the muscles on his chest and arms … this will help him to shoot straight, and to kill an animal with just one arrow … it is said that a good shooter will sometimes drop an animal in its tracks with just one strong and well-placed arrow.

From a small tortoise shell next to the fire Geutwe takes a black mixture of two sorts of burnt roots and smears this into his cuts. The roots are called //Alu and //Ale and can be used each by itself, but mixed together they are stronger. And this, too, will bring back his luck as a hunter, and make his family fat. When she is finished, they wipe their bodies with a mixture of stamped melon and seeds, to wash off the bad dirt so that fresh dirt can take its place … and so it is done.

I muse at Geutwe's earlier reference to Tgoo's first wife. This was the only case of divorce that I had ever encountered in all of my time among the Bushmen. We talked of it, and Tgoo himself said that it was because his first wife was such an angry person, that she complained all the time about everything, and a man could not live for long with such an unhappy woman. Those who were listening all agreed that she was indeed a very disagreeable person, and so, many years ago, she had gone back to live with her parents who had gone to the settlement.

Polygamy is extremely rare, and certainly something that I never encountered among wild Bushmen. A man has the responsibility of taking care of his parents-in-law, and it would be difficult to have to offer such a bride service to two sets of in-laws. Although permissible, it is simply not a practical option in a demanding environment. When people live together in harmony there is little need to change or sever the relationship, and so, in most cases, bride service from the groom to his in-laws seems to continue indefinitely.

Tired voices are carried in by the evening sun … the women return with skin bags half full, their legs scratched and slow. There is little to say … the last two years of drought have caused the Great Sand Face to suffer terribly. Everything they have found today is old and bitter. The /Gaa and Bie roots are roasted in the coals for a few hours before they are shared out, peeled and eaten, for they are our main source of liquid during this dry season, which lies four moons behind and still four moons ahead of us.

It has always been the way of life for the /Gwikwe of the Central Kalahari Desert, and it is no wonder that the alternative of life in a government settlement ... and water ... seems more and more attractive.

On these thoughts we sleep, and in the darkness of night I feel in my heart a great yearning for the Spirit lost in our world.

PASSING OF DAYS

Hunters on horseback pass by one morning ... they come from the settlement at /Xoie!om, riding to the west of our shelters on the outer circle of our snare lines. It is Seman!ua who brings us the news ... he says that they have leaf tobacco to trade for skins. He, his father and /Nedu khu kwe go out with some duiker and steenbok skins to trade ... tobacco brings pleasure in these hard times, and our bone pipes have been empty for some time now.

I do not wish to see the hunters from the settlement ... I have been where they come from, and I know the vulnerability that these last wild bush people have for the offered alternative of an apparently easier life in the settlement ... and the thought fills me with a familiar dread.

Too much human activity can place extreme stress on finely balanced natural ecosystems, and part of the reason that we struggle to find big game these days is because of these hunters from the settlement. They hunt from horseback and are able to run down and spear three or four eland in a day ... much more than they can use ... and having donkeys, they are able to carry vast quantities of meat back to the settlement to sell at a profit. We, on the other hand, take only what we need.

The settlement people are respectful of our immediate territory, but over the years they have hunted out most of the large antelope on which we depend for our survival. This is the oft unfortunate character of evolution and survival in a profit economy, and it is we who are left behind and must now consider the alternatives presented.

Even in an environment as harsh and dry as the Kalahari Desert, people have an obvious and natural reluctance to move or to be nomadic. The inference in most anthropological texts that 'the Bushmen are a nomadic people' is wrong! The earth's creatures are only nomadic of necessity, never by choice. In the olden days when these First People inhabited most of southern and eastern Africa, they hunted and gathered in areas abundant with water, game and veld food, and having thus no need to move, they stayed in larger groups and in permanent home-places.

But both time and history have run their course, and today the last free Bushmen eke out an existence in remote parts of the Kalahari Desert. It was the coming of more purposeful peoples, the African tribes from the north, and later the Europeans from the south that forever changed this age-old existence, for the newcomers were humans of a different consciousness, people with a different relationship to power and possession, who applied the pressure that drove the Bushmen to a forced nomadic existence, which in the end has come to this ... just a handful of people left in the harshest and most inaccessible of environments.

And still today the propensity for greed and material possession continues to taint and destroy the Soul of all that is good in humanity ... feeding the insatiable thirst for more and yet more, and when more comes then that too is not enough and the emptiness is never filled, for it is an emptiness of Spirit that can find no satisfaction in material gain.

In the desert there is no enemy outside of oneself, the adversary is found and confronted within each man alone ... we face only our own shortcomings.

The terrain itself imposes limitations ... not really a desert in the strictest sense of the term, the Kalahari is better described as sand veld, covered for the most part by thorn trees, grasses, and providing a variety of edible tubers, melons, berries and nuts that feed the many species that inhabit this dry, yet fertile environment. Such geophysical characteristics have always encouraged the survival of small, mobile groups of hunting and foraging creatures, be they animal or people. Small bands of between twenty and thirty Bushmen range within an area of roughly four hundred square miles within a radius of about fifty miles around their shelters, and these natural boundaries have delineated the unspoken territory of each band, a relationship both pragmatic and balanced, with a natural division and utilisation of resources.

Hunting and gathering within this territory still allows – in terms of daily distances travelled – for the return to a permanent home at night, and in an area this size the impact of thirty-four people on the resource base is not severely felt, thus allowing for the recovery of the prey and the natural replenishment of other food resources on an annual basis. Successful ecological adaptation remains the basic prerequisite for the survival of any life form, and for the /Gwikwe it is their adaptability to movement, and flexibility of band size within a supportive social structure, which has ensured their survival for so long.

There was a time when the earth gave more freely and there was more to be had ... the animals were many and the plant foods grew with greater abundance. The changes that are upon the world are because of changes in the spirit of men, for we no longer see the spirit of the world, and no longer do we evoke the assistance of the spirit beings in our tending of the earth and its creatures, and so we stand alone as never before. The Bushman people do not see the world outside of this place in the way that it is, they do not see the ignorance and greed that has laid waste to the great earth body ... they do not see that it is our doings that have brought this change ... they see only that something has changed. It is for us, who know, to carry the burden of shame. Life continues as we think and feel and will our way through the world, and for now the /Gwikwe do not surrender their relationship with the spiritual realm, for it is all that they have ... but this, too, is passing.

Here in the Kalahari, where the spirit is alone with itself, one can see what is true and eternal. To live in the vastness of the desert in this way is to face into infinity, and when there is nothing that reflects back at you, you are forced to look within to where everything you are and everything you are not stands before you; that you may choose ... knowing that your every thought will become a creation.

During the heat of the afternoon I watch as Geutwe and Se/twago tattoo a finger-long row of cuts onto the still cramped hip of Gening/u, who has remained immobile in his shelter for two days now. The appropriate letting of blood in any ritual triggers the impulse to change ... to invoke movement in the fluid body is to evoke the memory of a different state of being, and the body then follows the impulse to return to its original state. Sometimes this is not enough, and the pain continues.

Voices ... Geutwe says to Tgoo that he took a Bie root that she had put aside in their shelter ... he says that she must not worry about the root, because people must share, and she must not worry about water ... she says that the children need the water ... .

Seman/ua and the other men return in the evening, bringing news of relatives in the settlement and a government subsidy of mealie meal ... and water. The hunters have gone ... leaving behind some tobacco and an alternative to be considered.

That evening around the fire the men talk of /Xoie/om, the settlement, and the band reacts as if insecure and disturbed. After fifteen thousand years of living out this ancient relationship with life, these new considerations are significant. Through their long history they have always lived according to the old way, they have never had the choice of a different life ... but now they do.

Seman/ua says that he knows of a young woman in the settlement with whom he would like to visit ... and we understand his need. We are isolated out here ... the last band of wild /Gwikwe. In the olden days there were Bushman bands spread throughout the Central Kalahari, and so they shared in a broader social structure. There was interaction between different bands, and when a young man came to hear of a young woman in a neighbouring territory, he would hunt in that direction more often, and perhaps he would meet up with the women of the other band while they were out gathering. In this way, he might come to meet with the young woman and her family, and if she said that he was handsome to look upon, then in this way a young man could find his mate ... it was easier then.

The women play bow harp in the darkness, and their songs say much of the nature of these people ... the first song is played when somebody has been accused of something ... the second and third are the songs of a man walking who thinks he is very pretty ... and the fourth is about a man who is very weak because he has not eaten for a long time.

Silently we pass the bone pipes back and forth, and the enormity of the situation occurs to me ... I sit here in the middle of the Kalahari Desert within the last band of free Bushmen left on this earth. I know that in the great picture of life everything is as it should be, but here in our world it feels as if something terribly wrong is happening.

I am young ... I follow a vision that is not yet clear, but with enough sense to know that I must follow myself in faith. This is the beginning of a journey that will take many years to complete, and I trust then that I will understand what it is I must do. This life, however, goes on ... I make no effort to influence their decisions, but I do know that the more time we spend together the easier their transition will be. As if through some spiritual osmosis together we can better absorb the impact, which has in the past eroded and destroyed so many of the world's first peoples, so many fine cultures from whom we have failed to learn that which we need to know if we are to survive into the future.

Sadly now, this is the way forward from here for all of early humanity ... this is the earthly journey of cultural transition from the old to the new, and we are simply the last of the First People … our earth time is done … and our soul-journey must continue …

ONE DAY

The next day there are vultures in the sky. The sun is already hot as I follow Tso/tgomaa, Tgoo and Seman!ua across the barren and scorched sand face with that feeling of hope in our chests. As the sand burns my feet I think of Gening/u, the healing man, who cannot walk, who lies helpless in his shelter, and deep in my heart is the faint feeling not yet expressed in thought … that it is I who will have to bring the strength back to his leg, for over the last ten moons or so I have come to understand the nature of the invisible forces that bind all things in health and sickness … it is part of my learning to be a healing man.

We find a male wildebeest in a snare with vultures around the carcass … in silence we stand … it died two days ago when no one thought it necessary to check the snares … how could we forget that the earth would give us the food we need … give us each day our daily bread.

Even the vultures have come too late … the sun has already spoiled the meat, the flies have laid their eggs and the maggots have hatched … the stomach blown up and burst from the heat. Tso/tgomaa squats and puts his arm elbow-deep into the open stomach and pulls out a handful of chewed and fermenting grass. Squeezing out thick green liquid into his other cupped hand he drinks … it is necessary, and so we all drink, for there is no choice in this thirstland … bodies without liquid cannot live.

Tso/tgomaa scrapes maggots from the muzzle and out of the animal's open mouth. We others stand and watch, for even among these last wild people, there are few with such focussed will to survive, few so impeccably adapted to this relentless reality. I watch the man in awe … a pure human creature who survives with a grace that is wondrous to behold. He says that the meat is not yet poisonous and will be eaten ... and so it is ... and for three days the air around the shelters is filled with the stench of rotting, drying meat ... but this is nothing compared to the needs of hungry people.

ANOTHER DAY

The wind carries to my ears the sound of hands rubbing one against the other ... Magu sits hunched over an ostrich egg onto which he engraves with a rudimentary drill bit ... a small piece of sharpened metal in the end of a soft stick, which he twirls between his palms. He drills as many as two thousand small indents into the eggshell surface, and then rubs into each indent a mixture of fat and charcoal. The gradually emerging form takes the shape of an ostrich and two antelope ... /Tgoosa, female Gemsbok, with fat bellies and long, graceful horns reaching upwards to heaven. I see that they have human feet in place of hooves ... reflecting something in the memory that recalls the time when animals were people were as animals.

Images engraved on ostrich eggshells are beautiful expressions of the human relationship with the animal world, the creatures through whom we sustain our lives ... they that live in sacrifice to the human kingdom. Animal brothers and sisters, the gemsbok and the ostrich ... eland and wildebeest ... images of honey bees and the memory lines that bind one to the other ... reflections of a life.

Bushman paintings and engravings of animals are not drawn from cerebral memory, not of the outer shape or form of the animal, but from the artist's feeling or inner perception of the animal ... a recalling of the essence, the life-body of the animal. And the image need not always be especially significant or magical, it can simply be that which holds your heart on the day ... in the same way that anyone might draw or photograph those things most loved ... remembered in passing. We modern humans have the propensity for sometimes attaching undue significance to that which we do not know.

When you look carefully at any animal painting, at any number of gemsbok painted or engraved by different Bushman artists, then you will see that they all have the same feeling about them ... the same spirit. This is because the Bushman sees and feels the Soul-body of the animal, and because all the gemsbok share a group Soul they all reflect the same essence. So it is the 'collective' Soul of the animal that is always so aptly captured in the form painted or engraved by the Bushman.

There is much that is wrongly presumed in the interpretation of Bushman art and culture, for intellectual perception allows little appreciation of the super-sensible realm ... and so the opinion offered regarding these people who live in the imaginative world of feeling, is so often so wrong. This is not a deliberate error of judgement, it is simply that we do not know ... we modern humans have changed, our way of perception has altered ... we no longer perceive in the way that early humans did.

I ask Magu why he engraves a picture of gemsbok today, and he says simply that he does it for the rain ... if he prepares the container then surely the water will come? 'Kirre kwa khuusa /un ... I want the rain.' He uses the female word for rain because in his imaginings he feels for the coming of 'female rain' ... the soft rain that fills the earth with wetness ... and it is this simple wish, poured into the eggshell container, which will help to bring the rain.

In this world of cause and effect we should exercise great consideration with our thoughts and expression, for what we intend does indeed come to pass, and always at the right time. Rain-making can only occur as a selfless act. The relationship with the spirits of the watery element can only be evoked in absolute selfless reverence ... a barely conscious act of willing that calls forth from your Soul directly to those forces and beings that through divine grace will bring the rain. In time it will be understood that my interpretations are neither fanciful nor wishful, but rather that I am attempting to describe in pragmatic terms the nature of the actual relationship, which in an earlier time existed between man and the elemental beings.

I attempt here to affect a change in the thinking by which we come to know the truth of the 'other', for only in this way will we understand that which has been carried in ever-changing form in the human stream of consciousness for so long. Misinterpretation is seldom deliberate, but is nonetheless incorrect! It is the understanding and the opinion of an individual, based on the consciousness, thinking and language of that individual. In our physical material world of today, this has resulted in a vocabulary of thinking that is fundamentally inadequate to form the correct interpretation of what derives from a completely different human consciousness, from a different vocabulary and a different way of thinking.

Prejudiced observations seem to persist in the literature, and I quote here something I once read 'tremendous outbursts of elemental fury which sometimes visit the country, made their appearance, and the Bushman's superstition and dread were aroused, which among some of the tribes culminated in fits of impotent rage, as if the war of the elements excited their indignation against the mysterious power that they supposed was the cause of it'. If the author knew the people about whom he spoke he would not have made such an observation, for wild Bushmen have no 'superstition and dread' of the elements within which their lives are immersed. They have an innate sense of relationship with these forces, and it follows, therefore, that they have no inappropriate superstitions that would jeopardise the vital symbiosis of their living relationship with those elemental forces. The 'fits of impotent rage' are feigned, with a subtle and implicit humour. The nature and power of the elemental forces was never mysterious to the Bushmen, and there is no ignorance implicit in this relationship. Their relationship with thunderstorms holds far less mystery than it does for modern city-dwelling humans, not many of whom have experienced the full force of such an event unprotected in the open.

For us /Gwikwe, it is like this ... if you stand within a storm, a huge male rain, then you will know of the awesome power of that force which unleashes around you ... it is fearsome! You would not wish this force to be oblivious of you, but rather that it knows where you are and how you stand within yourself and all things ... for you would be Spirit-Man, and you have an I ... a Self. In this, you feel a strong inclination to stand both in reverence and in strength, and to shout your presence to this imposing force so that it can know 'that' you are ... so that it can know 'where' you are and not strike you! Such is the relationship between the elemental beings and the First People.

Now warmed by the afternoon sun, Magu lies stretched out on his stomach under the Old Man's Tree, his back stiff from sitting hunched over the ostrich egg for so long. He mumbles his feigned discontent into the sand, 'Come on, children ... climb on ... come, Seka, climb on like before ... we can't chase kudu in this kind of wind ... come, //Nale/twago ... if you were grown up you could stand on my neck. What kind of children are these who don't understand? Come, Seka ... come, my son ... climb on.'

Crowing their delight, two warm, fat, naked little bodies climb and clamber upon this weary invitation, with each prod or fall helping to massage the back and the mood of Magu on this day. His sister-in-law //Gama says to her little daughter, 'Take that digging stick and stab him with it.' And Magu lies there, softened by the pleasure of the little ones ... until finally ... 'Aiee ... leave me to sleep now,' he says ... and they do.

We are so familiar with the other, our nakedness a truthfulness in the way that we live together. We do not know the other through layers of clothing that hide and mask the form, we know the form of the other ... each nuance of shape and shoulder blade, of belly and buttock, limb and leanness ... an intimacy that binds us one to the other.

What we take in through our eyes nicely open is the gift of the other, the slope of the inner thigh of women, the fall of valley from neck to breast, and the man body on limb lean and strong. And from a distance we know ... we know the fall of light on curved stalking back, we know the shape of hunter's leg moving, and the lift of woman buttock as she bends for root or melon from the earth, and breast that hangs pendulous from lithe form as soft melon off bended body ... now she looks like an ostrich, an antelope, and he like an eagle in his eyes far-seeing, like a leopard ... the line of muscle, the crouch of sinew. We live together as one here on our earth place ... these wondrous nuances delicate to each individual ... the smells and sounds that come from these bodies painted into being by light and movement ... the human body given to the act of living in such a world is a sharing of truthfulness like none other.

I walk away from the shelters in search of a tree or bush that will give me the right piece of wood from which to make a dancing stick, for there are now things in our lives that say that it will soon be time for a healing dance. At the same time I check the snares ... they lie empty.

A relentless August wind washes in endless waves across the day, scouring the last tenacious leaves from every branch and bush ... the Great Sand Face cleansed for new growth, new life and all that comes with the Spring.

While walking I think of the many journeys that I have made to look at rock paintings, engravings and other ancient art. When approaching an old rock shelter or other place of power where these First People gathered and lived, I feel a quickening in my body and a mild trance-like state. A heightened consciousness comes over me, because of the memory lines that have been opened in my being ... the lines that bind us to more than we are. I remember to listen carefully at these times, for these opportunities become my moments of revelation ... in the way that I have learned, by listening through my whole being, I can know the age of the painting on the rock, and know of the person who painted the image, and of the circumstances at that time ... I can feel the thought that gave rise to the action. The residue of the energetic impulse that compelled the artist to put pigment to rock is held as a memory in the life body of that rock, and in the image depicted, and this memory I have learned to read.

In the same way, sacred artefacts throughout history have held the memory of the human spirit and of the events that gave rise to their value. If one thinks of those holy artefacts of antiquity, like the shroud of the Christ, the Spear of Destiny, the staff of an initiate druid, or the sword once wielded by a revered warrior king of an ancient culture ... these objects hold power, and sometimes great power, for the same forces that suffuse our own human form penetrate all that we touch.

I know that what many Bushman paintings depict is a reality very different to what we experience today ... a reality that we can now only imagine. What we interpret as 'painted in a trance-like or altered state of perception' was not always so, for it is said that the earth and all that lived upon it was different then, and that the strange animal forms depicted in many paintings were indeed real, for such were the old astral forms clearly revealed to humans in those times. These were the various winged and flying creatures ... the alites and the therianthropes ... part animal part human, and the great rain animals in the clouds, whose rain legs walked the African horizons.

And the records of great dances in ancient times ... bodies etched red and black on rock ... shapeshifting animal forms merged in and out of the human form as if part of the same physical entity. We should see these pictured forms as sublime conceptions of a spiritual world. The forms and figures painted on cave walls and rock overhangs throughout the African landscape are not imaginary, as supposed by those who seek to interpret the truth expressed within this vast heritage of story pictures. They are real perceived forms of Nature Spirits and other Spiritual beings encountered within the invisible world ... beyond the world of the senses. They are not some nebulous abstraction revealing itself to the trance dancer, but something real that provides an insight into the complex and beautiful nature of the archetypal human being. And when one comes to comprehend the human as a multidimensional being with more than just a physical body, consisting also of a Soul and Spirit-body, one comes to know more of the true nature of man. Do we really think that God would create only the dimensions of physical form within which we blunder about? No, we are more than we suppose!

That which expresses itself from within the realm of spirit does so with as much clarity as that which presents itself through the senses in the physical realm. It is our organs of perception that must be redeveloped, for we cannot see into four dimensions with three-dimensional eyes. It is evident that we humans are constantly surrounded and interpenetrated by a host of invisible forces and beings who constantly work within and through our lives, sometimes in empathy and sometimes in antipathy, for there are, indeed, dark forces that seek to distract us from the Light. And it is our denial of the existence of absolute truth, which gives power to these dark forces, a denial determined by the degree to which each man expresses his own lower animal nature.

So, with the passing of time, it is not only the human perception of the world that has changed, but also the world itself. We are surrounded by much that we could know, if we would only look with different eyes.

I think of these people ... of what it is that makes this stream of humanity so different. What impulse gave rise to their being in Africa, and what in their consciousness sets them so apart from the other African peoples. For the Bushman has a different inclination of Soul, a different manner of being, which does not express itself into the world in the way it does with the other African peoples. The Bushman makes no wrong use of anything in life, nothing is used in the service of dark occult, everything is inadvertently and only for the good. His relationship with the earth and himself, with the cosmos and with God is fundamentally different, revealing an inherent wisdom akin to that which each of us will find going forward in our own consciousness. And it is important to understand that the Bushman is not conscious of that which he bears ... but simply that, by the inclination of his pure Soul, he carries with no prejudice the archetypal blueprint of the full human being.

In the blood memory of these people is the primordial record of the fall of humanity ... the journey from old form and consciousness to new. The memory of our fall from grace is embedded in Bushman stories and paintings, recorded as a rite of passage of the human Soul ... a journey, which takes humanity from blindness in the light, to seeing in the darkness ... through descent to ascension.

If we look with more care at the pictures, and listen with more care to the stories, then through these last people of Eden our fall from grace can be understood ... brought into cognition from unconscious memory, so that we humans now can go forward with nothing forgotten ... everything redeemed.

A HEALING MAN

A few days of respite, but the feeling continues ... what is this bad luck that has come to the people? For two whole moons the hunters go out every day, and come home with nothing ... small things ... just enough for the children. Some say it is the abortion that has brought the bad luck. Dzero-O says it is the talk of /Xoie!om, the settlement that pulls the people apart ... and for a long time we have not danced ... and Gening/u, the healing man with the sickness in his leg, does not leave his shelter. I know now that it falls upon me to heal my friend and brother.

The last six difficult months have overtaken old /Tguikwe. She is now almost blind and must be helped to find her way ... she will not be neglected. When she needs to walk away from the familiar area around the shelters, one of the children holds the front end of a stick and the old lady holds onto the back end ... and so they walk.

Geutwe grumbles about her son Seman!ua, 'When a person talks to him he always looks the other way.'

It is Magu who comes to me when the sun already burns the sand. He sits in the entrance to my shelter. 'Tsamkwa /tge?' he asks in greeting. Are your eyes nicely open? I say, 'Yes, my eyes are nicely open,' for I know why he has come. He says that the women have asked if I will take away the pain in Gening/u's leg ... and so I know that I must.

He goes to the group of women who lie in the sun a little distance away from Gening/u's shelter, and tells them that I will take care of Gening/u when the afternoon shadows begin to grow.

I stay in my shelter through the middle of the day ... I need to silence myself and find in me the right feeling of pure intent. I have no clear idea of what I will do, but I know with certainty and with all of my heart that I really want to heal this man who has done much for me. I live in two worlds, ancient and modern, and have come to know that it is not the tool in the hand that does the healing, but the force that flows through both. I pray to the great father God as we humans often do in times of need ... I ask for help, and a stillness comes into me.

And when the shadows grow longer, I walk across the sand between the shelters. The women are gathered together under the Old Man's Tree ... close to Gening/u's shelter, and when I see their eyes filled with faith, I know that I have no choice, for such is the strength of our accord ... and so with clear purpose I enter the shelter of the healing man. I ask Magu to close the entrance with a gemsbok skin ... it is not that I would hide my doings from the people, but just that I am vulnerable with my newly taken responsibility of shaman.

Gening/u lies on his side with his left leg curled and cramped to the hip, eyes closed and body quivering in pain. I sit quietly behind him and speak a soft reassurance, 'Paul se habe ... I am here Gening/u.' I pray to the God of all humans to assist with this healing ... I place my hands upon him, and with my whole heart I intend that the sickness come out of his body, and that his strength return ... I will the forces of the earth and life up and through my body and hands and into his leg and hip, which burn like fire under my touch ... I feel the quickening in my blood and the n/um forces jolting up my spine ... a wind fills the silence behind my eyes and I become too big for my body ... a powerful wind builds up from inside, roaring and roaring in the shelter, and then I see from outside myself that I am above the ground ... I am sitting above Gening/u, who lies beneath me and the wind is thunderous around us ... forces ripping through my being and the body of my brother ... I am high above him and the space between us has no more distance, and everything is white, white light radiant, and I am lost inside the miracle of life and my heart would explode, and we are all one thing ... the wind, the shelter and Gening/u and I we are one thing ... and somewhere in the wind and the light Gening/u cries out the pain, and the roaring inside subsides and subsides and then we are in white silence inside of ourselves together and I have no thought of where I have been, but I feel that the wind has now come to rest inside of me and I sit with my hands on my brother.

After a long, long while I begin slowly to move ... I see that Gening/u sleeps and that the light in the shelter fades as I open my eyes ... I stand and push back the gemsbok skin and look out as if into a strange world ... the day has gone to darkness and the women sit around a fire under the Old Man's Tree and they watch me as I walk silently back to my shelter ... and sleep ... both Gening/u and I. We sleep in silent darkness with our Spirits far away ... .

In the morning I awaken still inside my dreams ... there are no thoughts in my head and no words on my tongue. Looking out of my shelter I see that the women are still under the Old Man's Tree and warm in the morning sun. I go and sit with them and make silent greeting. After a while they tell me that they did not know what was happening with me and Gening/u the day before ... and they say that all they could hear was the sound of wind, a big wind blowing, mixed with the roaring of a lion from inside of the shelter ... Ggamm. They say they were not a little fearful of looking, and so they just waited.

For a while we lie quietly on the warm sand, with soft murmurs of conversation and one unspoken expectation, and then in a moment of silence the gemsbok skin is pushed gently aside and Gening/u steps out of his shelter ... half asleep he walks around to the back of his shelter to urinate ... no one speaks. Water poured into the earth, he turns and walks towards us, and then, as it slowly dawns upon him that he is walking, he stops and looks down at his leg, stamps it on the ground and breaks into a wide and gentle smile as he stands above us and tells us that his eyes are nicely open and his leg is fine ... it is truly fine ...

I am humbled ... quietly I give thanks as I look at the sand beneath my feet and see only his smile in my heart and the power of faith.

It is a peaceful day.

I wander around inside my thoughts of the Spirit forces which work through us at times like these. Whether they be Nature Spirits or still higher beings and angels, there is only one source, one place of truth and light from which all life streams ... I have come to know from my journeys inside the Spirit realm that all comes only through one name.

HUNTER PREDATOR

It is now dry season in the Kalahari Desert and the hunter has returned ... he sits silently at a small fire a little way from the shelters and I see him ... lithe upper body, powerful and muscled like a predator ... long lean legs of an antelope, covered in fine scratches, dust and tiredness. He had left the shelters early this morning, at the time when the birds first awaken ... when the eastern horizon bleeds softly and tells of //Gammsa the Sun, which will soon be rising, and of how, when it does, it will burn ǂGuam/tge. Since olden times the /Gwikwe have called the earth ǂGuam/tge – the Great Sand Face.

Tso/tgomaa is a hunter, and now he sits alone ... contained in his own silence. When the people eat ǀKhaa, the wild cucumbers roasted in hot coals, he does not eat, for he holds the energy line that joins him to the wounded animal of whom he will not speak. Later, he will sleep ... alone.

I dream such dreams in the night. I dream that I am far away from our Kgoatwe place and the people, and I cannot come back ... everything unseen pulls at me and stops me from returning, and in my dream the struggle does not resolve.

I awaken early and lie quietly in my shelter waiting for the red sky, thinking of the part of me that I cannot find. Somewhere in my Soul is the memory of another life, of a journey unresolved ... and then I hear the old man, Dzero-O, moving around, so I leave my shelter and go to his fire. '/Tgeah?' he asks. 'Are your eyes nicely open?' My silence speaks my uncertainty. The August wind blows and sighs like my own breath, with the mournfulness of a long-remembered sadness for the sacrifice of being human.

The great sun rises and I walk with Tso/tgomaa and Tgoo towards the north. We walk for two hours and find the spoor of a gemsbok bull ... but we are not alone in our quest, for the sand tells us that three lions follow the same spoor ... they too, track the wounded animal. When food is in short supply, competition with other predators becomes fierce, and lions will scavenge whenever they can.

An hour later we find the gemsbok, but the lions have come before us. Two females and a male ... like golden shadows they disappear in the winter grass, and we stand hungry at the bare carcass. I think on how quiet it is, and somehow I hear the echoing beat of Tso/tgomaa's heart ... almost as if he would cry if he spoke too soon, and so we just stand in silence ... Tgoo at his side, and I ... brothers. 'This thing has happened,' he says.
  'There is no use in anger ... for the lions must also eat'.
  'Are we not all brothers?' I ask ... and in my heart beats the certainty.

We take what the lions have left and head back for the shelters. On the way we find a caracal caught in one of Tgoo's snares ... it had eaten a guinea fowl caught in a second snare, and had itself been caught.

Disappointment follows our footsteps today ... we need meat. The people are sad about the gemsbok, but not angry with the lions. 'It is the way of life,' they say ... and the caracal is skinned, roasted, and eaten.

The old people say that when they kill a jackal to roast on their fires, they will not eat the heart, for the jackal is a timid animal that runs even from the footprints of men, and so they do not eat the jackal's heart lest it should make them fearful in themselves. The /Gwikwe will eat leopard, cheetah and all cats except for lion, because lion sometimes kill and eat people, and Bushmen don't ever eat people ... even by association the thought of cannibalism is absolutely taboo in this culture.

If ever there comes the maturity of soul to look honestly into the 'struggled' past of black Africa, then know that the Bushman is wholly exempt from any custom of blood sacrifice or the eating of human flesh ... there is no inclination to the dark occult in the soul of these people. In Africa, the pure-blood Bushman stands as a beacon to what is right in the human Soul ... he reveals in innocence the very nature of 'That which must be filled with Spirit'. And that ... going forward ... is our task.

WHEN BOYS BECOME MEN

The older boys are learning to hunt. In the late afternoon they go with Tso/tgomaa when he checks the snares. Already quite competent at setting his own snares, Geamm shows all the promise of one day being the hunter that his father is ... and Tso/tgomaa is probably the finest wild hunter left on the Great Sand Face.

In silence the boys watch as he squats, predator-like and focussed, carefully reading the sand to see what he has missed ... to know what it is that he should do differently ... he must reset a snare that has been triggered by a duiker, but lies empty ... and //Guama must not escape the snare, for then the people will not eat.

The snare itself works on a fairly simple principle … a hole in the ground, perhaps twelve inches deep, a grass rope made from ǃGoie fibre, which forms the noose that is held under tension on a bent green sapling or bush. The noose with a sliding knot is held down by sticks across and around the perimeter of the hole. Carefully concealed with grass and lumps of sand the snare lies in wait … any pressure on the sticks releases the trigger stick, which springs the noose and traps the animal's foot … the hunters do the rest.

It is nothing to make a snare, the mechanics are simple and effective. The skill that must be learned from years of observation is in knowing where to place it. When you set a snare for any animal you must know the habits of that animal, how and where it walks, how and what it eats, and when. Every nuance of personality and behaviour that you understand helps to ensure your success as a hunter, and everything you need to learn is written in the sand.

On the way back to the shelters the boys lead the way … each proud within himself as he learns the ways of being a man.

In the morning Tso/tgomaa teaches his son how to scrape skin. He shows him the way of the old people, and tells him that whistling onto the blade of the scraper in a certain way will help to make it sharp, and to scrape cleanly. This is an old /Gwikwe tradition done only with scrapers, not with knives or axes. Whistling onto the blade in this way is not an arbitrary act of superstition, it is a deliberate enactment of a natural, energetic interrelationship … a relationship of forces that these people understand.

The role of ritual and tradition is easily misunderstood in the world today. If one thinks back, then one will find that many rituals originated in that olden time when relationships between all living things were more clearly perceived … more considered, and it follows, therefore, that the correct performing of the ritual is specific and critical to the outcome. The channelling of intent through light, sound and movement has a great effect on our lives and our surroundings, and it is from the realm of clairvoyant knowledge that many rituals originate and become tradition.

The /Gwikwe do not forget these ancient wisdoms, they live them, constantly reinforcing their very pragmatic relationship with the forces of life ... and today I see that the blades of the scrapers stay sharp ... and they scrape the skin of /Tehma the Wildebeest. The skin scrapings will be cooked and eaten together with /Gaa roots ... the dry earth still provides ... but little.

I remember the day we scraped the leopard skin ... it was a big male, !Ooema, and he had been robbing the snares. We men, we gathered around the skin which had been pegged out and dried, and we considered the spirit of that leopard on that day. We were sitting away from the shelters, because it was not a thing for women and children ... if the skin scrapings went into the stomach of a woman or child they would feel great pain, and it would be as if the leopard had come alive inside of their bellies and was tearing at them ... so it was work only for men.

And I remember, when we sat around that skin it was as if we became leopards ourselves, for something came over us and we did not speak with words, just the growl and rasp of leopard voice passing between us. We had been scraping from when the sun first showed its face until the time that the sun was in the middle of the sky ... each man with his own thoughts ... scraping ... just scraping and not talking, and we remembered that animal soul.

It was then that some of the smaller children had wandered away from the shelters and came too close to where we sat with that leopard spirit ... and suddenly, together, as one animal we leapt ... and, growling, we ran at them ... low and crouched, fierce as we ran, for we had become as leopards on that day ... and the children saw us coming through the grass, angry and fierce, and they screamed ... they just stood and screamed their terror of the leopard, and then the mothers came running out of the shelters with sticks and other weapons and, shouting, they chased us back towards the leopard skin, and we went backwards, growling and angry, for the mothers too were fierce and they took the children back to the safety of the shelters, and we leopard-men returned to scraping the skin of that animal.

It was a big leopard, from his nose to his tail he measured eight and a half feet. Long would I remember the spirit of that leopard.

DANCE THE HEALING DANCE

The sun passes through the day and I sit and dream in the space of open sand between the shelters ... the sandy hearth that holds us all together and to the earth ... I hear unfamiliar sounds ... voices raised in anger? Anxiety? /Gowsi is angry with his sister-in-law, Sema!nabi, and so he speaks with uplifted tongue! It seems from their words that she has taken a /Gaa root that he had put aside for his children ... she has taken the root for her own child, /Nana, who is not feeling well, for /Nana is not a strong child, and so who can blame her ... who can blame anyone?

Hunger changes people ... there is some quarrelling these last days, anxiety directed at everyone and at no one in particular. It is a general, almost instinctive insecurity, each of us caught in his own expression thereof ... triggering some biological mechanism that impels us towards conflict and then to the inevitable resolution wherein lies our security.

It is time for the healing dance ... .

It is the women who begin, with voices ... gently pulling us to the circle where we can be one ... that the outer rhythm and the inner rhythm become the same ... today they call softly, slowly easing the reluctance from our hearts ... they call with their voices and clapping, urging our feet to the circle and the dance ... tones, overtones and intervals ... sounds in movement and colour, which coerce and compel our immersion into a life-stream so powerful that it puts us in awe of the very idea.

Gening/u, the healing man, puts his rattles on ... recovered from the sickness in his leg ... he ties them on his ankles ... *tsshikk*! *tsshikk*! ... *tsshikk*! ... it is a good sound they make ... and the voices pull, and our feet stamp the ground of Africa in the way that we have for many thousands of years ... our heartbeat on the earth ... our Spirit in the world.

Before we dance there is much to say and much to consider ...

/Gwikwe spirituality is both communal and individual, and not, as in most modern religions, the sacred preserve of the medicine man or priest. Whoever wishes, takes part ... all you need is the inclination of soul.

The role of the 'priest kings' in human history is now obsolete. No longer do we need to be shepherded by priests and kings, for we carry the 'priest king' inside of ourselves, we seek our own council, we express our own knowledge, and have the freedom to choose, each our own way. The consequences of our actions are not preordained by another, but contemplated by ourselves, and of course our contemplation is sometimes lacking in wisdom, but slowly we must learn ... for only through knowledge imbued with Spirit will our consciousness evolve to meet the order of the cosmic day.

The medicine dance serves an important function in the band. Through dancing, our anxieties and fears are dissipated, scattered and absorbed into the forgiving arms of the universe ... through dancing we bring the people together again in communal spirit ... one circle one path.

What follows is neither mythology nor metaphor, it is simply their description of the physical spiritual foundation of our world.

And we believe in one Great God ... //Gamahma ... he is a father figure and capable only of goodness. He has two wives, and his children are the sun and the moon, who are said to be married. He and two wives ... in a genderless cosmos this reflects the relationship of the oneness of three ... a Trinity.

Considered the children of God, Sun and Moon are regarded as living beings by the Bushmen. The sun is not perceived as a lifeless ball of gas emitting light in the sky, but as a great celestial being who streams forth living forces into this world. One has but to pause for a moment, to see these forces of life-giving light evidenced in the world around us, and the forces of love reflected in the marriage between the sun and the moon in the giving and receiving of light, and so also in the interrelationship of giving and receiving between all things. And the moon is not seen as a lifeless lump of rock reflecting the sun's light to earth ... it, too, is a living celestial being, and in this understanding our relationship with the sun and the moon must come to be a living, Soulful relationship.

This marriage between sun and moon reflects a living relationship, for the moon has no light of its own. The light forces that stream from the Sun-being are reflected by the Moon-being to the Earth-being, even in the darkness of the night ... always somewhere, the light of the sun touches the life on earth and so further awakens, in reverence, the mystery of the sun in the human heart.

From the beginning these three great heavenly bodies are joined in a spiritual symbiosis that reflects in the living human, and our relationship with these celestial beings is part of the opportunity that was hidden from humanity, when, some four hundred years ago ... through the machinations of church, politics and science, we were led to believe that the sun was nothing more than a ball of gas, and so for us, a dynamic spiritual relationship was severed. And through this severance, this separation and the ensuing time of spiritual darkness, we begin to know the consequence of the fall of humanity ... of humanity's journey away from the Light ... even until today ... and the light shines in darkness, and the darkness comprehends it not ... for our relationship with light has now become no more than a calculation of quantity.

And so we see that what was in earlier times a conscious Spiritual relationship with a living cosmos, has today receded into unconscious memory, and it is this stream of wisdom, which must now be called forth in all of us, so that we may again come to know the true nature of the forces held in the cosmos.

This is the understanding reflected in the Bushman relationship with the sun, the moon and the earth … the founding human relationship with a living world. Our task now is to bring to cognition the ancient truth still carried as an unconscious wisdom in these people … the spiritual heritage of all humanity reflected in the soul-life of the last of the first peoples, embedded in their mythologies. In ourselves, it becomes the comprehension of Light, Life and Love as forces that permeate the fabric of the universe, and if, in freedom, we choose to make this affirmation, we will come to resist that which is held in the darkness.

The /Gwikwe simply 'live' the percept of 'God in Self', and in this they acknowledge the existence of good and evil and their own capacity for both … so bearing full consequence for their own lives. Such is their given clarity of Soul, that in their relationship with the world they are able to call God and the devil by the same name, //Gamahma. In this naming they imply that the forces of good and evil are bound together in a preordained relationship, a cosmic symbiosis that reflects in each individual human being.

They have a fundamental spiritual sensibility that surpasses that manifest in the prejudice of modern religions. And such is this spiritual sensitivity in the pure-blood Bushman, that in 'trance' he will acutely feel and root out this dark force, which at every man-given opportunity will invade the sacred sanctity of the human Soul. Evil must not be denied, it must be transformed through goodness … and the trance dance, then, is a dance of transformation of darkness to light.

Within each of us there arise those tides of darkness, dark thoughts and words and doings … those aspects of our being of which we are not proud … those feelings within that we would purge in order to better serve ourselves and each other. It is from within this feeling of dis-ease that the presence of the lesser and evil god makes himself felt in the trance dance … and the /Gwikwe say also that he is closely associated with the ancestors, the spirits of the dead … and that this evil presence enters and becomes as a darkness in ourselves.

Bushman spiritual belief reveals the understanding that a wrong relationship with 'ancestor worship' opens the portal for dark and demonic forces to gain purchase in the human Soul. No matter by what name you call evil, it manifests as a dark force in the lower human nature, either directly or through the spirits of the dead. And it is these dark forces, these demonic beings that are purged from the human Soul through the healing dance ... thrown back into the realms from whence they come. Healing in this way is a remarkable act of selflessness, of sacrifice and redemption, for to wrestle thus with the forces of darkness is an exhausting and draining process that often takes a huge toll on the wellbeing of the healing man.

In the consideration of 'African spirituality', we must clearly differentiate between the Bushman people and the black tribes of Africa. The Bushman people have a clear knowledge of what has passed before them, and have a simple respect for that reality. They do not practise any form of blood sacrifice or ancestor worship, and any inference, written or otherwise, is both irresponsible and a gross negligence of perception.

The practice of blood sacrifice, human and other, and ancestral worship by the black peoples across the African continent, is as a 'ball and chain' to their evolution. It is the cumbersome residue of an obsolete occult practice, which now serves only to bind Africa to its past ... to that which lies behind. To be bound thus, 'out of time' as it were, allows less inclination to forward evolution, and this is the tragedy of Africa ... partially held in what has become a stream of dark occult, and for the wrong reasons holding on to what lies behind, to the exclusion of taking itself forward.

The worship of ancestor spirits is an inappropriate reverence for what has passed ... the souls of the dead remain 'human' souls simply in another stage of their journey, and as such have no more or less wisdom than they possessed during the course of their lives on earth. Any guidance received from ancestor spirits may be right or wrong, good or evil. The very relationship with ancestor spirits holds one in bondage, and out of freedom, as it were, namely the freedom to think and choose one's own destiny, right or wrong.

And so, respect for ancestors? Yes ... even reverence for those among them who were great and wise souls in life. But worship through obedience? No! In undue obeisance to the souls of the dead, you hold back the development of your own individual 'I' going forward, and so Africa, through the perpetuation of ancestor worship remains held in its past and unable to move forward to where it might assume a more correct place in time and history.

I anticipate some confined academic opinion querying my right to speak the truth of another race! And what can I answer, but that I have lived through my lives in many cycles of time ... and that Soul has no colour.

Very few humans in their lives, are able to accept what lies outside of the parameters of their own prejudice ... I am learning. Very few humans are willing to see the 'whole' world, and grasp the thought of cosmic choreography ... to understand how the placing of peoples in time and space has everything to do with the purpose of evolving the human Soul and Spirit. The geography and culture into which you are born is a choice made with spiritual purpose.

Africa holds a great diversity of peoples and cultures in very different stages of development of body, soul and spirit. And these disparities may lead us either to our damnation, or our resurrection ... the spiritual world watches and waits. For those who cannot see beyond their personal or cultural prejudice, this knowledge may be a damning indictment, but for those who perceive that we are spiritual beings first, this knowledge is revealing and redeeming for the whole of humanity. The choice as always, remains with the individual Soul.

And now we dance the healing dance ... *tsshikk*! ... *tsshikk*! ... feet on the earth we dance the healing dance ... and the men, called by the voices and the movement, one by one, are pulled out of the body and into the astral ... the forces of sun-moon-light in fluid bodies moving ... dancing ... alive ... clapping sharp counterpoint with interval and rhythm which cannot be denied, and which spirals one and all into a space vast and full of memory ... singing voices resonant with remembrance of our sacred self, we dance long under the stars made bright by the darkness.

Tsshikk! ... *tsshikk*! ... we dance while the moon walks across the sky ... and the healing man Gening/u shakes and sweats as the heat comes into his body ... he feels with his trembling hands onto the heads, onto the backs and shoulders of the people in the circle, and in the name of the Great God //Gamahma he draws our pain, he draws the illness both known and unknown from our Soul-bodies ... primal sounds tearing from his own body, agonised cries that pull and pierce our hearts and souls ... and then shouting our anger and insult at the evil spirits, he hurls the sickness into the night, back into the darkness ... our wrongs banished into that place of redemption where there is only the way of God ... and in this way we are purged ... he collapses then, his forces spent ... and the 'sleep of death' overtakes him.

And still the women sing ... for it is their voices that hold the thread between the physical body, which lies spent on the earth, and the Spirit-body, which journeys in the astral realm. It is their songlines that call Gening/u from 'out there' and guide him safely back into his own body ... for a man can lose himself in the 'sleep of death'.

Someone brings a mixture of urine and juice from the Bie root ... this, too, will help to bring him back, and somewhere in his return is planted the seed of resurrection. Just as the blood has borne the memory through countless older generations of humans, it is the fluid-body that holds and carries the memory of earth-life and of all that has been before. In ritual like this, the fluid ... urine, water, wine or blood, is the bridging substance, re-enabling through memory and thus urging the re-awakening of Self ... and so it is that the healing man Gening/u comes back to the awareness of himself, and is reconnected with the group-soul of his people.

It is over now, and the people will sleep ... equal, as always, in the eyes of God. Trance dancing is our way of bringing heaven to earth ... raising our Spirit to that place where we can be touched by angels and seen by God, and then returned to our bodies filled with the certainty of who we are ... and in this, the truth of God in me, in God ... echoes of ancient wisdom ... 'blessed are they that have not seen, and yet have believed'.

The winter moons have passed, and we have called the sun light back to earth. Drawing closer it brings with it those forces which give life to all things, to all that lies as if dead but only sleeping ... for all life is borne of one light only, and that which was held and nurtured in the earth now expresses in outward form and movement on the Great Sand Face ... a physical expression of the will of the earth presented for our sharing ... how lucky we are.

COMING INTO WHOLENESS

The secret of a Kalahari spring ... furtive blossoms on one or two trees, but otherwise unannounced, each species holding onto what life force it has to sustain it through to the end of the dry season, to the coming of the rain, and only then to fulfil its purpose. In the shy opening of this small flower and that small flower, it is the stars that tell us that the spring has come ... every living thing carrying the order and will of the cosmos ... and so, too, we humans. In the seasonal cycles of life and death and new life in the plant and animal kingdoms, we are reminded of our own immortality of Soul. For just as the plant goes from flower to seed and then to flower again, so do we humans go from life unto death before returning again to new life ... a constant journeying of soul from the spiritual world to the physical world and then back to the spiritual ... and so onward through time, the fact of our immortality neither blessing nor curse ... simply fact.

There is something to be said of the sun during this time of spring equinox ... no matter where you live upon the earth, whether in desert, jungle or the cold plains of the north, there is a certain power that streams forth from the sun on this day, a power like no other, which calls the whole natural world to life. And there is something to be said of the first spring moon ... the nights before the new moon are dark and silent, as every living thing waits to respond to the forces that live and grow beneath the surface of the earth through winter, waiting in stillness for the first sign ... and then, as the moon turns, those forces rise up from out of the earth, and all that waits begins to move and live itself into the awakening world, responding as one to that magnificent impulse ... and the first sliver of moon on the western horizon, lying on its back like a slender grail cup facing upwards, as if asking the forces of the heaven down to the earth, to be held for the seeking and the rising of humanity. In the uncluttered starkness of desert, the workings of the world are so clearly revealed.

The days drag on ... the Great Sand Face becomes hotter and drier, and our struggle for survival more desperate. Spring has come and gone, and with it the occasional small gift ... a steenbok in a snare ... voice crying, dry heat, pounding ... no quarter asked and none given ... we eat for a day. The women forage far afield in small groups in the hope of anything that the earth might offer ... wild raisin bushes with small yellow flowers, like beacons of hope resurrected, for it is still four moons that must pass before the berries grow to ripeness ... and Tso/tgomaa, the great hunter, who searches alone day after day, finds nothing to shoot ... nothing.

And in the dryness, //Gammsa the Sun burns and burns relentlessly from the pale cloudless sky, and around the shelters no one moves during the heat of the day. We are thirsty, impatient and impotent ... each one trapped in his own heat ... small, still bundles in whatever black shade we can find ... a million miles of heaven and earth around us, and yet we breathe sparingly ... conserve energy ... and wait for the sun to pass.

And when the shadows grow longer, it is the children who first find the energy to move. The boys, Geamm and /Qua/tgara, still have the same determination to be great hunters ... one day. They walk away from the shelters ... bows in hand with clear intent and great self-awareness. No one would question them, for they require a certain privacy during their transition to young manhood, and it is plain to see that they take themselves very seriously at this time of their lives, for that is the way of boys who would be men on the path.

The great sun descends almost reluctantly, and the earth and we begin to breathe the cooling air ... soft voices and silhouettes of children against the fire-red sky. And later when I lie down to sleep, welcomed in the embrace of this great Earth-being ... I know that I will never be alone ... even in the darkness.

That night I dream that I am being born ... I am awake within ... touching the walls of a womb ... suspended warm and wet ... I see every little detail on the inside of the skin envelope around me ... the cells like stars in the flesh itself. At the same time I find myself flying through a realm of space black and filled with life ... touching the outer envelope of a universe vast and intimate ... flying like a giant eagle within the immeasurable womb of outer space, and then drawn willingly down ... down into the whirling vortex of a black hole to the very core of my being ... through threshold and unknown realm, and a journey through the stars that I choose to make ... as if each star holds a part of the memory of who I am on the course of my Soul-journey through this breadth of time-space ... dreaming my way to a sense of my own destiny ... and I am born.

I awaken inside the dark warmth of my shelter, and looking out through the silhouette of the doorway at the sun streaming softly onto the sand I remember that this is the day of my birth ... it is October the seventh ... and here I am on the earth, body and spirit bound together in my Soul. This dream is a revelation that I must not forget, and in the days that follow I think often of the feeling in the womb, the space inside as a mirror for the space outside, and of being reborn so as to understand my birth and its intended purpose. I know now that one does not need to seek purpose outside of oneself, for purpose is an opportunity of Soul, and your purpose will seek you out as and when you are ready. Your task is to prepare yourself, so that by the quality of your being, you have the strength to act on the opportunity ... no one is called for nothing.

RESOLUTION

Heat and the dryness ... the days go through the same endless pattern of waiting for the rain. The air becomes hotter, and closer ... the /Gwikwe wait, the rain must come ... it always does.

//Gang//gang roasts an old piece of leather thong ... to be ground up and eaten. The dried skin of the wildebeest killed in the autumn ... seven moons ago ... this, too, is ground up and shared among the women and children ... there is no other food. Always the hunger and thirst ... everyone suffers through this long dry season, and there is more talk of moving, of going to live in the government settlement.

On this same day, something happens that brings the first show of real anger that I have seen among these people, and a story unfolds, which reveals so much humanity and history, so much of all of us, for it is often old guilt that shows itself as new anger.

During the heat of the day we men urinate what little liquid we have into a large tortoise shell, and then mix our urine with juice scraped from a Bie root. When the late afternoon brings a small breeze we walk a short distance away from the shelters, and there we wipe our bodies with this fluid. Cooled by moving air, this liquid on the skin reminds our bodies to begin cooling down. It is as if the sustained and endless heat causes the body to forget how it is to be cool ... it gets into a heat spiral and loses its memory, and so at some point you need to remind your body to function, otherwise you just become hotter and hotter as if to die of heat stroke. On the other side of the shelters the women do the same thing.

What happens on this day is that one of the young boys, while squatting over the tortoise shell with the intention of emulating the men, accidentally does more than urinate. Later in the day, we drag our tired bodies together for our 'wash', only to discover that there is a small brown thing floating around in the tortoise shell ... no big deal ... it is the way of life.

The owner of the tortoise shell, Khaachiro, asks his youngest daughter if it was she who did the deed? At the same time //Gang//gang, who is listening, assumes that it is her child who has done this thing, and, taking up a piece of thick grass, she begins hitting him on the head and hands with it … the boy cries as he runs away into the bush behind the shelters … his mother is tired, hot, thirsty, hungry and stressed beyond patience.

And then begins a great commotion … almost as one, all of the other women begin shouting at her. They do not like this, and they are saying that Magu's wife must not hit her child without hitting all the children … they are saying that if one child gets beaten, then all of the children must be beaten. If this is not done, then the child who gets beaten will start to think that he is bad, and the other children will start thinking that they are good … and this is wrong, because all the children are the same … one is not bad while the others are good … they are all equal. The women then tell //Gang//gang that she should not behave in this way, and so she goes into her shelter to speak with her husband Magu.

Up until now, it is only the women who have accused //Gang//gang of bad behaviour … but now Khaachiro tells the women to stop their talking and to leave the matter alone. Magu then comes out of his shelter and shouts to Khaachiro to stop interfering and to leave the women to sort it out … can he not see that Magu's heart is sore because he has seen his son being beaten, and that he is not speaking, but just sitting quietly in is shelter?

Khaachiro says, 'Magu, leave it, let's not have an argument … can't you see that I have asked the women to stop?'
    Magu: 'I don't care … don't you tell me what to do.' He then begins insulting Khaachiro, who naturally returns the insults. Magu goes into his shelter.
    Khaachiro: 'Come out of your shelter so we can talk.'
    Magu to wife in shelter: 'Let me go out so that I can fight with Khaachiro.'
    //Gang//gang tries to stop Magu as he bursts out of his shelter with his bow and poisoned arrows … she hangs onto them and he drags her out of

the shelter as well. One of the other women comes to her assistance to stop Magu from shooting a poison arrow.

Khaachiro: 'No! leave him, let him come. I am fine, I am not fighting, so don't stop him.'

The women succeed in taking Magu's bow and arrows away from him, and then he and Khaachiro get into a heated argument. The women, too, continue arguing. Khaachiro's wife, /Tokwa, says that Magu once slept with her forcefully, and when she went to tell //Gang//gang about this, she replied that /Tokwa had been agreeable, and that was why Magu had slept with her.

//Gang//gang asks /Tokwa, 'Was it nice, is that why you allowed it?'
/Tokwa says, 'Magu did it by force while I was at the melon field and I could not shout because I was too far away.'

Khaachiro: 'Leave him, leave him … let him come and shoot me! You must not act like a brave man, Magu, because you are a coward! Do you not remember one day when we were tracking lion together, and when we got to the lion you ran away and went back to your shelter … and you stayed in your shelter all day because you were afraid of the lion? So don't you act brave because it is you who is the coward!'

Magu remains silent … soon after that he comes to sit at my fire … we do not speak.

Khaachiro:'You see, Magu … you get angry quickly, but you forget that day when you slept with my wife in the melon field, and I was going to fight with you and the people stopped me.'
Magu: 'Do you think that I can now be friends with your wife and you with mine? Because you are such an angry man I cannot do this. You were saying bad things about my son, and that is why my wife was beating the boy.'
Khaachiro: 'I was not saying bad things about your son. The women were shouting and I told them to keep quiet, and then you came and started fighting with me.'

//Gang//gang then says that !Tokwa had mentioned her son's name, and that's why she was hitting him. !Tokwa says that she did not mention any names.

//Gang//gang asks, 'Does !Tokwa hate my son just as she hates his father?'

!Tokwa: 'No, I do not hate the son like I hate the father!'

Khaachiro: 'I remember that day ... it was the boy's grandfather who stopped me from fighting you when you slept with my wife that time ... and you, Magu, are not stronger than me, so don't act like you are stronger than me. You should have left your bow and arrows, and fought with your mouth! That is a bad thing you did.'

Magu: 'You were talking ... that's why I was fighting.'

Khaachiro: 'Magu, don't tell a lie ... don't tell a lie.'

Magu: 'You should have told me directly that you were going to show anger against me for sleeping with your wife, but instead you take it out on my son.'

Khaachiro: 'I did not want to fight, because I am not a fighter any more ... I used to be a fighter.'

Magu: 'I am not a fighter ... you think that even when I am talking in a friendly way or joking with your wife that I am proposing to her.'

Khaachiro: 'I have a son who is not mine. Twenty-five years ago I shot a cow on the edge of the desert, and the farm people caught me and took me to a jail in Ghantzi ... I left my wife with a baby girl still sucking. After a long time the jailer let me go because he could see that I was dying in the jail, and so I ran all the way back home without stopping ... for three days I ran ... and when I came back I found my wife expecting another baby, which was not mine. So you see, all the children are now my relatives, and this business did not give me a bad heart. You will see tomorrow ... the children will probably do the same thing again. I am not a man who talks much ... only when someone does something bad to me. Do you know what was done to me before? ... Well, if someone does that to me now ... I will kill him.'

Magu remains silent. As suddenly as the whole thing began ... it ends ... someone plays a bow harp in the darkness and everything sounds as if nothing has happened.

A short time later ...

Khaachiro: 'You have seen that I never do bad things ... so how can a man take out his bows and arrows against a man who does not? But if you want me to I can, and we can fight the whole night!'

Silence ... dignity restored in the darkness. I reflect on what this whole argument was about. It was because //Gang//gang had implied by her actions that her child was not the same as the other children, that the children were not all equal. Such an implication threatens the stability of the whole band to such an extent that an argument involving all the people and many years of personal history is the result ... .

It all begins twenty-five years before ... when a Bushman kills a cow on the edge of the desert, a cow that strays onto land that has always been home to the /Gwikwe. The Bushman slaughters the cow so that his family can eat. In his life he has never understood or subscribed to the notion of ownership ... he believes that everything belongs to God.

The punishment by unnatural law is that this innocent man is put into a jail ... closed in a box where there is no light and there is no space. This is unlike anything he has ever experienced in his life, for he has never not seen the sky and the distance of the Kalahari. In this terrible closed place he cannot breathe ... he cannot see ... he begins to die ... as if his spirit has already left his body and the incomprehensible bewilderment of his situation. In the darkness of night he no longer hears the sounds of the living desert, the wind in the grass, and the whispers of all that is life to him. He has a wife and a baby girl who must think that he will never return, for no man has ever been away for so long.

And the mother ... what is she to do? ... she cannot comprehend her husband's absence, for there is no precedent in her history to explain the taking away of her child's father. She cannot hunt for food ... she and her child must find a way to survive ... and so now she carries another man's child.

One day her husband returns and their lives continue with sad memories. And that is the story of Khaachiro ... 'the peels of the wild cucumber'. After twenty-five years, the memories regurgitated today are the remnant memories of contact with a culture of inequality, a culture of pain and indifference, possession and greed, a culture to which we are all inexorably and hopelessly drawn ... the culture by which we may all be consumed.

In my heart I cry and I cry, for all of those humans and myself, who journey so endlessly through pain and suffering only to find that we did not have to hurt one another, we did not have to lie, deceive or fear ... we only needed to love.

We sleep with the echoes of our anger in the dark of night.

Light flows into the darkness with the rising of the sun.

In the morning the two families sit together at the same fire ... sharing a few /Gaa roots and whatever else they have, like old friends ... and of course they are.

THE CUTTING MOON

This next day is special. Khaba, a girl of thirteen years, has been budding visibly over the last six moons. She started bleeding this morning ... her first menstruation.

When she discovers that she is bleeding, she stays where she is and waits for the women to find her. If a man happens to see her first he will pretend he has seen nothing, and he will say nothing. When the women find her, they build a small grass shelter, and then begins an age-old puberty ritual exclusive to women. They begin to clap and to sing, and they will dance ... they will dance for Khaba ... for the woman spirit ... and for life.

They wait until the heat of the day has passed, and then, under cover of darkness, Khaba is danced into the shelter ... for there she will stay, in seclusion from the men, for as long as it takes for the bleeding to stop. Abeh, her favourite friend, will stay with her. The two girls lie down together face to face, and are covered with the same skin blanket. Khaba lies directly upon the earth, and into the earth she will bleed ... and that which is within her will 'come to life' through the exchange of blood into the earth, and earth forces into the blood.

It follows through every moon cycle, that this time of losing blood ... of losing iron ... of losing 'light', is a time of physical vulnerability and spiritual uncertainty for a woman. Do we men not all bear witness to this process time and time again, and then forget to bear wisdom?

And so it goes, this dance of puberty ... movement of dark forms against the red evening sky, utterly female ... the smell of women, and voices flowing, words of belonging ... on through the darkness to the moon ... fire-red light dancing on woman skin ... and I think of Khaba, and the sacrifice of iron and light through the blood of her body.

Through the night the women stay with the girls, female companions sleeping around the fire outside the small shelter as light in the darkness. At my own fire I sit through the night, thinking of iron in the earth and of our early ancestors, who found somewhere in their being the propensity to strike fire from rocks with a high iron content ... evoked by what wisdom I wonder? This alchemy reflected in all living processes, is indeed a dance of spirit like no other.

The rising sun brings light and warmth to the bodies of the women who sit around the entrance to the small shelter. They speak softly of that which must be heard by the girls ... and then, when their eyes are nicely open they begin to dance. They bare their buttocks ... always moving in a rough

162

figure of eight around and in front of the shelters. The figure of eight is the configuration of infinity ... the movement that compels the binding of the two sides of the body ... together the male and the female ... the movement that makes whole. Binding also heaven to earth, this movement evokes that which is within to express outwards, and that which is without to be within. Ancient invocation of collective female spirit ... this rite of puberty and procreation is a soul-journey that all women are compelled to make because it is the way ... the continuing of ourselves through time.

Cloaked in darkness under the gemsbok skin blanket, the girls have no eyes and they cannot see the sun in the sky. And because they cannot be drawn by the strength of the outer light, the are compelled towards the inner light, the light within themselves. It is this way, for when by choice or circumstance one cannot see the world outside, one is compelled to look for the world within ... and so they look within, and they see and hear with heightened perception the song voices of the women who dance and then stop to talk ... wisdom words that fill the darkness between them and inside of them ... and in this way they go from darkness to the light of understanding ... a safe passage into the realm of women.

I wonder, by what archetypal design and wisdom a ritual such as this is ordered, and what within these people compels them to call this ritual to life, over and over again ... even long after they have forgotten how it first came to be. I am constantly reminded that they carry inadvertently, in blood memory, much of the ancient wisdom.

The task of modern humanity is to take conscious ownership of this ... this wisdom of all humans, which is held in the memory of the world and reflected in these lives. From what is simple to the most complex, and to be cognisant that it is only through knowledge that we will come to transform life's mysteries to truth ... for Spirit has no partnership with ignorance.

They say there are no men allowed at this dance ... it is a woman's business ... and so now I must talk of my world.

For two years I have carried my camera like an extension of my body … with me all the time. These people see me simply as the hunter with a hunting set on one shoulder and a 'black thing' on the other. This 'black thing' has no bearing or effect on their lives and so does not matter. No one has shown the slightest inclination to look through my camera to see what I am seeing … save once … .

One day some of the children had asked to look through the camera to see what I was looking at, and in the ensuing curiosity all of the people had come for a look. Upon looking, they had not seen much of anything, because the camera was out of focus, zoomed in, or simply because their eyes were not correctly aligned to the eyepiece … and so consequently, from that day onwards, my camera was called 'the thing that cannot see is looking at you', and they continued to believe that as long as I was looking through the camera I could not see much of anything at all.…

As a man, I now bear witness to this puberty dance by invitation and blessing … the old lady Geutwe, mother of Khaba, has asked me to be here. She says that if I keep my eyes inside 'the thing that cannot see is looking at you' then I will not see anything anyway. I feel that on some level the women sense that I will record for posterity a truth, a truth about these people and their relationship with life through the cycles of time … and so with this trust, I immerse myself in the privilege. Only time will reveal and measure our trespasses. As a man I have known this female mystery which compels me to silence and respect … I can go no closer to that which I will never truly understand … that sacred place inside the female circle.

… and they dance the puberty dance with songs as old as the memory of the grandmothers. They dance with their digging sticks that are made of a hard male wood, and I watch as they sometimes place these sticks between the legs of the other women while they dance, and in this gesture they evoke and draw out the forces of procreation and abundance. And when they stop and talk they do this again, as if to draw out with word and intent the spiritual forces that sanctify this puberty ritual … in everything they do there is this wonderfully expressed spiritual alchemy.

On the second day, the old woman, /Tguikwe, comes to take part. She remembers and tells of how it was when she was young, a long time ago ... old legs following a pattern in the sand ancient and true ... voice raised in song celebration of a young girl's journey into womanhood.

/Tguikwe was born sometime in the late 1880s, here in the middle of the Great Kalahari Sand Face, and she talks often of that olden time. At that same time, two thousand miles to the south, there lived another woman called /Kweiten-ta-//ken of the !Xam people ... and she told the same stories, for they were sisters of the same group-soul. Joined by consciousness and the threads of a story, these two sisters lived in the same time on this African earth, and that is a remarkable thought. Old /Tguikwe still remembers and expresses that memory into our world today ... and I, with the privilege of being the man she calls her son, record that memory.

What is done to a maiden ... as told by /Kweiten-ta-//ken
They make a shelter for her to lie in
because she should not see people
that is why she has this shelter to rest in
a place where she may lie and rest
because if she walks around she will see people
that is why she has to lie down and rest and see no one
she has to rest so that she sees no one
so that she can lie quietly for many nights
while she is becoming a maiden
that's why the old women make her lie down
so that she can look at no one
because she will freeze them with her eyes
so that they can not move
that is why she has to lie there
the moon has to cut while she lies there
from the one that grows now

before the old women can take her out
the moon cuts while she is lying there
the other moon is the one from which life comes
the moon comes out while she is still lying

then the old women take her out of the shelter
and slaughter a sheep
and the old women eat the meat and the girl eats the meat
the young men do not eat the meat
the old women, they are the ones who eat the meat.

In between the dancing the women stop to rest and talk, and in their private darkness beneath the gemsbok skin blanket, Khaba and Abeh find their own truth. For Khaba, perhaps some anxiousness, and perhaps some pride ... for she is the one who becomes a maiden ... she is the one for whom the women dance. For Abeh, too soon for her own awakening, this is a time to understand and learn of that which lies ahead. And so in their sacred space they whisper the secrets of women brought to them through voice and song ... movement and smell ... and the dance ... an implosion of energy moving inwards into that dark and silent space under the blanket where everything mirrored between the two girls finds its way into the maiden heart of young Khaba, made open and receptive by the bleeding ... an encoded impulse awakened by the flow of life blood containing the memory of ancient purpose ... something that opens in her body, and into which place comes an unconscious knowing of her role as women procreator ... co-Creator.

Later when the sun moves to the west, the women resume their dancing and the red sky bleeds the sun to sleep through dusk and into darkness ... bodies further caressed and inspired by the light of the moon, N/aueema, and the forces of all the heavens reflect through the full moon upon the earth.

It saddens me that I live now in a world where these truths are barely known, and where humans are unable to draw strength and security from common understanding, which allows itself – like a soft blanket – to caress and make safe in those moments of aloneness when we cannot see and we do not have each other to remind us of who we are and how it really is. Puberty and adolescence in any young human are times of monumental significance. In the cycle of any life, it is as important as birth and death. Through puberty the young human first comes to understand the nature of his or her own Soul, and from that time forward in life, is compelled to find and express that individuality ... to know what it is and what it may become. In the blood, through the fluid body, comes memory ... and through the memory of the world in all women, Khaba is embraced in her time of changing.

She is only allowed to leave the shelter under cover of darkness to meet her basic needs, and even then must be covered by the skin blanket. She may not look upon another person under the light of sun or moon, for in this she will take something of their spirit and they will not go forward in a good way. Abeh may leave the shelter whenever she wishes.

Certain foods are taboo for Khaba at this time, and she is given medicine made from roots to protect her from the poison of these foods. She may not eat steenbok, gemsbok, hartebeest, springbok, springhare, porcupine, kori bustard and francolin ... neither sweet berries, nor sour berries and melons ... if she eats any of these taboo foods she will have terrible pains in her stomach.

The women make presents for her ... necklaces mostly, and I see the duiker skin aprons, front and back, made soft by her mothers loving hands ... for she will no longer be seen as a little girl. And they have made a digging stick for Khaba, so that she can walk about and dig for roots, and gather foods as the women do.

On the third day I go and sit with the men, and I see that while Khaba's girl life is changing into that of a woman, they hunt with little interest and no reward. 'The hunting will be bad,' they say ... and so it is. But, as all things are part of the same whole, the men are a reciprocal part of the puberty event, and to hold the luck in their hunting weapons they gather a certain root called Kghanabe, and a red stone called *Tgaago. The stone is ground up, mixed with fat and rubbed onto one side of their hunting bows and spears, while the root is peeled and rubbed onto the other side ... by this act they sustain their role and responsibility as hunters.

The heat is unbearable now, and the women dance only in the morning and late afternoon. To walk on the midday sand is impossible ... too hot ... arguments about nothing ... children crying ... hunger heat.

The endless thirst and dryness lead me ever closer to the primal essence of water, that living fluid which is as the nature of God himself ... substance without form that takes on all forms, which flows within and without, through all that lives and breathes on this earth. We humans are such an integral part of the cosmic architecture ... in our cold we long for the sun and in our thirst we long for rain ... and it is our very longing that compels the ebb and flow of the elemental forces, the cosmic change and balance ... the yearning of a million million creatures calls the water spirits to life and the rain to earth ... and such is the depth of our symbiosis with all that lives.

And then ...
    Khuu ... rain?
    There is a stirring in the west ... a wind.
    There is rain in the sky and the people see it coming ... but no ... it passes swiftly, it is nothing, only enough to wet the surface and to leave the small children wondering where it has gone.

And the dance for Khaba goes on ...

As the night belongs to the moon, so the day belongs to the sun, and this day is surely the hottest day I have ever known ... a huge sense of claustrophobia surrounds and presses us down ... we hug ourselves into the earth, the sand, as if to draw some coolness and strength from its depths. The heat feels as a weight upon us, and utterly crushed in stillness we lie waiting for life to resume … stretched apart from ourselves in coma we survive outside of our bodies … time itself stilled by the great burning sun.

They say that Khaba has stopped bleeding, but no one can care now … perhaps we will care when the sun has gone closer to the western side of the Great Sand Face.

The sun moves … so do we … the women wait for the moon … in the night that comes we see that N/aueema the Moon begins to cut, and so now the dance will end.

In the morning light the women are gathered around the shelter. Khaba's mother, Geutwe, scrapes Bie root for the juice … and Khaba is taken out from under her gemsbok skin blanket and washed with this juice to remove the 'old dirt'. After four days of darkness in the earthwomb she is born again into the light of life … like chrysalis to butterfly … like bud to flower, in this, the spring of her life. She wears her new apron … ǃToohsa … soft on her maiden skin. She wears the necklaces made by the women, and she says that her heart is pleased.

The older women now give her permission to eat the foods that have, until this time, been taboo for her. She eats a mixture of three roots called Saasa, ǀTgadee and ɎǁOuhee, and the forces carried in these roots lift all of the taboos, except for porcupine, springhare and steenbok … these she can only eat after she has had children and become a woman, and it is the old women who will decide when she is old enough and strong enough to eat these animals. ǁGama paints Khaba's face so that she can be beautiful and fat, and then she is taken out of the shelter to see the men.

Standing in front of the men and surrounded by the shelters, she seems so small … but nature has decided, and everything is as it should be. She does not speak … still held by the silence inside of her, she stands as if new in the world. Seǀtwago breaks grass in front of Khaba's eyes to help her to see clearly … and then she tells her, 'See … see with your new eyes ... these are the people you are always seeing ... your fathers and your grandfathers ... and Paul, who you always see ... these are the men whom you left ... now you can see them, bad luck must go away and good luck must come for their hunting ... animals must die, eland must die ... we must go safely and no dangerous animals must attack us. Yes ... it is good, it is nice, my niece ... you must be nice ... it is good to be that way ...'

Khaba stands and looks as if she has not seen this place before, as if the words she once used would not work in the same way if she spoke them now. And so she gazes in silence upon her world as if strange to it and it to her, uncertain of her next step, until her friend Abeh comes and softly walks her away ... together ... for now they know each the other as sisters forever.

At the end of the day old /Tguikwe looks long at me, and because of what I have witnessed in the last while, she asks, 'What has happened to this man?'

I have no answer, for we men, too, have our sacred circle.

WOMAN

It is noon and the day is hot. The women have collected a number of Bie roots, succulent and fresh, but too bitter for drinking. They spend some time scraping and pulping the tubers, and collecting the juice into various wooden bowls mixed with urine from their bodies clean and pure ... and then they call me. They say that I go with the men when they wash themselves, and so now, should I not also go with the women when they wash? I say that I should not look upon their naked bodies. They say that if I keep my eyes in 'the thing that cannot see is looking at you' then all will be well.

Again I question the invitation, but there is no objection from any quarter ... I know that my hesitation comes only from my own lack of innocence ... I have been alone for some time now, and am aware of my needs and curiosities ... perhaps there is another reason? They say that I have no need to hesitate because the other men are close by, and I see that to decline their brave gesture would be less appropriate than going along with them ... so I follow with respect and trepidation to where they lead me behind the shelters.

In childlike abandonment they remove their aprons back and front, and set about the business of washing themselves and their smaller children. They spare no intimacy, some laughing and giggling, others more conscious of what they reveal ... but the sheer joy of it contagious and beautiful ... the smell of wet clean bodies cooled in moving air ... woman shapes, and gestures offered in trust and laughter.

On this day I confess being witness to an intimacy of female nature that completely stills my words. The beauty expressed leaves me in awe and wonder at the truthfulness of a world that lives through humans in innocence ... a world that once was.

My sisters, I thank you for this sharing ... I will respect and hold sacred this day.

DAY OF THE RAIN ANIMALS

One whole moon has passed, and now, at last, on this day the east wind comes, gently at first, banking up clouds in the western sky ... layer upon layer of grey upon grey ... and then a silence descends ... no insect sounds, no bird calls ... the greatest silence I have ever not heard – stretched like a blanket across the whole earth ... a darkening silence beyond all of us and all things. The grass itself stops growing and the earth waits, and we wait, caught between day and night ... all power being out of ourselves and part of another dimension now, for the 'rain animal' waits in the sky.

For the first time ever I have become the calm before the storm ... trapped inside an enormous vortex of imploded energy ... holding ... suspended somewhere between the cosmic in and out breath ... reminded that all arises out of silence. And it stirs again ... wind moving waves of countless millions of grass stems, swaying and bending in unison like a great ocean over the face of the earth ... energy lines of enormous magnitude stretching across our Great Sand Face ... the air between earth and sky charged with an imminence almost frightening ... so much bigger than our greatest need, this display, which stirs my Soul to the joyous realisation of my own physical mortality.

Thank God that we live ... thank God that I live ... that I can give myself over to this power ... for if I am to know the wind itself I must immerse myself within the feeling of this enormous breath, which holds the power to heal or harm. If I choose to understand the wind through my intellect it stops blowing right there, and I have only the word 'wind' ... but when I feel it through the power of my imagination, open myself to the primal force that compels and shapes that wind, then I have more, so much more ... and in this way, I too will come to know the spirit beings of air and wind, of whom people once spoke ... and so it blows and it blows ... wind breathing rain-laden clouds out of the blackness before it ... the opening of the heavens pouring tears of our joy into the waiting thirst. The rain has come, and the earth, and we begin to move.

Tso/tgomaa's youngest child ... this is the first time he has ever seen rain ... and so, too, for all of us, for the first summer rain in the Kalahari is like the first rain you ever see ... each single drop carrying the memory of all since the genesis of life on earth ... for everything, everything derives from living water, and everything remembers the rain.

The children dance, a weaving circle of little brown bodies washed yellow gold by big soft drops of water heaven-sent ... laughing and shrieking out the joy and acknowledgement from all of our hearts. And we smile as they offer their souls with pure abandon to the earth and sky ... lost in the wonder of a day.

Voices ... 'We have been wishing for the rain and now it is raining on us ... leave that skin there to catch the rain ... first it was raining water, but now the hail has come and I will swallow one ...'

Inside the shelters bone pipes are filled with the last of our tobacco ... everyone smokes and the gap between ourselves and ourselves is bridged, for we return with the rain, bound to the rhythms and cycles of life. Carried in water memory, the unending cycles of dryness and dying through the winter, the rain resurrection through spring and summer ... and the journey of human souls through Spirit become clear, for we, too, continue in changing form through all seasons and cycles. Dying in our winter, our Souls are held and nurtured in the world of Spirit between the time of death and new birth, and then born again into a new cycle of life ... to live and grow until our next winter of rest. And so it continues, this endless journey of seasons ... each cycle closer to the truth as we ascend to Light through life ... death ... rebirth ... life ... death and life.

Behind the blanket of rain the invisible sun sets, and in the coming darkness we hear the great voice of the storm ... Khuuma, it is 'He-rain', thunderous, fierce and powerful it comes ... and the people are afraid of the thunder, and they shout at the lightning so that it can know where they are and not strike them.

Voices ... 'Aiee ... the rain is throwing drops of thunder and lightning ... Aiee ... stop thundering here, go and make a noise in a far-off place.' Rain is a living entity ... the /Gwikwe believe that the rain is like a person, or a lion, or anything that is dangerous, and so if you shout at the lightning with conviction, it will hear you and go away. They say that if someone is killed by lightning, then it has been sent, either by the devil or by black medicine men ... it is never random.

Voices, voices ... 'The rain is raining on us ... it is killing us ... people, we are in trouble, the rain is coming through the shelter,'... it is //Gama and her family who run from their leaking shelter to that of her brother,

Gening/u ... the first rain has made them wet ... as was meant to be.

The rain holds back for the rising moon ... a voice sings, and then more voices ... a foot stamps, and then more feet. Tonight we rejoice in the simple fact of life ... so tenuous ... so powerful ... so precious. Under the light of the moon, on wet earth we dance our thanks long into the darkness, and then later when we sleep, we dance in the darkness of our peace.

But Khuuma is not yet done ... sometime in the night he comes, out of the black roaring he comes ... the fierce male-rain animal comes again with his legs and hurls himself into the earth ... blinding blue light shredding the black blanket of sky, such that there is only one reality in each primal moment ... the storm within the storm without, like a man and woman caught in that frenzy of lust and love ... no victory, no defeat ... there never can be.

It rains, hard and long through the night. No one sleeps, for our small shelters are scant protection, and tonight we are inside the belly of the Rain Bull ... the lightning spears tearing and splitting the vault of black sky, and the roaring of thunder that rends and shakes the ground of our existence, and the rain, are all that exist.

Voices from the blackness shout in fear, pretending anger ... one storm only ... and somewhere in the rain face of my sleep I see the dream face of Khaba ... girl who became maiden on this day ... and then it is over.

For us creatures out on the sand face, it is a display of power so absolute that it renders us utterly vulnerable, our mortality and immortality coalesced in each moment. For the great earth, as it journeys through the heavens, it is a passing gift given and received.

The rain courts the maiden as she lies in her hut
the rain smells her and comes to her and the whole place turns misty
the rain comes to her for her fragrance

he comes trotting, as it were, while the maiden lies in the hut

as she lies and smells the rain
everything becomes fragrant
as if the breath of the rain encloses
as if everything takes place in the mistiness

the maiden becomes aware of the rain
as it touches her and lets down its tail
the maiden sees him and asks:
Who is this man here with me
who first squats and then stands up?

And she takes buchu and presses it against her head
she makes a kaross and knots it across her shoulders

she mounts the rain and the rain takes her away
she sways with him and looks to the trees.
'Put me down among the trees as I am hurting.'
The rain goes at a slow trot in among the trees
and puts the maiden down next to a trunk
the maiden rubs buchu onto the forehead of the rain
she rubs and rubs and the rain falls asleep

when the rain sleeps, she softly climbs into the tree and goes away
far away from there she climbs down and silently goes back home

behind her back the rain awakes, because the heat of the maiden is gone
but when he bends down at the spruit, he feels her on his back again
she rubs herself with buchu until she is green
she rubs and rubs until she is fragrant.

This story of *The maiden and the rain bull* is told from two thousand miles away by a young /Xam Bushman called /Han‡kasso, who lived in the Cape in the late 1800s, in the same time as Dzero-O, who still lives here on the Kalahari sand face under the Old Man's Tree … and today, we /Gwikwe, we live this story of the rain, and of the maiden who comes to taste the fruit of the tree of knowledge. Is this not the archetypal story of Eve and Adam?

I will reveal one small chapter in the life of this man /Han ⁄kasso, so that you can better understand how it was for him at that time.

There were five men bound to each other by shared history … the first, A!kungta, was imprisoned for eating some of the meat of an ox which had been stolen by another. I will say here, that no Bushman ever stole an ox so that he could possess that ox, but only so that he could eat and feed his family.

The second man, ‖Kabbo, was imprisoned for cattle theft by the race of people who had parcelled the land of his ancestors into farms for the settlers, and who had hunted and slaughtered every wild creature that he had depended on for his food.

The third and fourth, Dia!kwain and ⁄Kassin, were imprisoned for 'murdering' a farmer who had threatened to kill them … at the time of their retaliation, they had each lost several members of their own families to violence from these same settlers.

The fifth man, /Han ⁄kasso, was imprisoned for cattle theft and later released. He left Cape Town after a short stay in 1871 to go and fetch his wife and the wife of his father-in-law, ‖Kabbo. He found them, and set out on the journey back to Cape Town with the two women and their children. ‖Kabbo's wife fell ill and perished on the way, and then his own baby died. His wife and ‖Kabbo's child were beaten to death by a policeman in Beaufort West. Only /Han ⁄kasso survived the journey … and in this way we all continue with the stories of those who came before us.

AFTER THE STORM

A new day begins on the Great Sand Face, and we begin again, like always after our storms ... just the simple joy of being alive. The earth breathes out the scent of the universe brought down in every drop of rain, and little Seka plods his body across the sand towards my shelter, coming to see that I have not been washed away.

Spanning the heavens in the eastern sky is a rainbow of such colour and beauty that we humans who stand upon the earth with all that lives, pause one and all to reflect on this fire-water bridge between heaven and earth. This bow in the clouds, first given as a covenant between the great God and every living creature upon the earth 'that never again shall there be a flood to destroy the earth' ... Gazing at that radiance I ask, what force is it that so shines in this beautiful bow of colour? The rainbow is a phenomenon of such magnificence as to reawaken and nourish the human soul ... a resolution of primal forces reflecting perfect balance between earth and heaven, the part and the whole. Beneath the bow the whole sky is wet and grey with soft showers falling here and there across the sand face ... a gentle 'She-rain' that soaks the inside of the earth, so that those forces gathered in the ground, now blessed and nourished by rain and moon, will stream outwards and give rise to all that grows out of the earth. I have known this day before.

Voices ... 'The people who are hunting the eland will be alive from this rain ... come, let us drink water from the tree behind Paul's shelter,' ... and so they come, Gening/u and Magu, and with a reed straw that they take from one of their hunting bags, we drink the rainwater held in the fork of the Camel thorn tree behind my shelter.

Later I walk with the old men, Dzero-O and Kamageh, and we go with /Gaiekwe and her children to where some of the rain water has collected in Kgoatwe pan. The earth is soft and open from the rain, and we walk with a lightness of being on the Great Sand Face, where everything that lives today is filled with the spirit of water. We carry many ostrich eggshells and skin water bags made from the stomachs of large antelope.

We come to the pan when the sun is in the middle of the sky ... a small herd of wildebeest moves off into the heat haze ... they have already been through the water, drinking their fill but leaving enough ... green-brown earth liquid. We drink. This is the only water that we have seen in the last twenty moons, and by tonight it will be gone. //Gammsa the sun is thirsty. Rain in the Kalahari does not mean that there will be water to drink, it is very quickly soaked up into the sand or evaporated. Its coming only ensures that the creatures of /Guam/tge can live for one more year. Using tortoise shell scoops we begin to fill the ostrich eggs, our animal stomach bags and our bellies.

Geamm's little brother, /Gaie, who is one year old, has never seen or touched water before yesterday's rain, and it is with some uncertainty that he now approaches Tsahsa, this pool of living water in the sand. As with all children, he walks that delightful path from the unknown to the known, where today's trepidation foretells of a reverence for tomorrow.

This is a time I will long remember, for I have thirsted greatly ... I have longed for water when there was none ... I have ached with my whole body for water ... I have thirsted in my bones, and there was no water ... I have thirsted in my whole being, until my very Soul ached for water, and still there was none to be had. I have gone beyond the longing, beyond the thought of water, beyond the feeling of thirst to where there is no such feeling, no such idea. I have come to understand that either I have water, or I do not, and there is nothing in between these two separate moments of reality. When one is compelled to live in a world so harsh, one is compelled to go beyond the idea of things, and into the essence of the thing itself ... and so, in abstinence, I have learned of the nature of water.

Sitting now on the edge of this rapidly evaporating pool, I watch as /Gaiekwe and the two old men push aside the green-brown scum on the surface to get to the murky, but cleaner water underneath ... scooping it carefully into tortoise shells and pouring it into the containers. It is a slow but comforting process … just to be near water, the sound, the smell of it … basking in the force of it rising upwards and absorbing into my thirsty body.

I see that one shell is from the tortoise that we roasted three moons ago. I track through our time with the tortoise, which is a 'creature of the rain' … I remember how we gathered it in the hunt … how the women roasted it in the fire … how we listened to stories of the tortoise, and our eyes were nicely opened … and the rain animals came, both male and female, bringing rain to the earth … and now we scoop the water with the shell of the same tortoise, for I remember its colour. And I see how the tortoise came to us … from sacrifice to redemption, I see how all things go full circle.

I cannot easily say how it is to see the rain animal come to earth … I have seen the force, the form painted on many rock faces throughout the land … male and female rain animals, spirits of the water, and know now that they were never illusions or imagined creatures, for they are as real as the rain that fell in the night and the water that lies before me as sustenance for my Soul.

It is said that the rain animals depicted in Bushman art are 'conceptual' creatures, but that is not so. This is an opinion borne of the confines of intellect, which I dispute and will adamantly remind anyone who truly cares to look through a Bushman's eyes that to the Bushman the rain animals are perceptual … they are actual … for they see with eyes that are closed in you … into a realm that is closed to you. And the very fact that water rains down upon this earth is a miracle that we do not fully comprehend.

Says Kamageh, 'I have collected bark from the /Gaa tree to tie up my water bag … hold, so I can tie it, and then we can go … for this is the way I am going.' After filling all the containers and drinking our fill, we begin our journey back to the shelters. The great red sun sits on the western edge of the earth, and in the east the full moon hangs, fat and redolent with heavenly forces.

ALL CREATURES

Birdsong in my morning ears, and the world awakens ... the air like colour itself ... cerise orange pink yellow hues that defy any one description, but fill my Soul-body with feeling.

Tso/tgomaa shot a gemsbok yesterday. Gening/u, Kamageh and I will help track the animal, and so we walk with the rising sun on our backs towards Gantam//nau ... the place where we brought fire to the grass in the winter. It is a long walk, but there will be water held in the trunks of hollow trees, and so we will not thirst.

The idea of burying ostrich eggs filled with water in the sand for long periods of time is an absurd one. It is seldom that a hunter will walk the same path on two hunts, and in a world where we are thirsty every day, it would be an unnecessary temptation to keep water stored for the day when you might be 'more' thirsty than today ... and how do you refuse a child who asks for water? Thirst is simply the name of the fear that lies between having and not having water, and there is no need to name or indulge that fear when there is nothing you can do about it. Everything is just as it is.

Today there is no conserving of energy ... the earth and we celebrate the gift of life-blood rain, and I see the face of God in every living thing brought forth in the natural world. We pass fresh kudu spoor ... female and young, browsing the seed pods of the Giraffe thorn tree. Gening/u says that eating these pods helps the mothers to produce more milk for their young, and so one day we will have nice fat kudu to eat. We walk, and our bare feet in touching the earth know the spirit that lives in everything that lives ... and the birds ... like flying flowers that sing.

Many miles ... and the sun dries the earth as we walk. Tso/tgomaa shows us the place where he wounded the gemsbok ... /Tgoosa, a female. It was a bad shot, into the rump ... and we see no blood. But the sand tells us that we have a chance because the animal has separated from the herd, so it must be feeling the poison. The sun crosses the sky, and our bodies carry the tiredness of six hours of fast walking … perhaps fifteen miles. Still we follow the spoor, and two hours later we find the animal resting under a tree, and the chase begins.

Blood coursing through tired muscle and limb … running … running … the gemsbok slows and we close in … Tso/tgomaa indicates that I have the first spear throw, and in this simple gesture of friendship he offers me the world, for this means that I shall have the task of dividing and sharing the meat among the families, and in this responsibility there will be much to consider … many lessons. During these times of hunger the people are less inclined to generosity and sharing … and so perhaps he feels that I, having no family of my own, will divide the meat more fairly and so prevent disagreement between the families.

Little by little we close on the animal … /Tgoosa stands and waits, for she has run as far as she will. Crouched and focussed we come slowly within range … it is a long throw … I aim for the chest … the heart, but my spear pulls to the left … towards the neck. She sees it coming and parries with lightning speed … catching the spear between her horns she deflects it away and over her shoulder … I must retrieve my spear for a second throw. One man on either side … they shout to distract the gemsbok while I dart in and grab my spear, moving quickly out of range of her long, sweeping, rapier-like horns … formidable weapons that have impaled many a creature more powerful than I.

My second spear goes between the ribs and finds her heart … blood-breath sighing, and two more spears finish the task … something shared between us in the knowing of our living-dying relationship, and I see into the distance with her departing spirit.

Kamageh cuts the forelegs and we skin the animal, roasting the liver, the kidneys and the udder … sustenance for our worn bodies. Tso/tgomaa throws the gall bladder to the ground, splattering what it holds onto the earth ... asking //Gamahma to help us, as always, so that all the animals we shoot with our arrows can die in this way, and the people can grow fat.

We have time ... we have food. We rest and talk as we work ... the skin spread underneath the carcass to hold the spilled blood ... it will be dried and softened into a fine cloak against the cold. We cut and hang the meat on branches set onto forked sticks in the ground and in the trees around us ... slowly, methodically we work our way through the whole carcass ... the skull and the leg bones to roast in the fire and to crack open for the feast of marrow held within ... the thick sinews from the back of the neck for binding arrow and spear to shaft, the fine sinew for thread. The horns are used to push through the intestines to clean them from the inside out ... and so it is done. Anything we leave will be sustenance for our animal brothers and sisters who will come in the night for their share.

By late afternoon the sun has dried a protective skin around the strips of meat ... by nightfall each of us has walked a rough circle around our camp, looking for all signs of animal movement on the surrounding area ... the sand face tells us who may or may not visit in the dark hours.

We sleep this night away from the shelters, and in the warmth of the fire I dream of /Tgoosa the Gemsbok ... the antelope with distance in her eyes ... the one who always sees you coming, and who reads your intent with a primal awareness that has lived and died a thousand times before. This is my totem animal and I hold my thoughts for long into the night. I know that she dies so that we can live, and inside that shared moment I wonder which one of us lives and which one of us dies ... for what is death but a birth into the world of spirit? There is much that I would understand ... rationality has its boundaries, and we must come to believe if we wish to see beyond the threshold.

In the still darkness we sleep.

Somewhere in the silence of night I awaken ... the only human on earth

... big half-moon in the sky shining down the wisdom of the world ... sleeping forms around me, held and caressed on the enormous silver blanket of sand. In these nights I am reminded ... all that arises in this world comes out if silence ... the silence of nothing before the thought, silence filled by the word and the deed. It must be with great care that we choose how to fill the silence.

The fullness of life in light or dark ... whispered bat wings through night air ... the faintest rattle of porcupine quill ... small creatures of the night ... soft rustling around the carcass ... no matter, we have taken what is ours.

From the far distance the voice of a lion rolls endlessly across the sand face ... earth-voice huge in the darkness ... reminding all who listen of the power of Ggamm ... and in my mind I see a huge and powerful cat padding softly across the desert sand with a majesty absolute ... just he and I in a shared universe. I reach out, quietly pushing wood further into the glowing coals ... the others, they sleep ... gentle breathing surrounds me ... the sound of wind over everything like the breathing of the earth, and the grass whispers the name of the Great Sand Face ... and such is the extent to which we are joined one to the other to all.

The memory of lion voice hangs long after in the silence, and in the darkness behind my eyes I see a world filled with creatures great and small giving voice in a common tongue, a language understood by all, a landscape of sound and movement held in the palm of the hand of God. For how many nights must I listen before this becomes a part of me forever ... my Soul immersed in this universal current of life, the place where the lives of all creatures are one, and we are able to know everything because it is written.

Jackal voice calling quavering through night air ... then silence ... then again ... trembling through the darkness as if to reach into my Soul ... evoking an inexplicable longing for the purity of aloneness. I hear your voice, brother jackal ...

The soft pattering of feet and the sound of breath, and suddenly they appear ... two moving spirits of the Jackal clan ... black-backed with silver-haloed aura. They stop almost within touching distance ... in stillness, my eyes join with eyes of the male animal, and something dances in my heart ... I will not forget you, little brother, for your coming tonight is no accident, and what you say is true.

My /Gwi brothers are utterly at one with the earth ... even in sleep they know there is no danger, for it is only the jackal and his mate, and they too must eat. And in their dreams they run together on the Great Sand Face in moonlight silver ... God's light.

I lie in silent reverence of the Divine force that compels the moulding and shaping of forms in the kingdoms of nature. I know that there are many who deny the existence of such a principle, who insist that it is merely chance mutation that gives rise to the wonders of natural form. But to live in denial of such obvious truth is to renounce your own Divine nature, and then you have nothing ... no purpose ... no meaning.

And the night takes me softly away.

In the morning we eat and rest ... I muse on the image of sleeping Bushmen, with their arms folded up under their heads as a pillow. I remember reading somewhere something thoughtlessly written, which said that the Bushmen slept this way in order to prevent insects from crawling into their ears. I wonder which insect would be so stupid as to crawl into someone's ear and not be able to crawl out again, and to what purpose in the first place? Bushmen, and any man in the bush who sleeps directly on the earth, will sleep this way simply for reasons of comfort and to prevent himself from getting a stiff neck.

I have long since learned that there is always a down-to-earth reason for everything that these people do. Living this close to the earth, they can only survive if they are pragmatic in all of their ways.

Wind soft on our skin as we lie in the shade of Grewia and Camel thorn ... wallowed into the sand ... slow-roasting a piece of meat every now and again ... no hurry ... we have food, we have life, and to live immersed in the skin of the earth as we do on days like this is a wonderful thing.

Kerrak-kerrak-kerrak sounds across the sand face ... it is !Gae the Black Korhaan, and he tells the world that he protects his nesting mound ... *kerrak-kerrak-kerrak* ... always the sounds, the endless alchemy of sounds permeating everyone and everything, each frequency and tone touching and nurturing a different part of one's Being. A natural symphony so arranged that every invisible niche or space is filled with the substance of these sounds. So much is determined by our perceiving and understanding of these sound-meanings ... life-messages, both in the audible frequencies that we hear with our ears, and the frequencies that we hear with our bodies ... the infrasounds, the ultrasounds, all carrying volumes of information critical to our relationship with life. And equally critical is the process of learning to hear, to listen without prejudice and hear the essential sound itself without any predisposition, so that it can permeate and fill your Being with the chorus of meaning that it carries.

When working with any and all of the outer senses one must consciously transform the way in which one processes the endless in-streaming of life-information. Like a child again, but consciously, one must bypass the filters constructed from both positive and negative life experience, the veils of prejudice that so fundamentally change the value of that which would come to you. In the black night of aloneness, it is this that makes all the difference between listening to the voice of a lion with fear, or listening with reverence.

By midday the weight of the drying meat is reduced sufficiently for us to begin our journey back to the shelters ... it is always hot and it is always far. Before long, we are met by Dzero-O and two of the women. They say that when we did not return to the shelters last night, they knew that we had hunted well and there would be meat to carry ... and so our burden is shared. As we walk, I wonder how this astonishing old man finds us so easily.

We did not follow a straight line while tracking the gemsbok and neither do we follow our own spoor back to the shelters. Somehow he always knows, as if he carries in himself an eagle's vision of the Great Sand Face ... a vastness inside of him equal to the vastness around us.

When we talk of it later, he puts his hand on the ribs beneath his heart and says that he felt as if the blood was flowing down his left side, and it is this feeling that gave him direction. Such was the way of the old people.

The days follow ... the heat returns, and with it all those feelings evoked through our struggle to survive ... a tireless circle within which we beg just a moment of respite.

THE OLD MAN

One evening two weeks later we see that when the sun sinks below the earth the old man has not returned to the shelters. He left early this morning, at the time of red sky before the dawn. We watch and wait as the darkness covers the earth like a silent blanket over our thoughts ... no one can say why Dzero-O has not returned. //Gama, his daughter-in-law, lights a fire under the Old Man's Tree and there she sits into the night. His son, /Gowsi, irritated by his own anxiousness, finds many things to do ... and even the children speak softly.

There is no moon in the sky, and voices in the darkness say many things ... perhaps he has walked too far and cannot find his way ... the lions may have been in his pathway back to the shelters ... perhaps he is hurt ... who can know, for the darkness always gives substance to our shadows.

I think of a story told by //Kabbo of the /Xam people ... a story told to him by his mother:

The Girl of the Early Race who made Stars
My mother was the one who told me that the girl arose ... she put her hands
into the wood ashes ... she threw up the wood ashes into the sky. She said to the
wood ashes, 'The wood ashes which are here, they must altogether become the
Milky Way ...'

The darkness comes out ... the stars wax red while they had at first been white.
They feel that they stand brightly around ... that they may sail along while they
feel that it is night. Then the people go by night ... while they feel that the
ground is made light ... while they feel that the Stars shine a little.

The Milky Way gently glows, while it feels that it is wood ashes ... therefore it
gently glows. While it feels that the girl was the one who said that the Milky Way
should give a little light for the people, that they might return home by night, in
the middle of the night. For the earth would not have been a little light, had not
the Milky Way been there ... it and the Stars.

I see that tonight the stars shine luminous in the altogether black
sky ... perhaps they will show the old man the way home. In the middle of
the night I awaken to see that the fire still burns alone under the Old Man's
Tree. I lie in the darkness thinking of Dzero-O, his place in the band, and of
the sense of comfort we all draw from being able to see his familiar sleeping
form whenever we look out of our shelters in the night ... even in sleep he
binds us together, not by his words or deeds, but simply by what he holds
in his being and consecrates in his old memories. Tonight, the dream lines
extend outwards from each shelter ... across the sand face, to envelop the
old man wherever he sleeps.

We greet the morning with silence, for still the old man has not returned.
I see that some of the hunters have already left ... today they find many
reasons to hunt in all directions around the shelters. No one would voice a
negative thought about the old man's absence, for he is one of us, and this
might weaken his resolve wherever he may be. The day hangs empty around
us as we wait without waiting.

When the sun hangs above our heads in the middle of the sky, just at the time when we think of other things, Dzero-O arrives back at the shelters. I see that his legs are filled with tiredness and his old body covered with dust and exhaustion. He would not have it that anyone should worry after him, and so he arrives as if he has only been gone for a short while.

Quietly he sits under the Old Man's Tree, and takes from his shoulders his carry bag filled with !Nan!te bean pods, some melons and gemsbok cucumbers. No one asks … for we see that he has returned.

Tschk … his digging stick splits a melon in two. He pulps the insides with the back end of the stick, using the front end to scoop the contents into his mouth. He rests for a while and then tells us that he could not find his way in the darkness, and that he slept the night at !Omchoro, the place of dead locusts. So be it … all is well.

The name !Omchoro came about many years ago. Sometime in the early 1940s and before … there were many locusts in the Kalahari, especially at !Omchoro. The people would sometimes roast and eat these locusts, but they were many, and big piles of locusts would rot in the sun until they began to cause a sickness … a kind of ulcer under the skin. Gening/U says that many people died from this sickness. He shows a round, dark scar under his right shoulder blade, which was caused by the locusts when he was a young boy.

Dowgwi comes from gathering with a bundle of wild shallots … they will be roasted. 'These are the ones that come after the rain,' she says.

After a while old Dzero-O stares into the space around us, and asks of the universe, 'Can the taste of this melon be mixed with the taste of animal blood a little later?' Who knows … perhaps the hunters will be lucky.

And so it is … /Nedu khu kwe shoots a hartebeest on that same day, and the next day Tgoo finds an ostrich caught in one of his snares. The earth provides and we give thanks, and for the next half-moon we rest, we share and mend our weapons. We talk of many things, joining with our words in truth, for it is only truth that can bridge the gap of difference.

In the days that follow I often walk with the old man across the sand face, and simply by the manner of his being on the earth he teaches me many things. Hunting with a Bushman bow and poison arrow is not easy, and so by cultivating other ways of seeing, we close the gap between ourselves and our prey.

He shows me how to read the sign of the creatures on the sand, and how to listen through my body. In the years that follow I learn to hold my hand on animal spoor, days or weeks old, and know the animal that walked on that place. From the feeling in my body, I know the age, the gender, the exact time, and even the disposition of the creature on that day.

To read the earth in this way is to cultivate a companionship with the invisible, to see into a living-world map that expresses the life-forces and the doings of all living creatures ... walking a path that compels a spiritual relationship with the world ... knowing that all I perceive, whether visible or invisible, has existence. In a world filled with feeling ... billions of humans compelled by the ebb and flow of their daily feelings, it is both fallacious and stupid to deny and separate ourselves from these feelings. With so many things, it is not necessary that we plod laboriously through the process of step-by-step proof through demonstration, simply to arrive back at what our feelings told us in the first place ... it will take too long to unravel the mysteries of the universe in this way. Through intuition one must learn to trust the essence of feeling, for intuition is not simply a chance happening, it is a real process by which we come to knowledge, and in this re-educating of oneself, it follows that through intuition the physical becomes imbued with spirit, and so one should not look for spirit somewhere 'out there' as it were, but rather focus on the transformation and understanding of one's own inner life, and in this way make space for Spirit in the Soul. True feeling of something is proof enough of the existence thereof ... and so it is with the universal idea of God.

It is this thought that holds me more than any other as I continue my Soul-journey on this earth. Sometimes I think I only dreamed of walking with the old man ... but then why can I still smell the sun on the sand, and why do I feel his voice? ... And how can I know that the earth so loved the touch of our naked feet?

WISDOM OF THE WORLD

Many days pass ... we hunt, we gather, we dance, we talk, and we live out this time on the Great Sand Face as if there were no other world but ours, and I forget that I come from another place ... I live now in the thinking, the language, the doings of these people as if held in that warp of a time that nurtured and bore the archetype of the Soul of Man ... a place of enormous, endless comfort.

The new moon brings a night sky black and filled with stars, and many are the secrets held in the stars, for their courses and constellations are much more than calculated numbers and movements ... they present the living spiritual countenance of the cosmos, and no matter on which part of the earth we stand, we humans remain connected to the whole cosmic Being. We have life only because of this connection, and as we sever this contact, by degrees, we cause our souls to die.

There is a thread of magic and wisdom that comes into our lives every now and again, as if to remind us of who we once were and who we might be. We must give thought to what it is from olden times that we do not remember, what cloud veils and obscures our memory ... and to what end? The paradox is that our descent is a journey towards the light ... but first through the veiled darkness we will go, for only in darkness will we come to know the true nature of Light. We began our journey together in innocence ... we will complete our journey together in knowledge.

In the realm of nature we will come to know the secrets of our own creation. The Ten Commandments plainly define the laws of nature, first written so that humans could begin to consciously examine and understand the human relation with natural law. In this knowledge we learn to exercise choice on our path going forward, to form a wise and willing partnership with what always was and always will be.

So here we are all, lost or found somewhere on the same road from selfishness to selflessness.

MYSTERY TRUTHS

It is said that among the //Xo/xei people there is a clan called the Jung/uasee ... an elder clan of the First People who are great medicine men. It is said that one of the many things they can do is turn themselves into lions ... Ggamm ... and so this is a true story.

It was in the middle of a summer about thirty years before this book was finished. There was a Batswana village with many cattle, which were kept in the safety of a thorn boma at night. One dark moonless night, two lions came into this village and jumped into the boma, where they killed a young bull. The men of the village awoke and chased them away, with much shouting, and throwing of sticks, and fire. With a spear they managed to wound one of the lions in the ribs ... and the lions disappeared, hungry in the darkness.

As serendipity would have it, camped not far from this village were three hunters, a young white man with two old Bushman trackers of the /Aiekwe people. In the history books of today, these /Aiekwe people are called the Naro Bushmen ... but that is an insult, for it is not the name they give to themselves. Rightfully, they are called 'the people who walk on stones' ... the /Aiekwe.

So in the morning, the villagers came to these three hunters and asked if they would track down and shoot the lions. For a small consideration they agreed and set out on the spoor with the sun behind them. It had rained the evening before the lions had come, and so the spoor on the sand was easy to follow. They followed the lions for most of that day, westward towards the land of the //Xo/xei people, and in the late afternoon came to a thicket of trees still ripe with Mongongo fruits. Sitting at a fire in the shade of these trees were two old men who waited quietly, watching as the hunters came towards them.

The lion spoor went directly into the circle around the fire ... and there it ended.

Tsamkwa/tge? ... the afternoon greeting passed between them. The hunters searched the sand face all around, but there was no sign of the spoor, and no lions ... nothing, just two old men sitting at the fire. They asked the old men if they had seen the lions, and in reply the old men smiled softly, as if in a dream-space.

After a while the young hunter asked one of his older companions what could possibly have become of the lions ... but the man gave no answer. After a further search he again asked what had become of the lions. The old hunter stood looking at the two old men, and then he spoke softly. 'These are the lions,' he said pointing to the two old Jung/uasee men sitting at the fire. The young hunter looked carefully at the two old men, and saw that one of them had a fresh bark bandage around his chest and ribs, as if to heal a recent wound. The hunter repeated softly, 'These are the lions,' ... and there was no reason to doubt his word.

And then a strange silence descended into the space between them, and it was as if they were now all part of the same dream, and there was little more to say. So they shared and roasted the Mongongo nuts collected from under the trees, and slept that night around the same fire, dreaming dreams of a time when the world was different.

In the morning, when their eyes were nicely open, the three hunters went home ... the two old Jung/uasee men stayed at their fire, and the lions roamed free in the land of mystery truths, where there is no boundary between visible and invisible ... for it is only one place.

A HUMAN TRINITY

I remember once travelling northwards through the western Kalahari in Botswana ... from nowhere to nowhere. I had journeyed simply to take myself to where other people had not been. On the map there was nothing recorded beyond a certain point, and that was the way I went.

I had gone many days without seeing a single soul, passing through two or three long-deserted small villages ... just remnants and residues of the people who had once lived there ... lying broken in the dust ... an old skin water bag, fragments of ostrich eggs, a leather sandal that spoke of many miles on a foot that was once small, soft and dimpled, becoming strong for walking the path of life, and then old and gnarled skin cracked until that human journey was done ... just the wind and the silence of forgotten times, of people who had once hunted and danced and lived upon this land ... people of an older time who might have been me, and who might have been you. I could still smell them in the bone and ash heaps, their bodies embedded in smoke from a thousand fires into the wood and grass domes of old shelters, where they had slept and spoken of their lives and their simple dreams. I walked with reverence through these old people-places, for it was as if they knew that I, or some other, would come to remember them, for they would no more return ... their time here was finished, their earthly task ... lived ... and in their dying, they too would have ensouled the earth, the memory of their lives forever written for those who followed to see.

And then, in the brownness of wood and grass turning silently to dust, I saw a splash of turquoise blue ... a cluster of old beads threaded onto grass string hanging from the roof, beautiful hand-crafted shades of blue and turquoise once treasured by someone gone. I asked and the silence said yes, it would be right for me to take them, for I would hold them as a memory of that life ... and so I left that place and went on northwards with those blue beads held in my hand.

Miles and miles of nothing and everything all together ... I saw no creature for seven days ... until I came upon one single grass shelter some way off the track ... one single dwelling in the middle of absolutely nothing. I approached with caution and care for there were signs of life around ... footprints in the sand and the smell of fire in air ... and then I found them ... they were sitting, just sitting and watching this man who came from out of nowhere and approached with hands raised in a gesture of greeting. They were three ... an old woman, one in her mid-life, and an infant girl ... a female trinity sculpted from the stillness of desert.

I squatted ten feet from them, for that was the invisible boundary of their safety.

They sat in utter silence, inside of an equanimity so profound that it was as if they had never known of anything else, no other way of being ... the sun would rise and then it would set, the wind would blow and then it would stop, and the rain would come and then no more, and life would continue as it does, simply for its own sake ... and after what had come had passed, they would still be sitting. There was no question, no asking in their eyes, no expectation ... nothing ... they sat with their eyes nicely open that I might enter, that I might bring what I was, just as everything came or did not come to them. And I saw that they had nothing ... absolutely nothing ... no sign of food or sustenance of any kind ... just three souls alone in the middle of life. We spoke a few words in the old tongue and they told me that the man, the son of the old one, the husband of the woman and father of the child, had left two years ago to look for food and that he had not yet returned.

They carried on with their lives for there was nothing else, and perhaps he would return and perhaps he would not ... who could say? With my old camera I took two photographs as they sat ... and these I show to you ... three generations of women ... an old blind woman, a mother who was the only source of sustenance for the three, and a suckling child.

I shared what food I could with them and went away, and when I had passed from their view I knelt alone in the sand and asked God to care for them as he does for all life, that they would live or die in peace ... and I knew that it would be so with or without my asking, for they were there before I came and they were there after I had gone.

SPOKEN WORDS

So many nights, so many fires and so many stories. Oral tradition evokes a different relationship with the world. Among the First People and all the root nations, everything learned begins with an understanding of the whole, each person then gradually reinforces this fundamental perception with specific life experience ... moments of revelation and clarity in context with the original holistic perception, so there can be no misconception.

In Bushman culture the concept of 'misunderstanding' does not exist, and in /Gwikwe language there is no word for it ... every human, from the youngest to the oldest, always knows exactly what is being said.

In this root language there is a delightful and trusting open-endedness in every story or narrative ... it reflects the deep certainty that everything can pause, hold for a while, and then continue as living narrative when it is time. This propensity allows for an instinctual response to living in a moving, changing world, a life that demands this flexibility in order to adapt and sustain. Language is expressed from the innate nature of the being, and the way that one speaks oneself into the world is the way in which one lives oneself into the world. As a living entity, language grows or diminishes in the mouth of man.

We modern humans seem to learn backward, going from the part towards the whole. We isolate each component, separating all the bits of information in the hope of one day accumulating enough bits to add up to an understanding of the whole percept. Seldom do we reach that point of understanding. In modern language we process everything through our intellect, using words for which we have no feeling, words that come from now obscure roots and from other beginnings with which we have no conscious connection. We have scant relationship with the origin of our sounds, and subsequently with the meaning of many of our words.

The language of the /Gwikwe is a root language, and so everything remains connected to the source ... earth, air, fire and water. Words derive originally from an elemental sound or expression of cosmic energy ... from the primal phenomena themselves. A force of life becomes a sound, which, with added human meaning, becomes a word. Every word has a common and understood beginning, sometimes even originating from a remembered experience in the history of the people.

Every living thing has its own unique essence, and to know the essence of a thing is to know its meaning, and hence its name. The 'name word' leads back to that of which it speaks, and so before anything can be named or spoken it must first be known. And so, in this way, when you name something according to its essence you become bound to that thing through knowledge. All language derives from knowledge of the essence, and from this relationship the first language was born.

I know that if I am to understand this /Gwikwe language then I must hear the life force inside of the words. In the word /Tehsa ... Fire, I must feel the nature and the force of fire itself, and in this way come to know the phenomenon that is held in the word. This ancient language was not born out of intellect, it was born through imagination and inspiration ... powers that were far stronger in olden times than they are today. It is the nature of ancient languages that they express more directly the spiritual meaning, evoking greater spiritual response than do modern languages ... the closer to the root in language, the closer we get to the original impulse expressed from the spiritual world into the physical world ... that which gave rise to the word ... of life ... from which all things arise.

Too often we speak when we should be silent ... too often we speak without meaning and so in compromise of the truth. Both in our thinking and in our speaking, we indulge the concept of relativity – to deny that which is absolute, we have become a world of people drowning in the compromise of relativity. What chance when we know not even which gods we serve, the relative or the absolute? 'On earth as it is in heaven' means in the relative as in the absolute ... in the part as in the whole ... as one.

If one thinks further then, of the nature of the collective human voice, of the vocabulary of life ... it is an endless streaming of the whole truth of humanity to the ears of the angels. The 'cosmic word' incarnates and evolves, along with humans, from emotion to intellect, from subconsciousness to consciousness ... thought becomes matter and words become flesh, and this impetus of creation carries on through eternity with every thought and word we express back into the cosmos. It is the nature of this expressed human truth that determines the guiding response from the spiritual world. In this way, right or wrong, we have always been co-creators in a universe in constant creative evolution.

The evenings here in Kgoatwe are filled with moon and music ... //Gama, //Gang//gang and Se/twago play the harp with a gentleness and beauty that silences our talk and opens our ears. //Gama plucks melody from the sinew strings with her fingers, and the others, one on either side, play beautiful percussive counterpoint by striking the strings with long stems of grass ... //Gae khu //gaa, the grass that can be thrown like a spear.

The instrument itself is carved from the whole trunk of a softwood tree ... beautiful, hollowed out and shaped like an ark, with engravings of eland with fat legs and giraffe shaded in charcoal. The soft resonance of sinewed strings touching life chords ... they sing ... voices raised to the spirit of the world ... calling forth a deep and ancient sadness ... memories of a long human journey ... so long ...

... and in my mind after so many years ... //Gama's face ... haunted and silent still, her eyes filled with a longing for something that we all cry for in our moments of truth ... just one moment of eternal peace ... just one place of rest.

Under the soft blanket of full moon light we listen to stories of how lucky we are ... and indeed it seems that way.

GOD'S CHILDREN

And in the morning ... sun ... child of God, rise and fill the air with light. The first golden rays touch the edge of the earth, and then each and every living thing, touched and filled with the same light ... the same life.

Still held in sleep, we sit as we have since the beginning of human time ... each in the dawn of our day, waiting for the full return of our soul spirit from sleep ... waiting for our own awakening. And as we sit thus, do we humans not all ask with unspoken words for the same gift of life ... of love? Do we not ask, each of us, for our daily bread?

Later ... voices on the breeze ... the children have built a small grass shelter in the nearby bush where they re-enact the stories and songs of last night. I am drawn to watch and listen as Khaba begins a song that she has heard only once before ...

'I am just learning it,' she says. It is a /Gwikwe song, and the owner of this song is at /Xoie!om. Some people came through this way many moons ago on their way to the settlement, and we shared a healing dance. There was a famous dancer called Abama who made this song, and that was the first time it was sung with other people.

As with all the world's children, stories and songs evolve and change in the wake of their free-flowing imaginations, and then, as if to bind the spirit of each story into their collective consciousness, they begin their own healing dance. The girls clap and sing and the boys dance the circle ... young gracile bodies filled with the forces of life expressed with such compelling intensity. They become embarrassed by their own severity and collapse in heaps of self-conscious laughter ... the smaller children running around in spontaneous delight until they, too, find reason to wander off to whatever the day will next place before them.

I am left holding the echoes ... thinking in silent sadness that this little band of children has no way forward from here, for they are, indeed, the last of the first. I ask the Great God to guide them, so that they might be the bridge that leads the past to the future, and that the wisdom carried in their blood holds the truth for long enough that we all may learn. These are the journeys of souls through time ... each choosing its own course and the lessons that journey will bring. I am reminded that each successive generation must carry forward the life lessons of their parents, and I have seen that some of today's children carry, effortlessly, a light within that they nurture as a chalice for the Holy Grail of humanity, and which, now more than ever, must be held against the dark forces that have so come to prevail in our world.

Shrieks come from behind /Gowsi's shelter where the little ones now hang and swing on thongs from a tree, their constant pleasure in small things a source of joy for all. Says little //Nale/twago to Seka, 'Come, let me bite your cord!' (/Uamm, which is belly button). More shrieks follow.

On a second tree hangs a thick twist of wildebeest and gemsbok skin strips, but on this swing they do not play ... the spinning log is heavy and dangerous, and the /Gwikwe are mindful of the safety of their children. Attached to the bottom of these thongs is a weighty log, which from time to time is wound up tight with a long stick by one of the men and then released to spin out, thereby stretching and softening the thick strips of skin that are otherwise impossible to work ... a simple and effective technology. It will be two or three months before the thongs are soft enough to use for carry-nets and rope, or be traded for tobacco and metal.

It is afternoon, and some of the hunters bring meat given to them by horsemen who passed on their way back to the settlement. There is delighted laughter as Kuramatso chases little Seka across the space between the shelters, his plump little legs, straddling a crudely fashioned stick-horse, run as fast as they can to stay ahead of the older boy who pursues him with a play-play whip.

That evening around the fire the men talk of a different animal ... they have begun to wonder how it would be if they, one day, had their own horses. These would be the first animals they own, and in a culture that has never acknowledged the concept of ownership it would be a fundamental transgression of their way of life. The concept of ownership would give them 'status' ... a false importance never before assumed in their lives. It would herald a change in their living philosophy which insists that all things are different but equal, and in their age-old symbiosis with the animal kingdom they would be adapting to a concept of 'dominion over' rather than 'relationship with'. And they talk also of /Xoie!om ... the settlement.

For a while I think of the Bushman state of 'beingness'. More than anything else, it is a purity of heart that these people have, a benevolence of Soul. There is a mutual kindness expressed in all of their relationships, and the security that comes with this condition of Soul is everything. Something changes as they come into the world of greed and possession, a new expectation arises, and what was always plenty is no longer enough ... and so begins the fall from innocence, that journey of descent that all humans must make ... and it is a long journey through darkness to light.

The days pass and the sun burns us to stillness ... we burrow into small hollows of black shade under bushes where we lie waiting for deliverance, for any movement of wind on scorched skin, any movement of air that will bring respite. We lie still ... mortal and fragile ... each in his own silent relationship with the sun ... breathing small and shallow, for the air is too hot to take deep into our lungs. There is nothing else at this time of the day ... only the heat ...

I think of the sun and all that it brings, and I am reminded that there is also a world without light, a world of darkness with its own power ... but I know, too, that true power lives only under the light of the sun. I think of how completely our lives on earth are ordered by the course of the sun ... whether it be in the daily rising and setting through cycles of light and darkness, or the yearly journey of seasons governed by the sun's passage through equinox and solstice ... through spring, summer, autumn and winter, and then by the precessional cycle of the great year spanning 25,920 years, as the sun moves through the twelve ages of man reflected in the heavenly constellations, so ordering the evolution of humans on earth.

Slowly the sun passes, and we make our way back into the world and the closing of day. The evening fires are surrounded by silence for there is much to think of. For some time now the people have talked … why must they be hungry and thirsty when they hear that their relatives in the settlement eat mealie meal and drink water … why must their children be without?

And then almost by subconscious accord it is resolved, a decision is made that heralds a time in history when the last of the First People, by their own choosing, begin a journey away from the innocence of Eden towards what will be their final fall … and their winter.

The waning of the moon begins.

EXODUS

It is a silent morning in the world of men, for these are the last days of the wild /Gwikwe.

I stand in stillness as they gather their small belongings and set off on a sad journey to the government settlement, /Xoie!om. They take with them everything that they have, it is a long walk, five days to /Xoie!om.

My legs refuse to follow … my voice would call them back to make promises that I cannot keep, for I cannot change the course of the world. And so I watch them go, beautiful first human creatures gliding away through the yellow grass, voices lilting, drifting into silence … silence … they go … that part of myself that I love the most. I will catch up with them before they cross Kgoatwe pan and the water hole.

I stay behind, standing under the Old Man's Tree for a while to hold the memory ... feeling pictures in my heart, my tears on the sand ... I struggle to accept that this precious time has come to an end. I know what lies ahead, and so my eyes can see only behind me, holding onto every moment of the time that we have shared ... my Soul filled to the brimming.

For so long now this Kgoatwe place has been our home ... //Gau//gae, and now, around me, it stands empty ... silent shelters with doorways black vacant, for my people have gone ... no voices, no fires ... only the bone and ash heaps remain to tell the story of those who lived in this place.

And so I leave without my heart ... how can I tell you of the emptiness of every step ... how can I tell you of the aching sadness that begins even now.

That evening, together, we cross Kgoatwe pan ... the water hole is dry, cracked mud. People voices call and echo across the dryness and a small band of humans walks into the northwest and a setting sun ... a band of souls journeying through time from one place of meaning to another, and only at journey's end will we know what we have done.

We sleep that night in a strange place far from home. The smaller children are quiet and subdued, staying close to the comfort of their mothers ... the older boys express snatches of hollow bravado from time to time, unconsciously reflecting the fear and anxiety held silently by their fathers and mothers ... and so we sit around our night fire as strangers in ourselves, wanting to give something to one another but not knowing what to give, for we are all caught in the changing.

For so long together our evenings and our darkness have been filled with the reassurance of the other, of voice sounds, laughter and teasing, playing back and forth between the shelters, our hearths and our hearts in Kgoatwe ... but now, silent and still, we are afraid to say what disquiet beats in our hearts and what thoughts we hold in uncertainty.

I sit as silent witness in the darkness outside of the ring of firelight, my eyes searching into a world of humans that passes before me … watching how they reach across to one another … small gestures given as if to bridge the separation that lies ahead. My only comfort is that there are eyes greater than mine that, too, bear witness on this day. And in the sky … something of all of us in the chalice moon … held in hope between the forces of Venus and Jupiter … love and wisdom, with Mercury between as the messenger to awaken us to the possibility of ourselves in the time ahead, and the thought of what it is that comes to us now from out of the cosmos … what is this possibility, and how has it been foretold throughout history?

In the morning we help one another to shoulder heavy carry bags, and then we walk. A sadness bears down as a weight upon every step … some with feelings of anticipation, others uncertain … but we are together.

It is mid-morning when the hunters find some ostrich eggs. They say that /Gerusa was nowhere to be seen, and the sign on the sand tells that she was killed on the nest by a lion, dragged away and eaten before the coming of the sun to the sand face … Tgoo says it was lucky that we came upon the eggs before the hyena and the jackal.

And so we stop and rest under a small umbrella of trees … the great sun burning from above. Today there is no joy in the making of fire … the flame will come as it does … the eggs will be roasted in the coals … we will eat.

I cannot bear the unspoken sadness … it is as if the very purpose of our existence is taken from us … to be consciously doing a wrong thing and yet compelled to continue because it seems the only way forward … holding the pain of those countless human souls who have been forced at one time or another in history to cross this threshold from the old way of life … to leave behind the comfort and surety of an age-old existence … to be dragged onwards by the undeniable compulsion of evolution.

What is there to say … Tgoo … Tso/tgomaa the hunter … and his wife,

Dowgwi … my brothers and sisters with whom I have shared the Earth. The children are silent now … they begin to understand that a change is coming into their lives and it is not a change that they would choose. It seems strange that no one laughs when Tgoo burns his fingers … silence and a wry smile … Geutwe … Kamageh … we share the roots and the other foods collected along the way … we shoulder our loads and we walk.

As if from afar, I think of the historical significance of this journey … in these five days the earth bears witness to the final exodus of a people. This is the last band of free and wild Bushmen left on the Great Sand Face, and they walk their last mile towards a brutal uncertainty … gone forever are the ancient ways for which we shall mourn.

Walking, walking on the ground of the earth … two days later we reach Kia//nau, halfway to the settlement … another day … tonight we sleep at //Xolo, the place of the big wolf … just one more sleep to journey's end.

The last morning comes with a muted reluctance … we are blessed with an overcast sky … the sand will not be too hot for walking … but what on earth are we doing? What on earth are we doing?

And so I witness … that after four days and many miles the last band of Bushmen find themselves at //Xale … the big pan … only a few hours from the settlement. These little people of the Great Sand Face who share the world … they hunt together under the light of the sun, they gather food and watch the same sun setting at the same time, and they sit together under the night stars around the same fire … always, in all ways, they have been equal.

In silence suspended I watch as they cross the sand face … from freedom they come … lithe, beautiful bodies clothed in the skins bequeathed by animal brothers and sisters … their weapons and tools on their backs … in each face the memory of what lies behind, the uncertainty of what lies ahead … and the sound of feet touching softly and reverently upon the earth so that it remembers their passing, for this day, this moment in time, is a turning point in the history of humanity.

They come to the road that leads from the pan to the settlement ... soon they will be there. Carried on the wind they hear the sound of the borehole engine. It breaks through the silence of the vast sand face and their own thoughts ... dogs barking ... donkeys ... and many people.

And so it is ... finally they come to the settlement and the end of their ways ... unnoticed by the world ... and I, born to witness and someday make sense of this time in history and of these humans with whom I have shared my life. Small feet in the dust stand reluctantly in a strange place ... /Xoie!om, the place that from now on will be their home. No one is speaking ... a clinic ... soccer posts ... a school for the children ... and at the centre of everything, a borehole ... and water. I am swamped with a despair that has no deliverance ... a sadness for everything that is wrong in our lives, and carried on the face of this sadness I am as helpless as the next.

In the eyes of the settlement Bushmen, dressed in cast-off clothing rags, echoes the silent derision of mocking laughter, for we newcomers, dressed in skins, cluster around the water-running tap like wild animals thirst-weary, from far away, and we are now here in this place where all are not equal, for some already know many of the irrelevant things that others must still learn.

My heart aches as I watch Kamageh ... archetypal primitive human, his hands clutched tightly around an ostrich egg filled with water. He stands mesmerised by the water-flowing tap, the breath heaving in his chest ... caught in the momentous fear of this new and strange reality ... and I am held in the moment inside his breath ... in and out ... and in ... and out ... the quintessential anxiety felt by the countless human souls who have, through the ages, walked this same path forward into uncertainty. In this place today, and in this one human, sounds the heartbeat and breath of all humans, so small and vulnerable, and yet sometimes so great in time and space.

It must be said that for as long as Bushmen have lived in the Kalahari Desert, they have known thirst ... a thirst almost genetic in proportion. And so when presented with a tap that constantly runs water, clean water, it is understandable that a man's whole being is drawn to that place and the water ... the Bushman nemesis.

I cannot tell you how filled with sadness is my Soul, a sadness I will hold forever or until the understanding comes that all is, indeed, as it should be in the eyes of God. For do we humans not choose our own way? Do we not do all that we have done of our own free will?

And now in this place of darkness we must somehow hold onto what was light ... our freedom, and the voices of our children, for it is they who must go forward to a new way in a new place. In our bellies we carry the fear of survival in an unknown future, but it is what has come, and so here we are now, utterly mortal and standing on a threshold too big to comprehend ... a threshold on which all of humanity has stood at one time or another, on our journey through the disparities of history and time. What is there to say? ... if we do not stand together now, then we have nothing, not even ourselves. In reverence and on bended knees I ask God to somehow make this right ... for I cannot ... not today.

And the government of this land? Like any government, they are not the design of free people ... they are nought but the manifest failure of humanity to understand the nature of true power. They have done as much as any government will for a small minority of people who, for so long, have been so different in all of their ways ... they have done nothing. They and the mineral-mining monoliths, who, behind the lip service, only continue to perpetuate the genocide of innocence.

So the first people are dying. This fact alone is not important in our great living world, for many are the physical forms that have lived and died, and many are the sacrifices of soul. What is important is that we remember, that we honour that which came before us, that we take forward the knowledge for our children. What is important are the lessons of Spirit, so that we might live and go forward with a clear vision of who we can be.

When we speak of our earth it is plain to see that we have contaminated the waters, poisoned the air and destroyed one forest too many ... the degree of our trespass is enormous. Those who care have used many human tools and resources in the hope of protecting what is left, but, alas, it seems late for such measures ... too late for us to heal the earth's wounds by physical means.

The way open to us is through Spirit, for only in spirit will we find the means to make the difference, and what makes this difference is how we acknowledge our trespass, how we mend our ways, and how conscious we are in the doing. If we but lived as humans together, if we understood what it means to love one another, we would, in shame, restore the dignity that we have stolen, and the truth that we have buried in the prejudiced record of our history.

I have always believed that my journey to this place was a blessing ... there was a purpose greater than I, which would be revealed in my life. Here on the sand face I have learned through an unconscious osmosis, in breath, blood and bone ... a transmutation of ancient wisdom vital for the human journey forward ... the wisdom of a Divine principle ... God in the beginning ... a God who will not be explained or denied with any cerebral dexterity, and who cannot be defined within the parameters of our physical existence. At this stage in the evolution of humanity, our relationship with God can only be one of faith ... a knowing faith.

Past truth serves future knowledge, when we no longer see life as a series of disconnected beginnings and endings, but rather as an eternally interconnected continuity of events ... each period woven out of the spiritual memory of what came before. There is much that has stirred within me ... I have remembered. I understand the soul relationship between myself and Dzero-O, and Gening/u, and many of the others. I think of who we have been before ... what history have we shared on this earth? Why have we come together in this place and time? And what is it that I must take forward?

On this earth, many an epoch in time has passed. Great orders of humanity have lived through different stages of earth and human evolution, and passed onwards through the spiritual realm to return in changed form in different times ... each successive order adding what it must to the evolving human spirit. And in these great cosmic comings and goings there is neither right nor wrong ... no one is to blame ... for all of us here and now a time has passed.

I stay for one moon in the settlement ... I see the destiny written, and I know that it is time. I look for the old man, Dzero-O ... it is a difficult goodbye because we both know the same thing ... gently into my hands he places a necklace that he has made from the claws of the antbear ... so that I can be strong when I am alone and away from the people. Tso/tgomaa gives me his hunting set that I may hunt well as I go to *Oooohga!noo ... the land of the white people.

I said goodbye and made the promise to return. What followed were two years of consternation, confusion, adulation and despair in the land of the others. Heralded as the White Bushman, and unduly praised for doing what many said they could never do, I wandered around in a world of incidental alternatives, a world that seemed without anchor and root. For me as a bush man, I had done no more than follow myself in the hope of finding my way ... the door had opened, and I had been made aware of how I might continue ... with my eyes nicely open.

ALL CIRCLES CLOSE

It was late afternoon in the autumn when I returned to the Kalahari. I had been gone for twenty-four long moons. I had been in a world so opposite and filled with people so different ... a winter in London. I had walked Park Lane barefoot in the snow with a gemsbok skin draped over my shoulders for warmth and comfort ... utterly at one with my place in the world, and mildly bemused by the strange responses of my human brothers and sisters. So many people who insisted that I came from a world different to theirs, when I was from the same world as all of us. It was just that I had walked a different path, taken things a little further, and carried within me my beginnings ... the power of earth, sun and moon in my Soul ... I was a lucky one.

And now I was going home into the vast sand face, filled with clamouring memories, like a ball of pain in my stomach'... finding my way back to myself and back to Kgoatwe ... to a memory too precious to hold.

I am alone in the southern Kalahari, with that enormous, familiar stretch of empty fullness before me. I have driven for two days, and now I leave my Land Rover who has come to be called 'Martha of the lonely hearts'. I leave her under a giant Camel thorn tree just outside of the northern border of the Khutse Game Reserve. From there I will walk for three weeks and four hundred kilometres north-northwest into the central Kalahari to where this story began.

There is a fear in my belly and a madness in my blood, but this is what I must do. No one knows where I am or where I am going ... it always seems to be this way in my life. There was always so much that I could never tell ... was it me so used to my own silence? ... Or was there simply no one to tell? ... Perhaps it is this way for all of us.

I take from the vehicle my favourite hunting set, the one given to me by Tso/tgomaa ... a spear and a good bow. Inside my quiver bag are fire sticks, five arrows with old poison, a digging stick, some snare ropes and a knife. Stripping sweated shirt and jeans from my body I stand unfettered and free once more, blessed by sun and wind. My old skin moochi smells like I used to smell. My balls fit snug into the familiar moulded leather, and once more

I feel like a hunter-man, and it is time to run ... predator, wolf, wild man.

I run for an hour until my body is wet, and then stop at the edge of a pan where I once found the skeleton of an old bull giraffe ... !Nabehma ... I remember you well. I roll in soft sand until once more in communion with the Kalahari earth that I have so missed, until the fine dust covers every inch of my body and I know that the sun will not burn me.

And then it is time to walk ... my Soul soaring heart bursting for what lies ahead.

Endless miles and miles of Eden ... the earth clean as it always was ... ripe grass showering seeds onto my feet as I brush through virgin plains of untouched land, redolent with sacred memories. I know that I am blessed beyond what any human could hope for ... holding the feeling of each step and the cool breath of autumn wind on my skin ... how can I ever tell of this privilege .:. how can I ever tell? And so I walk within this blessing, and I know utterly how it is to be held in the hand of God ... how can I ever tell?

Passing through the southern part of Gantam//nau seven days later, I begin to hear the voices ... I remember, we men had hunted here ... !Nabehma ... the Tall One ... how we had run ... and laughed ... so much joy and life ... and I walk on ... and then I cross the first cut-line, and the voices stop ... a fear tightens my belly and pounds in my heart, for I know what this means ... there is an evil come into this last Eden ... a darkness between the Sun and the Earth.

Standing naked on this diamond mining cut-line looking to the east and the west of me, along an endless, brutal, straight line ploughed through virgin desert, fresh earth stripped of all vegetation and baked to death by a merciless sun. Machines driven by eyes that cannot see, cutting through the flow and contour with an impunity both terrible and absolute ... and a greed that has no boundary. And for what? Nothing more than money in the hands of another earth-consuming, world-governing crime syndicate. Is there nothing that they will leave alone ... is there nothing that cannot be raped, cut, used and passed over on the way to their next atrocity? Forest, desert or ocean ... the seawater itself will die when it no longer carries dolphin voice and whale song, and without living creature and the touch of human feet, the land will die of a great aloneness. And how long before we learn that there is another way? How long before we finally come to understand that our purpose is spiritual ... and then, will there be anything left?

I walked in this way for many days, just one little soul come to remember the end of a time in our history ... one soul coming to understand more of the reason for being human. So many feelings rekindled in my body ... my heart singing and crying at the same time.

Thoughts ... and miles ... my feet on the earth.

After twenty-four days of walking in this way I came finally into the Kgoatwe area ... I was going back to the place where we had lived, and to the shelters that had been home. With each step bearing me closer, my heart filled to overflowing with a pain and loss that I could not bear. For two years I had held my memories as if nothing had changed, unable to accept that the end had come and that, never again, would the Great Sand Face be graced with the flowing spirit of free people. Tears began to pour from my heart and from my eyes, and I became lost both inside myself and without ... and how I searched for mile after endless mile, but my eyes could not see and I could not find the shelters ... I could not find my way back.

Filled with a desperate sadness I found myself running ... running ... looking for //Gau//gae ... the place that we had called home. I ran on in this way, searching for that familiar circle of shelters that in my mind were still standing as we had left them ... in a circle around the ash heaps and the memories ... but I could not find them ... and I was searching, running ... running like a child in the pain of everything that I had ever lost.

And it was then that I ran into the smell … into a solid wall of reality … lion smell … and lions! Blinded by tears and my broken heart I had forgotten myself entirely, and now I stood paralysed on the spot, stuck in the middle of thick lion smell. Drifting in the air in front of my face were tufts of lion fur floating inexorably earthwards, my eyes following their course to the full realisation of where I was. I had run right into the middle of a pride of Kalahari lions. I had run into a space that was not mine but theirs on that day, and I had done so with no awareness. Startled by my sudden appearance the lions had backed off. I stood rooted, and around me they crouched … eight of them that I could see. I looked at each in turn and they at me as if waiting for my next impudence. I knew that whatever I did next would be critical, but I could think of nothing clever or brave that would change the circumstance of my foolishness. I could think only to apologise with absolute and humble sincerity, for it was I who had trespassed. And so I quietly told them that I was sorry, and that I really had meant no rudeness … and they, crouching and waiting in the curious disbelief that a human was suddenly and inexplicably standing in their midst … and now talking to them. No doubt a first for them, too, this strange human running smack into their day and then standing there, possessed, with tears streaming down his face, looking at each in turn with utter respect, but without fear.

I could see which lion held the power on that day … a large male on my right-hand side, and the closest to me. It was he who had been involved in the dispute that left that tuft of fur floating through the air, and it was he who led the pride. I held his eyes with my own … no challenge no fear, again voiced my humble apology, and then began slowly to step backward the way that I had come. With each step I took backward, the lions took a step forward … and so nothing changed. In their manner there was no intention, just the curiosity of this strange encounter … and so I stepped back, and they stepped forward. With utter sincerity I again said that I was sorry and that I had truly not meant to be careless or disrespectful, and then it ended … I stepped back and they did not follow.

Within the grace of nature there is always an empathy for that which is true, and on this day no harm would come to me, for I was held in the wings of angels and my journey was not done. From a distance I gave thanks and set off again, but this time with more care ... running a two-mile circle around where the lions were, and towards where I hoped at last to find the shelters.

And then again I stopped in bewilderment, for now there were human tracks on the sand ... and they were my own? Something had compelled me to double back in a full circle, into the lion pride, and then back onto my own tracks ... and so I stopped, for my feet would go no further. Once more overwhelmed by feelings of huge and inexplicable loss I began to look around me, and I could almost smell something that I had smelled before ... some memory ... something familiar in the back of my brain ... a residue of smell in the sand that evoked the sounds that now echoed faintly as voices in my memory. And then I saw it ... just a little hump in the ground covered in purple autumn flowers ... and then another little hump ... covered in flowers ... and yet another ... and I saw that each flower-covered hump was once a bone and ash heap that had been scraped up in front of each little shelter that had held the lives of the last wild Bushmen ... and there I stood ... surrounded by the shelters, as I had stood so many times before ... //Gau//gae ... I was home.

It was an enormous time for me ... my heart bursting with feelings more powerful than anything I had ever known, and tears of memory running down my cheeks, my heaving chest, and onto my tired feet. And then at last, when I looked down, I saw the sand grooved in a ring around me, I saw that I was standing in the middle of the dancing circle. I had walked through twenty-four days of remembered dreams ... alone through four hundred miles of Kalahari to find myself ... utterly lost and then found, standing exactly in the middle of the dancing circle. Resurrected into the heart of the sacred circle from where our lives had been dreamed, felt, spoken and danced and danced and danced so many times ... the woman melon dance, the man ostrich dance and the people healing dance. It was here, together, that we had seen the face of God in one another and each in his own heart.

And as I stood there the sounds came ... layer upon layer filled with the laughter and voices, of children and women content, men voices low, and fire smells and story-songs ... everything held in the memory of the earth, held in the life-body surrounding this place where we had partaken of each other and of life as humans do in their fullness, in their finest hour. We had lived here in Kgoatwe, in a truth and harmony that would resonate forever in the memory of the world. This was our entry into that book of records, which holds for eternity the thoughts, words and deeds of all human Souls, and of all life lived.

I would be no place else ... for here I am.

And then, in the last stillness of daylight, I hear the sound of an animal coming through the bush from the north, from behind where Tso/tgomaa's shelter had once stood. Crouching in silence behind the bone and ash heap, I wait to see what creature walks here with such carelessness, as if this Kgoatwe place belongs to him! I see light glinting off the straight black horns ... gemsbok ... from fifty yards he comes directly towards me, and there seems something familiar about this animal, something I know in his walk, his manner ... and looking right at me he just keeps coming. I think that perhaps he cannot see me and yet he looks straight at me, and I at him ... and still I do not move. He walks between the ash heaps and comes to within ten yards of where I crouch in silent awe. He begins to walk in a circle around me, from the northeast around south of me and then right around to the northwest ... all the time looking over his right shoulder at me. I want to stand so that he can see me ... I am overwhelmed with an emotion that I cannot fathom, and can think only that I should talk to him, tell him who I am, and that I have returned and that I used to live here, and that I know him.

So I say to him, 'Paul se habe ... /nee, Paul se habe ... look, Paul is here ... I have come ... I am here.' Slowly I stand as I speak to him, and all I can say is that it is me and I am back, and more than anything in the world I just want to know that this wonderful creature sees me as I see him. There is nothing in his movement or in his eyes that shows any fear or confusion ... he simply looks ... and then he stops, and still looking at me he turns and begins to walk back on the same circle around me again. I understand that he does see me, and that in the interconnectedness of all things he comes as the messenger ... for God knows that I am back, and so the animals know that I am back ... and the sand, and all that I have known returns, for everything is as it should be and all is remembered in the world of Spirit.

And even as it happens I cannot believe what I see ... this gemsbok that walks in a circle around me, and who looks at me as if he, too, has come to this place for a purpose bigger than both of us. He walks in the other direction still holding my eyes. Spirit brother animal, I see you, and I remember now that it was you who first stood under the Old Man's Tree ... I remember it was you who showed us that this would be good place to live ... and that it is with you that this story begins.

When he comes to the Old Man's Tree he turns off the circle and walks away towards the southeast, every now and again looking back over his shoulder ... I follow in wonder, trying to hold the contact for as long as possible. He goes ... for it is done, and I return to the Old Man's Tree. I know that this is the same gemsbok bull who, five years ago, had stood under this same tree, so that four men could see that this Kgoatwe place was to be the place that we would call home. And now he returns at this time to bring me to the understanding that I am not lost, but that I am found, and that equally with all things I am held in the consciousness of God.

I stand in awe, I kneel in reverence ... I will always know this day.

The sun has gone, and I sit exhausted under the Old Man's Tree. In the enfolding darkness I have neither the will nor energy to make fire or shelter for myself ... the day has been too strong for my little Soul. I know that the lions are not far away, and that they are aware of my presence ... but I am without strength.

And then, through the twilight, they come ... small dark forms filtering quietly through the tall grass and across the sand towards where I sit in vulnerable stillness ... watchdogs of the wilderness ... guinea fowl. Utterly unconcerned, they surround me as if I were invisible. Thirty or so birds, they flutter and climb into the trees around and above me, and into the Old Man's Tree ... some of them almost within touching distance, and I know that nothing will move through this place in the night without these birds giving ample warning.

Guinea fowl are wily and cunning, they do not come close to people in wild places. I do not fully understand what is happening, but I do know that they have come, or that they have been sent on this day, to keep me safe ... for today I am surrendered. I curl into the sand among the softly twittering good-nights of my feathered sentinels, my keepers through this night.

I know not why or how these wonders occur, but by these happenings I am made certain that there is no accident in any of our doings ... in the eyes of God nothing is invisible, and there is consequence and meaning in everything that we do. Sometimes we are given through grace the revelation of a special moment in time ... the revelation that brings to clarity our place and being in this great cosmos, and the wisdom of the world, which seems so impossibly far, becomes ours ... becomes our own wisdom for that time. And if it is this way for just one moment, then it must be this way for all moments and for all of us through eternity. We have only to remember to live our lives in such a way that we open ourselves to our own revelations, our own miracles ... each one of us.

I know that I belong absolutely on this earth, in this life and under the eyes of God, and that I am seen and heard, and that this will never change ... only my awareness of that truth may change from time to time. Alone under the moon in this great wilderness I vow that I will learn to hold each moment, to nurture each revelation and know the miracle. One man standing ... in the middle of the night in the Kalahari Desert in a land called Africa on the earth ... somewhere in a solar system in a far galaxy ... a universe in a world immeasurable ... and yet it fits so easily into my heart ... and /Tgooma the Gemsbok has come to remind me that all is as it should be.

I lie in still darkness holding a wish that cannot come true ... for a time has passed and that is the truth of it. In sleep I travel far into the realm of spirit ... I know, because in the morning I bear gifts that were not mine the night before.

Awakened by sun and soft bird voices ... my feathered companions descend from the tree above me as if I were part of the earth, slowly scratching and chirping themselves away into the golden grass. If ever I was held by angels, then it was this last night ... one man alone on the Great Sand Face under the Old Man's Tree, in the middle of a vast wilderness ... utterly safe and utterly blessed.

I think of my people gone ... I stand in remembrance of the souls who lived in this Kgoatwe place, of the words that were spoken, the feet that walked and danced upon this little place on the earth, which we humanised for a time, for that was our return gift, our redemption for the sacrifice. We ensouled this small piece of earth ... our words and deeds remembered in the trees, the sand, in the bone and ash heaps now covered with flowers ... a blanket to hold the memory of our shared lives.

In the silence of my Soul I hear the voices of a people who have passed ... Our Souls have lived on the earth for the time that was ours to live, and now in this time of our winter we return to the world of Spirit from whence we all come.

My heart yearns.

BROTHERS AND SISTERS

I could not face the settlement and the sadness I knew I would find ... I walked onwards through the desert, passing Kgoatwe pan ... dry and empty, but I recalled that day and the rain ... I could still smell the water ... I thought of many things.

I stopped at //Xolo, the place of the big wolf. I met with a small party of women who were out gathering the last of the summer foods, knowing they would tell my people that I had come and was camped nearby.

Night falls ... I wait under the full moon, my heart filled with questions. They come out of the darkness ... Seman/ua ... I hear you from a distance ... your voice singing from the fire to the night sky, and Tgoo ... the snare man ... your whole face smiling happiness, and Tso/tgomaa ... the hunter ... your shy silent joy, and the truth of your relationship with the earth, which kept us all through the dry seasons ... how much I have missed you.

Soft voices, old friends ... '/Tgeah? ... Kiri kwa /tge.' ... My eyes are nicely open ... Yes, I see you ... Yes, I am here in this moment in time. After greeting we do not say much, for we know that we have left a better time behind us and the memory of that time is suddenly heavy in our hearts ... when one has too much to say it is best to say it in silence. We sit around the fire ... four men ... as it was in the beginning. We have not forgotten how we first found our Kgoatwe place, and how we had come together ... the many miles and many things that we have done.

It is the strangest of nights, the Great Sand Face is alive with spirit and remembering ... and then a thing happens. Across the sand they come ... scorpions, big scorpions ... one after the other out of the darkness, crawling towards us, and over and between our bodies ... coming from all sides and going in all directions ... trailing luminous energy lines across the silver sand. In our lives none of us have ever seen anything like this, there is no aggression and no anxiety. It is not even that they have a singular purpose or destination that we can see, nor are they attracted to the fire. Just dozens of these amazing creatures responding to some compelling force under the full moon, called to move, to seek, to gather together. And for us, what message comes from the earth? ... Is this a living metaphor foretelling of a great gathering of Bushman spirits, a last coming together of the First People? ... A family of humans held in the hand of God ... we will know in time. And as strangely as they come ... they go.

When N/aueema the Moon reaches the top of the sky we sleep, dreamlines joining us one to the other ... cradled and made strong by the earth we dream of another time. What had happened in our lives together was significant beyond anything we could understand at this time ... we had indeed been the last of the First People, and it was no accident that we had shared time in such a way. Through our coming together we had lived a story, that in the telling, might show a way forward in a time when all seemed hopeless on the earth, when the forces of darkness were so relentless that the face of God in humanity would be forgotten ... this was our dream that night.

The others came in the morning, each as the day would allow ... gently coming into the space around our fire ... never invasive. The children were shy, for Paul had returned and they knew not what to expect. The women came last, for they had stopped to gather veld foods on the way so that they would not come with empty hands ... and what can I say, my sisters and mothers, as I see you and hold you in my arms ... if the world was mine I would give it all to you.

We sit for the day under a familiar tree mostly just touching and talking through our bodies ... legs entwined, arms and shoulders rub and brush, hands holding and sharing, eyes filled with all we would say to each other and the questions we know we cannot answer ... but we are here at //Xolo ... together again. My breath fills with the smell of people I have missed so much, and in my heart ... never before have I known such love. The women have filled their carry bags with the last of the wild coffee beans and shallots, and these they roast. We share food and stories with eyes nicely open so as to take in all that we can of this time together. //Gang//gang tells me that little Seka has climbed onto an anthill every day since my departure and, looking into the distance towards the south, he asks for me. He asks every day where I am.

So much has happened, so many things have changed. In the settlement they found themselves immersed in a life so different and cruel. Each soul challenged to adapt and survive, and I knew by what was unsaid that it had been difficult beyond my experience.

THE LAST GREAT DANCE

By the next afternoon it was as if we had never been apart. Gradually then, a feeling came upon us, and we knew that it was time again for a healing dance.

One or two women began to clap, to call the dance together ... hesitantly at first, clapping ... waiting, and then starting again ... and the men, almost fearful of coming into this dance, sensing the unusual enormity of it, and holding back ... the air becoming thicker and thicker ... the forces of spirit almost palpable.

Magu is the first of the dancers today, and the people say that Magu has not danced as a healer for a long time. They say that his trance became too powerful and there were times when it seemed that he would not come back. He then became ill from the dancing, and so he stopped working as a healer.

When you trance you shift dimension, perhaps, in a way, like breaking through the light barrier. The exertion is enormous, and the stress placed on the body can leave one drained and exhausted to the point of sickness. In all humans there is a seeking towards higher self, an innate compulsion that we can deny only for so long, and then our lives choose a course that takes us inexorably homeward ... within.

Today there is power in the sand face and the sky coming down ... this will be no ordinary dance. We feel it, one and all, a gathering of spirit forces ... the air, almost luminous, becoming one with earth ... and we, bound to this act of consecration ... drawn to a higher dimension but holding back, almost afraid of the enormity of the spirit realm and the event that unfolds around us. Compelled also by the longing to be together again in the soul world, where all that took us apart can be reconciled in our reaching upwards.

Again the women clap and one or two men begin to dance, and then pull back to the edge of the circle ... holding, and then urged again to dance ... bodies drawn by the invisible power that compels us to something greater inside of ourselves and which wants to be ... and so we must.

It took a while before the dance became full, for we knew that once we began there would be no turning back ... and the voices calling, until the rhythm of the one becomes the rhythm of the other, until the sounds turn to colour ... and so this is how we danced a great dance ... that day at //Xolo ... our bodies painted red-yellow by the light of fire, and we without fear into the realm of Spirit ... .

Dust ... voices ... red sun and we dance, feet on the earth ... rattles ... *tshk*! *tshk*! ... through the day and into the night ... through the sun into the moon, sacred and silver ... *tshk*! *tshk*! ... we dance our sadness and our longing, cleansing our spirits and each other with a selflessness that has no boundary ... a purging of all that is wrong and held within. There has been so much holding and hurting over the last two years of separation ... so much that has challenged our lives and everything we had known for so long.

I recall taking pictures as if in a dream and then I remember only feelings and myself alongside Magu crawling across the sand towards the fire ... voices calling and hands clapping so insistent that we cannot stop ... and from his body a roaring and bellowing ... and from somewhere inside the belly of the earth and the red warmth of the sun I remember, for I was there, my heart bursting ... bursting ... body moving of its own volition, heart pumping, surging cosmic pulse ... immersed in a primordial cry sound that I cannot hear but which fills my every cell to exploding with a longing that shreds and soothes my soul at once ... healing ... healing ... and that sound ... and again.

Bodies moving, shifting ... shape changing ... animal forms merging into and out of the human form as if still part of the same physical entity. Dancing between dimensions ... dipping deep for pure soul sustenance ... emerging back into the trance process of healing and transformation, and then drawn back into the immeasurable realm of the absolute ... immersed in Spirit-stream ... utterly washed ... together in healing and wholeness, in and out, and in and out until all are renewed ... and a great stillness ...

The little death comes and passes, and we sleep under the round moon ... our spirits filled with all that we have asked this night.

ACROSS THE THRESHOLD

In the morning we rest ... there is little that has not been said, and we sit together in the comfort of silence. When you trance you have no need of your thoughts, no need to choose, for you become the direction you seek ... you breathe in perfect synchronicity with the great cosmos, and in that place there is no wrong or right, only the doing ... and then you have no need of breath, for your breath stops as you become the breath itself ... and then, an immeasurable silence, as you as Soul-body are breathed in and out and in and out with the world ... and for us Bushmen, now in our earth evolution, there is no place beyond this, it is as far as God wants us to go on earth ... the rest of our journey will surely follow when we no longer have the need to ask whether our eyes are nicely open.

I think the social mechanism of trance dancing among the First People is remarkable ... it allows their inherent relationship with the invisible, giving rise to the propensity to experience the Spiritual world in altered states. The trance dance is a cosmic referencing ritual born of the pure instinct to survive and sustain, refined by the unconscious will of a people who know that there is no other way to live but by acknowledgement of the individual within the group, and the group within the greater cosmos ... people who know that there must be correspondence between what takes place in the heavens and what takes place on the earth.

This healing dance serves as an intuitive truth commission, and in the altered state the interchange of energy takes place on a level of complete nakedness. There is no expression of the lower human nature, no place for verbal dexterity and manipulation, just a total submission to unconditional truth. The dance allows for the admission of our trespasses, and it is trespass that brings about separation from Self and others ... separation in any environment, physical or spiritual, leads only to isolation and extinction. The healing dance brings that which is separate together ... through a transubstantiation of matter and spirit. The Kalahari Bushmen are among the few remaining peoples who still practise this ancient ritual of resurrection.

We humans are responsible for the evolution of earth, our consciousness the interface between the physical world and the world of spirit. It is this balancing of life, which the Bushmen have always known to be utterly important to their wellbeing within the greater environment. The very fact of the healing dance, and the manner in which it takes place, is perhaps the sole reason why these remarkable people have survived for so long ... the trance realm is the sacred space that none can take from them ... it is the realm within that the spirit of humanity is defined, and once you have touched this place it becomes you, and can never be lost or taken. It is this, which defines these people.

I have long considered this particular condition of consciousness that enables the wisdom of the world to yield to human understanding. It is because, when in deep trance, the human etheric body accompanies the shaman into the astral realm or the realm of soul ... aspects of the spiritual are brought back from the astral realm as memory in the human etheric body, and in this way the wisdom of the spiritual is brought to the physical ... the Bushmen call this journey through the astral 'the little death'. Similar practices have found form in many cultures around the earth, and in the time of the 'ancient mysteries', through the initiates of old and a ritual known as 'the sleep of death', the wisdom of the world was brought to memory in humans.

We were all once 'first people' ... all somewhere on the same path. We come after those who shot their quartz-headed arrows into antelope, and after those who threw their stone-tipped spears into mammoths. One must imagine the early race of whom the Bushmen speak, as the root race, the earth's first humans. They extended right through Africa, across much of Europe and Southeast Asia ... emerged from out of the ancient land mass once known as Lemuria now covered by the Pacific Ocean ... just the island tips of mountain ranges left behind, and old words like 'lemur' from an ancient tongue ... and now, legends of this stream of primal humanity come from Semang, Aborigine, Waitaha, and Bushman, in whose mythology this ancient race lived before and after the time when the moon separated from the earth ... now in faded threads of stories ...

The Sun had been a man, he talked; they all
talked, also the other one, the Moon. Therefore,
they used to live upon the earth; while they felt that
they spoke. They do not talk, now that they live
in the sky.

The /Gwikwe are the last remnants of this old order of humanity, from that time of dreamlike consciousness, when the requirements for evolution were different. They carry, still, the inclinations of that ancient order, just as each succeeding order of humanity, in turn, carries the evolutionary response appropriate to their own time on earth.

We modern humans are compelled to understand what we know, compelled to become fully conscious, compelled to take a will-full part in the education of our Souls. Our place in time requires of us a clarity of purpose, and nothing less will take us forward from here. We must come to understand the nature of true power, for it is not the egoistical illusion we pander to. We must resolve our innate need to conquer and control the physical world, for the origins of this destructive response are archetypal, stemming from our separation from oneness ... as we descend deeper into matter and materialism, we see ourselves as separate from 'Spirit' or 'God', and so by inference, separate from our Selves. It is this gap that we spend our lives trying to close, and from this stems the primal insecurity that creates the need to control that which is outside of ourselves. The purpose of our Soul-journey here on earth is to consciously traverse and reconcile the disparity within ... to close the gap between lower self and higher Self, and so effect the spiritual evolution of humanity.

There are a thousand race memories, stories and metaphors that show the way, and as we know the nature of that which we leave behind, we will know more of the nature of that which we take forward.

THE CONSECRATION OF HUMANITY

It is not by accident that we share the earth with so many who are different from ourselves. It is not by accident that we see our own light only in the eyes of another. The simple act of living in relationship with other humans is an act of consecration. Each human life reflects a spiritual essence that affects the surrounding whole to a greater or lesser degree, and we must be utterly aware of the quality of what we add, each with our own unique essence determined by the degree of consciousness with which we live our lives ... and it is this thought-full participation that binds us so irrevocably to the consequences of our every word and action, to the laws of cause and effect. The consecration of man is the constant transforming of the physical into the spiritual in each living human relationship ... the act of 'making sacred' through life.

I think of the seven years of my life shared with Bushmen ... of the miles walked and the dances danced. I think of the hunger and thirst, the voices of children, the joyful beating of our hearts and the shared memories we hold in trust. So often have I heard the question: 'What can we do to help them?' And I answer that ours is not the responsibility to preserve what is past ... it is not our task to physically resurrect a people and a culture that has lived its own time and served its own purpose in the grand picture of human evolution. The greatest sadness is not the passing of a people, it is our failure to remember, our failure to bring forward the knowledge, our failure to consecrate the wisdom and so redeem the sacrifice of those who came before us.

My own act of consecration, then, is that I take forward the truth, the beauty and the goodness of these people, for it is this knowledge, consecrated in each of us, that will redeem and give 'life' to their gift ... the past held in the essence of the future, and nothing lost from the circle of life.

I ask for these words to touch in you what is touched in me, so that I might tell this story of a people, and show a truth that belongs to all of us.

Each man is unto himself his own way, and only in death will we know the life that we have lived.

This book stands as a consequence of my deeds ...

BUSHMAN WINTER

So I have spoken for the /Gwikwe ... the scattered remains of a people who could once claim the earth as their own.

We have never really known just how different these First People are ... they live just one small step removed from nature spirits and other spirit beings, and their language expresses that truth. When we look at them today, among the remnants and residues, it is easy to look past what we should see.

My life shared with these people has taught me to seek for the truth of things ... to know that there is no finite right and wrong, for we humans just do what we are in our time. I was granted this last window into a time that has now gone from this African earth, and it has taken me a long while to see past myself ... but I have seen.

And why, as a people, have they waited, why have they stayed so long? So that unconsciously, the archetypal wisdom could be held long enough for us to know who we were, and so see who we are.

And in which way do they need us? ... They don't, for the need is ours, not theirs. Never in their long history did they ask for the patronisation that is now their nemesis. Life does not ask to be saved, preserved or protected ... it asks only to be known ... for how do we honour anything, or take anything forward? ... Only through knowledge ... to truly know something, anything, is to take it forward in its own truth. The gap we ask these people to bridge in order to justify our own evolution is an abyss that will not be bridged in the way that we ask it, and in their pretended attempt their physical mortality bears witness to their failure ... but equally, to their spiritual success ... for their purpose has been served.

The consciousness gap will only be bridged through knowledge going forward, and that is our task. I am not speaking of the way it should or could be, but of the way it is ... and this is a Bushman truth. The God of all humans and the collective consciousness of all humankind has evolved and left behind these, his First People, for their work is done ... and it is for us now to close the circle, and through our own knowledge to offer redemption for their sacrifice.

May we remember the purity of heart of the /Gwikwe, and in so doing come to know our own true human heart.

There is no blame, it is neither right nor wrong ... it is just that a time has passed ... and the Bushman Winter has come.

THE END

/GWIKWE CONVERSATIONS AND CLICKS

The /Gwikwe have a tendency to what I call horizontal conversation, as opposed to the vertical way of communicating that is a hallmark of Western 'civilised' peoples. One could also describe it as non-linear conversation, compared to the linear way of talking we modern humans employ.

In a horizontal conversation everyone always listens to the other, gives consideration to what was said, and then adds their own comment in turn. In this manner there is no competition of ego, and no misunderstanding is possible, for it is not a squabbling of concepts and personal opinions, but rather an expression of percept and truth. This propensity comes both through the Soul inclination of these people, and from the fact that they live within the same life context. They speak from common ground as opposed to the often disparate nature of conversation among modern humanity. There is no concept or word for 'misunderstanding' in the /Gwikwe language – misunderstanding is an unfortunate characteristic of modern conversation.

CLICKS – A DESCRIPTION OF HOW TO MAKE THE SIX PRIMARY CLICKS

/ – indicates the dental click, sounded by pressing the tip of the tongue against the back of the front teeth of the upper jaw, and then suddenly and forcibly withdrawing them. A soft implosive click, it resembles our interjection of annoyance.

! – indicates the cerebral click, sounded by pressing the tip of the tongue against the roof of the palate behind the front teeth and withdrawing it suddenly and forcibly. A hard implosive click.

// – indicates the lateral click that is sounded by pressing the back of the tongue against the side teeth of the mouth and then withdrawing it. A similar implosive sound is made to urge a horse forward.

* – indicates the palatal click, sounded by pressing the flat of the tongue against the palate and gently withdrawing it. A soft implosive click.

Y – a strong explosive ejective from the back of the throat.

V – a gentle explosive ejective from the back of the throat.

There are various ways of expressing these clicks; sometimes tone is the only distinguishing feature in words that have different meanings but are spelt the same.

LIST OF PEOPLE

Gening/u (m) and Se/twago (f)
their children: ǀQua/tgara (m); Kuramatso (m); Pelo (m)

/Gowsi (m) and //Gama (f) (sister of Gening/u)
their children: /Nau//tge (f); ǀOie/tge (m); //Nale/twago (f)

Semaǃnabi (f) (sister of of Gening/u)
her daughter: /Nana (f)

Magu (m) and //Gang//gang (f)
their children: //Nae/tui (m); Seka (m)

Tgoo (m) and Geutwe (f)
their children: Semanǃua (m); Khaba (f)

Tso/tgomaa (m) and /Gaiekwe (f)
their children: Geamm (m); /Damegu (m); ǀGaie (m)

/Nedu khu kwe (m) and Dowgwi (f)

Khaachiro (m) and ǃTokwa (m)
their children: Abeh (f); Beh/tebeh (f)

Kamageh (m)

Dzero-O, the old man (father of /Gowsi)

/Tguikwe, the old woman (mother of Magu)

GLOSSARY OF /GWIKWE WORDS

* for animals, the female name appears in brackets behind the male term.

//Aauuma	kaross; blanket	
//Ahmahma (//Ahmahsa)	red hartebeest	
//Annsa	tsama melon	*Citrullus lanatus*
!Auuma (!Auusa)	antbear//	
//Auusa	hunting arrow (plural: #Auudze)	
Bie	edible root	*Raphionacme burkei*
Denku	thumb piano	
/Ehnuma (/Ehnusa)	bow harp played by a man (woman)	
/Gaa	wild cucumber	*Coccinia rehmannii*
//Gae khu //gaa	'the grass that can be thrown like a spear'	
!Gaema (!Gaesa)	black korhaan	
/Gaema (/Gaesa)	steenbok	
!Gaima (!Gaiesa)	springbok	
//Gama (//Gamsa)	kudu	
//Gamah	the lesser god; the devil	
//Gamahma	the Greater God	
//Gammsa	sun	
//Gau//gae	home	
//Geema (//Geesa)	aardwolf	
/Geruma	fire sticks	
/Geruma (/Gerusa)	ostrich	
Geuma (Geusa)	eland	
Ggamma (Ggamsa)	lion	
!Goie	mother-in-law's tongue	*Sansevieria hyacinthoides*
//Guama (//Guasa)	duiker	
#Guam/tge	earth, the Great Sand Face	
Juaneeh	mole snake	

Kanna	kougoed	*Sceletium tortuosum*
Kghanabe	a type of root	
#Khaa	gemsbok cucumber	*Acanthosicyos naudiniana*
Khordze	skins	
Khuuma (Khuusa)	rain	
Kiam!ah	poisonous spider	
Koranna	!Xam Bushman name for the Hottentot	
Kwhootse	Kalahari truffle	*Terfezia claveryi*
//Xa (!Kung word)	Mongongo nut	*Ricinodendron rautanenii*
!Nabehma (!Nabehsa)	giraffe	
!Nabehma/Ono	the Southern Cross	
!Nan!te	edible seeds	
!Nauu	gum arabic exuded by various species of acacia	
N/aueema	moon	
Nn!oduu	porcupine (old language)	
/Nooni	Hook thorn tree	*Acacia detinens Burch.*
!Oba	edible succulent	*Pachycymbium keithii*
!!Ono	stars	
!Ooema (!Ooesa)	leopard	
!Oom/tge	region (area)	
//Oooohga!noo	white people's country	
!Ou bea !aba	devil's claw	*Harpagophytum procumbens*
#//Ouhee	medicinal root	
#Ouii	the 'sound' of a bitter taste	
!Outsi/noro	crested barbet	
Peetsa	edible root	
Po	kori bustard	
Saasa	medicinal root	
songololo	millipede	
!Taema	man's loincloth (moochi)	

/Tehma (/Tehsa)	wildebeest	
/Tehnu	bow harp	
/Tehsa	fire	
//Tgaago	red ochre stone	
/Tgadee	medicinal root	
/Tgara	succulent edible bulb	*Vigna lobatifolia*
/Tgooma (/Tgoosa)	gemsbok	
!Toohsa	woman's back apron	
//Ua chorooma	poison grub	*Diamphidia*
//Uaasa	poison	
/Uamm	belly button	
//Xam	wild potato	
//Xane	brandy bush (sour berries)	*Grewia flava*
//Xann	tsama melon	
//Xau#ede	the planet Venus	
/Xoie!om	the government settlement	

ACKNOWLEDGEMENTS

It has taken me twenty-eight years of searching and learning to bring this book to print, and if anywhere in it I have reflected the thoughts or words of another person, then I thank you for your wisdom. I have great respect for the work of Wilhelm Bleek and been endlessly inspired by the wisdom found in the work of Rudolf Steiner.

I give thanks to you my /Gwikwe brothers and sisters ... I pray that in the fullness of time I have honoured your spirit in truth. Magu Tamai for the road shared, my fine son Talon, and my further acknowledgements to the Souls who travel this life with me ... I have learned from those who have brought me joy and from those who have brought me pain. Mine was the freedom to choose ... I have failed and I have succeeded ... for I live.

BIBLIOGRAPHY

Bleek, W.H. & Lloyd, L.C. 1911. *Specimens of Bushman Folklore*. George Allen & Co. Ltd, London.
Stow, G.W. Reprint 1964. *Native Races of South Africa*. Cape Town, Struik Publishers.

Run to exhaustion by /Gowsi, the kudu stands as if in trance while Gening/u cautiously retrieves the first spear, and then from close range pushes it through the kudu's ribs and into its heart.

'Nedu khu kwe – One must imagine oneself back into a world inhabited only by the first people, a time of elven-like humans who lived within the realm of spirit as easily as they did within the physical world.

Geutwe and /Gaiekwe return from a gathering trip, their carry-bags
filled to bursting with gemsbok cucumbers or ǂKhaa.

The women build my shelter ... 'The grass is smelling very nice even though it is old, says //Gama, it is because it caught the dew last night.'

In the morning I go north with Tso/tgomaa and Gening/u. The sand beneath our feet tells us that /Tehma, the Wildebeest, have not walked far from the place where they were shot.

The joy, the innocence, the uninhibited beauty which flows from these children is a reminder of truth for all of us.

These /Gwikwe boys relate to hunting just as soon as they can walk, and hunting within
a radius of about two miles around our shelters, their prey, is anything that moves.

These boys ... immersed in everything, secure in their
own identities, they share one and the same reality.

The harmony mirrored in these forms holds my breath.

So many days spent living under this African sky on the earth with
God's first people. //Gang//gang and //Gama … sisters in Soul.

The boys, Geamm and ʏQua/tgara, have come to help with carrying meat saying,
'We are old hunters who can walk any distance and never get tired.' So be it.

//Gama and her husband /Gowsi had talked long into
last night, and we could hear their words in the deepening darkness.

If anyone epitomises the fundamental nature of the First People,
it is this man, Dzero O, the most human being I shall ever know.

Four women, one day in the Kalahari … Dowgwi, !Tokwa, //Gama and /Tguikwe.

/Geruma … filled with the spirit of our lives. We dance the
ostrich dance that day, a celebration of male victory.

Orange sun cuts through dust crouching hunters, thrusting, twisting,
turning in pretended battle … the age-old companionship of predator and prey.

These /Gwi women are extremely able plant ecologists, an old knowledge
carried in the blood. I know that my purpose here is to awaken that ancient
knowledge within the place of memory in my body.

I drink from the pocket of crystal fluid between the skin and the flesh … I no longer think or
consider the alternatives of another life, I have gone beyond the boundaries of that existence.

//Gama returns to the shelters with a stack of wood as heavy as herself …
I marvel at the power of will in her small and beautiful body.

With a snare rope made of !Goiee, the dead antbear is secured to a pole
and carried back to the shelters by Genin/u and Kamageh. I follow.

Dzero O has asked Gening/u for the claws of the antbear …
He says that there is something that he would use them for.

Old /Tguikwe has lived her life on this Great Sand Face, as a child,
as a mother … and now the grandmother speaks, 'My old body is tired,
the hunger and the thirst have killed me … and now the Winter'.

/Tehsa … the fire that we make today must burn out the old grass and make way for new grass, so that the animals can return to this place and the hunters can be lucky.

A strong wind will take this fire through many hundreds of square miles, and when the spring comes with the new grass, this will be a good place for hunting.

The cuts on Tgoo's forehead resemble the black mark on a Duiker's forehead, and these will bring him luck. The cuts on his chest and arms will make him strong when pulling his hunting bow.

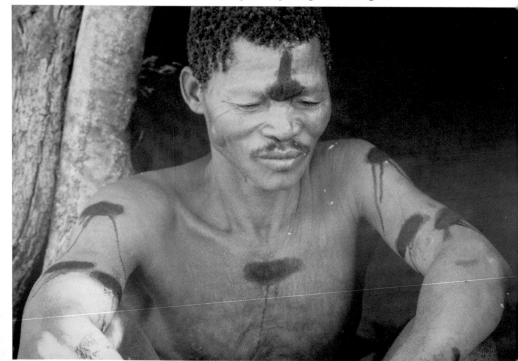

When Geutwe is finished with the tattooing they wipe their bodies
with a mixture of stamped melon and seeds … and so it is done.

Squeezing thick green liquid into his cupped hand, Tso/tgomah drinks ... and so we all drink, for there is no choice in this thirstland ... bodies without liquid cannot live.

Crowing their delight, two warm, fat naked little bodies climb and clamber upon
this weary invitation, to massage the back and the mood of Magu on this day.

Sema!nabi had taken a /Gaa root which /Gowsi had put aside for his children. She had taken
the root for her own child who was not feeling well, for /Nana is not a strong child.

It is the women who begin, with their voices … gently pulling us to the circle where we can be one … so that the outer rhythm and the inner rhythm become the same.

/Gwikwe spirituality is both communal and individual, and not as in most modern religions, the sacred preserve of the shaman or priest … whoever wishes, takes part.

Each one trapped in their own heat, small, still bundles in whatever
black shade they can find, waiting for the sun to pass.

This rite of puberty and procreation is a Soul journey that all women are compelled
to make, because it is the way … the continuing of ourselves through time.

In between the dancing the women stop to rest and talk.
Little Seka catches his beautiful mother in time for a re-fill.

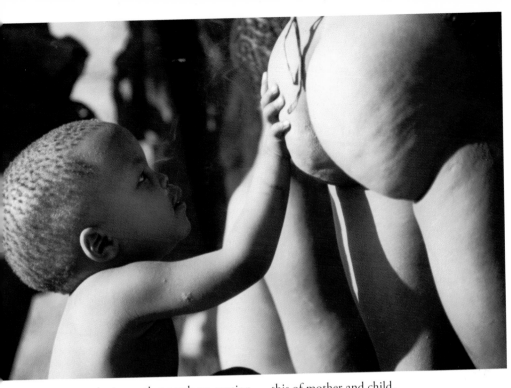

A picture that needs no caption … this of mother and child.

Spanning the heavens in the eastern sky is a rainbow of such colour and beauty that we humans pause one and all to reflect on this fire-water bridge between heaven and earth.

A picture now gone from the Great Sand Face ... the women
of the band dance the melon dance ... they dance the melon dance ...

My second spear goes between the ribs and finds her heart ... blood, breath, sighing –
something shared between us in the knowing of our living dying relationship.

Dowgwi brings a bundle of wild shallots for roasting in the coals –
these small elongated bulbs grow soon after the first rains.

Archetypal mother in the stillness of desert.

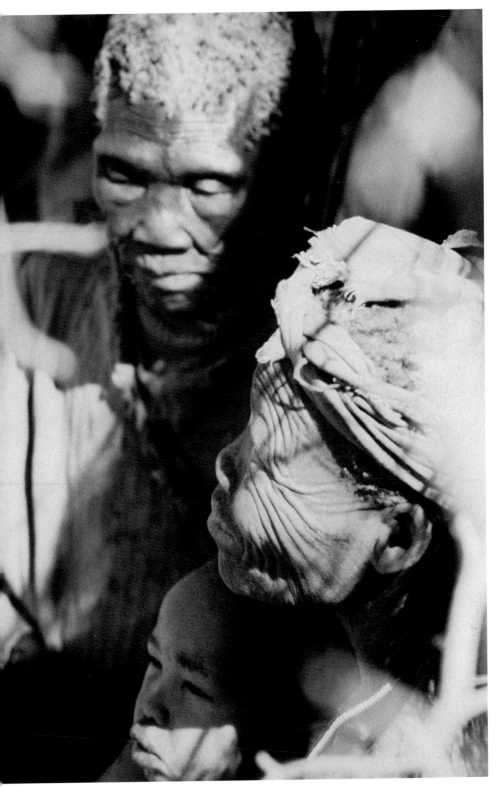

With my old camera I took two photographs as they sat. Three generations of women.
An old blind woman, a mother, and a suckling child.

The eggs are filled with ostrich embryo … It is not the way we would choose to have it, but it is food … they will be roasted in the coals, and we will eat.

Two days later we reach Kia//nau, halfway to the settlement. Tonight we sleep at //Xolo, 'the place of the big wolf' … just one more sleep to journeys end.

And so we come to the settlement from a far off place, now standing between
two worlds, almost as strangers amongst our own people.

Trance dance – bodies moving, shifting … shape changing … animal forms merging into and out of the human form, as if still part of the same physical entity.

The little death comes and passes, and together we will sleep under the round moon.

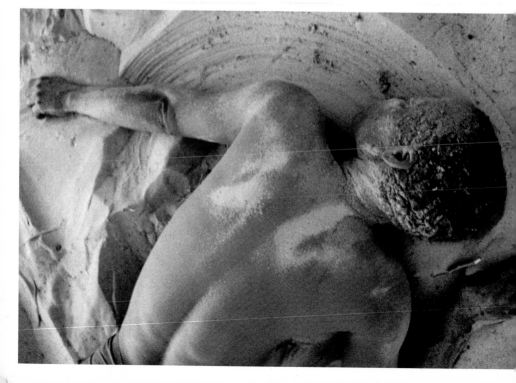

Magu became ill from the dancing, his journey into the astral was too deep,
so for a long time he had stopped working as a healer.

Gone from the African landscape … this form of man,
held thus upon the earth and under the sun-filled sky as it was in the beginning.

It was late afternoon in the autumn when I returned to the Kalahari. I had walked for many
days … one soul coming to understand more of the reason for being human.